THE WORDS OF CÉSAR CHÁVEZ

THE WORDS OF

César Chávez

EDITED BY

Richard J. Jensen

John C. Hammerback

Texas A&M University Press
College Station

The paper used in this book meets the minimum requirements of the
American National Standard for Permanence of Paper for Printed Library
Materials, Z39.48-1984. Binding materials have been chosen for durability.
♾

Library of Congress Cataloging-in-Publication Data

Chávez, César, 1927–
    The words of César Chávez / edited by Richard J. Jensen, John C. Hammer-
back.— 1st ed.
        p. cm.
Complements the editors' earlier study, The Rhetorical Career of César Chávez.
Includes index.
    ISBN 1-58544-169-4 (cloth : alk. paper)—ISBN 1-58544-170-8 (pbk. : alk. paper)
    1. Chávez, César, 1927– 2. Chávez, César, 1927—Oratory. 3. Discourse
analysis. 4. Persuasion (Rhetoric) 5. Labor leaders—United States. 6. Mexican
American migrant agricultural laborers. 7. Migrant agricultural laborers—Labor
unions—United States. 8. Mexican American labor union members. 9. United
Farm Workers—History—Sources.   I. Jensen, Richard J. (Richard Jay), 1943–
II. Hammerback, John C. III. Title.
    HD6509.C48 A25 2002
    331.88'13'092—dc21

                                2001006994
    ISBN 13: 978-1-58544-170-9 (pbk.)

Contents

List of Illustrations

Acknowledgments

This book is the culmination of nearly twenty-five years of teaching, research, lecturing, and writing on César E. Chávez. It should serve as a fitting complement to our earlier book on Chávez, *The Rhetorical Career of
César Chávez,* and we hope that it adds usefully to our published work on
Mexican American rhetors who were active in the protests that began in
the 1960s. As is almost always the case for editors of a book, we received
considerable assistance from others along the way. We would like to thank
our students for their many ideas and continuous support—contributions
that gave us valuable intellectual capital and emotional motivation for
this project. We owe a special debt to the many individuals who provided
valuable documents during our research; although we cannot here name
everyone who lent a hand, we will mention two of the most helpful: Marc
Grossman, Chávez's speech writer and press aide, and Kathy Schmeling,
Wayne State University librarian who over the years supplied essential information and documents on Chávez. Particular thanks are given to the
César E. Chávez Foundation for allowing us to use the speeches and writings used in this text.

As always we must express our love and thanks for the support of two
splendid supporters and critics, Carol Jensen and Jean Hammerback.

Introduction

In 1998 our book *The Rhetorical Career of César Chávez* marked the culmination of some twenty years of research and writing on César Chávez, extending our previous work that had been published in four articles in scholarly journals and five chapters in books.[1] Our focus on rhetorical analysis, meaning an analysis of Chávez's speaking, writing, and nonverbal communication (picketing, marches, fasts, etc.) designed to influence audiences, seemed entirely appropriate for a leader whose extraordinary accomplishments relied primarily on the art and practice of communication he placed at the very center of his long career. His extensive and unrelenting campaign to improve the lives of farm workers and bring social justice to the oppressed consistently featured speeches—sometimes as many as a dozen or more in one day, and frequently at least one during every day in a month—but also included written documents such as public letters, proclamations and printed plans like the Plan of Delano, newspaper columns, book chapters, interviews, and pamphlets, as well as nonverbal forms of communication like picketing, fasts, and marches.

Our book was not confined to a history of Chávez's words. Instead, it told the story of his career from a rhetorical perspective, a perspective he had painstakingly developed over many years, a perspective through which he saw the world and upon which he based so many of the acts that made up his life as a leader. Two models and an approach to rhetorical criticism were created and applied in order to identify and explain what motivated Chávez to speak and write incessantly, what directed him to his most characteristic and enduring rhetorical qualities and elements, what made up the complete rhetorical profile that characterized his speaking and writing throughout his career, and what rhetorical dynamics accounted for his startling effects on audiences—effects that translated into the primary means through which he accomplished goals that initially seemed impossible. Thus, our book served not only to record and document Chávez's life as a rhetor, but also to show the vital place of public address in his worldview and career and to account for the spectacular rhetorical successes which this unlikely persuader achieved against-all-odds goals few thought could be accomplished—most notably the first permanent union of farm workers, the first collective bargaining legislation for them, and the many farm-worker–union contracts with growers. In so doing, the book advanced a critical approach that addresses those baffling cases when orators transform the identity of audiences, reconstituting the character of auditors in a way that impels them to enact a speaker's agenda.

At the time we wrote this introduction all published reviews of our rhetorical analysis in *The Rhetorical Career of César Chávez* have been favorable. Its reviewers have ranged from scholars in communication and history to journalists and activists who had close-up experience with Chávez. These men and women who worked with, followed, and studied Chávez or protest discourse or both have credited us with accurately capturing the essence of the rhetorical aspects so central to Chávez and his cause. We are grateful for their confidence in our work.

Our study profited from our use of some 160 texts and tapes of Chávez's speeches and writings, the vast majority of which had never been examined by scholars. Copies of most of the written texts were made during research in the United Farm Workers Papers at the Walter P. Reuther Library of Labor and Urban Affairs, Wayne State University in Detroit. The written materials in the collection are well organized and easily accessible; however, copies of audio tapes and other audiovisual materials are not catalogued at this date, but researchers do have access to them. Some materials are also available in the San Joaquin Valley Farm Workers Collection, Special Collections Department, Fresno State University. In preparing this book, the editors transcribed several audio tapes and have made few alterations in these and other texts; the attempt has been to make the texts as authentic as possible. Copies of all the texts and audio tapes used in this book are in the possession of the editors. Some of these written materials had Chávez's handwritten comments in their margins. In addition, the texts include copies of speech notes—some in his own hand and used while delivering his addresses—that afford special insights into how he intended to relate his ideas to audiences and his audiences to ideas. Together the texts and notes offer a valuable mirror into the man, his movement, and his times, a record of what mattered most day by day in the struggle of farm workers for their union, a map of the changes that occurred and challenges that endured in the union struggle but also in the broader struggle for civil rights for Mexican Americans and others. Our original textual sources also allowed us to build a rhetorical profile of Chávez and helped in the development of a critical approach to explore the underlying rhetorical dynamics of the charismatic interactions with audiences by a speaker who in person seemed anything but charismatic.

Almost from the day our book appeared, we began to receive suggestions to consider a companion volume of Chávez's most significant and representative speeches and writings. We well remember Fernando Delgado, a professor at Arizona State University–West, asking at a panel during the 1999 convention of the Western States Communication Association: "When will your anthology of Chávez's speeches come out? When will those of us who teach and write about Chicanos be able to read Chávez's main works?" This anthology, with our introductions and analyses, is meant to address that question, to satisfy a need we believe is pressing. Its many speeches and writings represent the discourse in each of the most important periods of Chávez's career. We have included his most notable addresses and those to which he devoted the most preparation—some addresses having gone through several drafts, a few read word for word, such as his 1984 speech to the Commonwealth Club in San Francisco.

Together the texts in this book reveal the history of a remarkable man and his movement, a significant piece of our nation's experience during a particularly unsettled time, a record of what mattered most and why to *la causa* (the cause) of Chávez and farm workers, and a wealth of detail attending the history, goals, challenges, successes, and defeats for farm workers specifically and Mexican Americans in general—in all, nothing less than a portrait of what is best about humanity. To us, telling this history is enough to justify the existence of the book. To understand the career, impact, and indeed the very meaning of Chávez is to understand the rhetorical discourse upon which he consciously based his career as organizer/leader and to which he devoted so much of his life.

But *The Words of César Chávez* contributes more than history, undeniably valuable though it is. Here too is the story of Chávez as an extraordinarily effective and skilled communicator, for his abilities as a rhetor as manifested in these texts are present for all to discover and evaluate. His consistent use of some themes, arguments, evidence, appeals, strategies, and techniques is obvious, as is his adaptation of substantive ideas and rhetorical qualities to particular audiences and occasions. There is plenty here, particularly when supplemented with our extensive and detailed analyses in *The Rhetorical Career of César Chávez*, to begin to account for his success in persuading some audiences and, more startlingly, for the redefinition of other audiences so that those new-found or newly energized supporters could take on his own communicated qualities—qualities necessary for enacting his demanding agenda. Thus in this book resides not only a story of Chávez and his rhetorical discourse, but potentially a larger story of how specially gifted leaders can transform audiences.

As is the case with many busy leader/rhetors whose canvassing is extensive, such as political and corporate leaders, Chávez on occasion worked with other people to create rhetorical works under his name. In particular, some of his texts reflected his collaboration with Marc Grossman, who served as Chávez's primary and only full-time press secretary/media consultant/general aide from 1975 to 1981 and who assisted Chávez with his speeches off and on until Chávez's death. A graduate student in Journalism at UCLA where he met Chávez's oldest son, Fernando, and through him César, Grossman typed early versions of a number of Chávez's speeches and essays and worked extensively with him on several major addresses. Even in those texts, however, Grossman was expressing Chávez's ideas, form, and style—content and techniques that dominated the texts.[2] Thus with the exception of the Plan of Delano, which represented a team of writers working with Chávez, the labor leader was the primary or exclusive author of the texts in this book. That his signature rhetorical qualities characterized the texts and that audiences attributed the discourse to him and were persuaded and transformed by the merger of the man and his message are more important to our purpose than whether Chávez alone composed all of each address.

To provide background for understanding Chávez and his discourse, we will now review his career, discourse, and worldview and discuss the events in his early life that prepared him for his long journey as a leader. In 1962 Chávez quit his job with the Community Services Organization (CSO), a group dedicated to grassroots organizing, and moved to the central California valley town of Delano to start a union among farm workers. He faced a formidable task. The contest pitted the uneducated, poor, and largely itinerant ethnic minorities who picked crops against the wealthy growers whose power dominated every stratum of local life and extended into the inner workings of statewide politics. The image of David vs. Goliath is apt. "Few thought he could succeed," wrote Chávez biographer Jacques Levy: "He was just a farm worker, one of the thousands, easily lost in a crowd, small of stature, quiet, self-effacing, soft-spoken, poorly educated."[3] Against massive odds, lengthened by his own absence of financial or organizational resources and by a long history of failed attempts to organize California's crop pickers, Chávez built the first successful farm worker union in the history of the United States. That success vaulted him into national prominence, making him a hero to many people.

It was clear from the beginning that Chávez was a unique leader. That he reached heroic stature is not in doubt. His former secretary, Susan Samuels Drake, sweepingly described him as "a powerful persuasive speaker, labor leader, charismatic hero; American-born farm worker of Mexican descent; the Mexican Martin Luther King; America's Gandhi."[4] Representative depictions in newspapers and magazines labeled him "one of the best-known American labor leaders, and probably the most controversial,"[5] "the militant farm worker leader,"[6] "the UFW's charismatic leader,"[7] and a "charismatic 1960s hero," "a folk legend," "a symbol of social justice." President Clinton summed up the sentiment of many by referring to Chávez as "an authentic hero to millions of people throughout the world."[8] Reverence for Chávez was probably deepest where he lived out most of his career: on August 18, 2000, California Governor Gray Davis signed into law a state holiday to honor César E. Chávez one day each year.

Chávez had detractors and powerful enemies as well as admirers and awe-struck supporters. Critics called him a "'Communist,' 'Alinsky-dupe' [referring to the controversial organizer Saul Alinsky], 'opportunist', 'phony civil-rights worker,' 'outsider,' and 'colossal fraud.'"[9] One of the most frequently used but far-fetched attempts to tarnish Chávez was that he was following orders from Communists or that he was a "red." In several of the texts in this book, Chávez refers to this preposterous charge. Toward the end of his career, with no evidence ever supporting the claim, few took seriously the desperate effort at guilt by association. Upon his death, however, even his critics noted his rhetorical skills and lasting effects. One such adversary admitted: "He was a worthy advocate for his cause. . . . He was no saint, but he certainly changed the face of California agriculture." [10]

Whether revered or reviled, Chávez was a different type of hero. Soft-spoken and quiet, he did not call attention to himself. He resisted celebrity status and maintained his fundamentally modest manner throughout his career. "To this day," wrote Luis A. Solis-Garza in 1972, "Chávez remains unchanged. To be sure he has a certain messianic quality about him which draws people to him, and yet Chávez denies being a great leader."[11]

A signature label for Chávez became "quiet charisma."[12] Chávez biographer Eugene Nelson attempted to identify that charisma when he stated that Chávez had "a great deal of personal magnetism . . . as well as an undeniably keen intelligence and exceedingly pleasant if not handsome appearance. . . . He is one of those persons one feels [one] has known all [one's] life."[13] That warmth and electricity characterized his speaking. *Time* declared that the quiet spokesperson's charisma made him into "a liberal hero and his United Farm Workers of America a power in the grape and vegetable fields of the Southwest."[14]

Chicano activist José Angél Gutiérrez captured the special relationship between Chávez and Mexican Americans. Assessing that the earnest Chávez's commitment to farm workers was "total and complete," Gutiérrez related how Chávez was one with the Mexican Americans whom he led:

> He looked mestizo. He was dark skinned, short, with high cheek bones, piercing black eyes, and sparse facial hair. He was the embodiment of a Chicano. Chicanos could see themselves in César: clothes, personal style, demeanor and commitment. Chávez inspired himself. And, his inspiration moved Chicanos.[15]

Identifying one of Chávez's means of identifying with and inspiring Chicanos, Gutiérrez described him as a speaker:

> He usually spoke in Spanish. He spoke in English to staff, non-Mexican audiences and reporters, and on college campuses. He was bilingual and bicultural. He didn't have an eloquent, grandiose or verbose speaking style. He was plain speaking and monotonal. Rarely did he raise his voice to make a point or command attention. He was tireless in all his roles as father, husband, Catholic, leader, Chicano, organizer, staff manager, and man. In his personal simplicity he was poignant. The simplicity of his message—justice for farm workers—made him eloquent.[16]

The mysterious link between Chávez's quiet speaking manner and often electrifying effects caught the attention of many close observers. Marion Moses, a nurse, first heard Chávez speak in Berkeley in 1965. "He wasn't a good speaker at all," she reported, "but there was something about him. I always say the word 'charisma' which is often used but it doesn't begin to describe it." The Berkeley speech inspired her to volunteer at union headquarters in Delano, and she later became a UFW doctor.[17]

Susan Ferriss and Ricardo Sandoval, authors of a recent book on Chávez (*The Fight in the Fields: César Chávez and the Farmworkers Movement*), reported some of the feeling of listening to his speech to farm workers in 1973 in the Coachella Valley. The workers and Chávez were "taking a rare moment of rest between picket lines and meeting to talk about their union." Chávez was "in his element" among workers, who "listened intently as he talked about his life, trying to fuel their determination." He connected deeply to them as he told them how he had "stayed in the same kinds of run-down labor camps with filthy outhouses as these workers, and paid too much for the privilege." In Spanish he related that his grandfather had come to the United States from Mexico "when the frontier was more an idea than an actual border." But the family lost their land and had to become migrants. Moving to the turning point of his own life, he recounted how in 1962 he went to "Delano with the idea of organizing a union. Of every hundred workers I talked to, one would say, 'It's time.' Everyone said no one could organize farmworkers, that it couldn't be done. But we got a group of forty or fifty, and one by one, that's how we started. . . ."[18]

Eliseo Medina, a union organizer, remembered when he was nineteen years old hearing Chávez speak at a United Farm Workers union meeting. A tall, distinguished looking man with a mustache was speaking. Medina thought he must be Chávez, but the speaker concluded his speech by introducing Chávez. At first Medina found little that was inspiring in the small labor leader: "And then César gets up and he's this little guy . . . very soft spoken. I say, 'That's César?' You know, I wasn't very impressed." But as Chávez spoke, Medina's perceptions shifted: "The more he talked, the more I thought that not only could we fight, but we could win." When Chávez finished his speech, Medina volunteered to work for the union.[19]

In 1974 Dorothy Rensenbrink caught the essence of Chávez's speaking in public after hearing his address in a ballroom in Los Angeles. "I have heard César Chávez speak many times," she began; and she pointed out that "this time, as always, I am puzzled at the power of such an uncommanding person to command so much loyalty from so many." Chávez "entered unnoticed; when he is announced, he appears suddenly on the platform as if he'd been hiding below it all the while—but of course he wasn't, one realizes with surprise." As he began to speak, she noticed that he had improved as a speaker: "His English is getting better—less sing-songy than when we first heard him in the mid-60s—and he lightly touches the lectern. He speaks as though he is resuming a friendly conversation" with his audience.[20]

In this speech Chávez initially assumed too much knowledge from his audience. When he recognized their confusion, he adroitly adapted his message to the audience by simplifying it. Eventually he struck a responsive chord, prompting Rensenbrink to exclaim: "I am finally hooked by recognition. It is hard to describe why. It is not self-recognition, just a kind of kindred recognition; as it is with thee, so it is with me." At the end of the meeting she spoke with a friend who described Chávez's appeal in this manner: "You sit there and wonder where he's going and after a while his personality sneaks up on you."[21]

The puzzling power of the rhetorical magic that "hooked" Rensenbrink, the fully unexpected impact of Chávez's words on Medina, and the undeniable charisma of the improbable persuader whom so many observers marveled over, all of these mysterious rhetorical processes were the hard-earned product of Chávez's early experiences and painstaking efforts—and each grew out of his worldview and can be explained by rhetorical theories and principles. The discourse that powered Chávez was not the product of luck or mystery, as we showed in *The Rhetorical Career of César Chávez*.

CHÁVEZ'S PREPARATION AS LEADER/RHETOR

Although when Chávez first arrived in Delano in 1962 he appeared decidedly unsuited to the challenges that would face him, his early life had provided superb preparation for his destined career as rhetor/leader. César Estrada Chávez was born on March 31, 1927, in Yuma, Arizona.[22] His family lived on a small farm originally settled by his grandfather. His father, Librado, ran several businesses including an auto-repair shop and a poolroom about twenty miles north of Yuma. During the depression the family was unable to pay its taxes, forcing them to leave the land and become migrants to survive. The loss of the land planted the seeds of rebelliousness that would one day grow into César Chávez's willingness to protest against injustice to farm workers. He later recalled: "I bitterly missed the ranch. Maybe that is when the rebellion started. Some had been born into the migrant stream. But we had been on the land, and I knew a different way of life. We were poor but we had liberty. The migrant is poor, and he has no freedom."[23]

Like other migrants, the Chávezes had a difficult time but eventually learned to do what was necessary to survive. During those years young César never received a sustained formal education. He once calculated that he had attended thirty-seven different schools and learned little in any of them. He quit school after the eighth grade. The education of this leader would be from informal sources.

The Chávezes frequently faced racial discrimination. He and his siblings often attended racially segregated schools where Anglo teachers treated them harshly. The racism extended beyond the classroom. Chávez remembers being forced to sit in segregated sections in movie theaters and being denied service in restaurants. Such demeaning experiences left anger that later would provide energy necessary to build a union dedicated to eliminating those injustices.

During their migrant years Chávez's mother kept the family unified. She taught her children through traditional knowledge contained in *dichos* (proverbs and sayings), *consejos* (advice), and *cuentos* (stories) that often carried a moral lesson. They covered a wide range of subjects, some telling of miracles, others promoting obedience and honesty. The sayings and stories, an integral part of the Mexican American culture, would later appear in his speeches and writings. He used them to teach all audiences and especially to instruct and identify with his Mexican American audiences.

His travels as a migrant brought Chávez into close contact with unionism. His father and uncle often joined unions; most proved to be ineffective. Chávez joined his first union, the National Agricultural Workers Union (NAWU), when he was nineteen. Although that union failed, he pointed to the experience as the beginning of his career as an organizer.

Chávez tried to escape from migrant life by joining the Navy in 1944. He was unhappy in the Navy and was particularly struck by the discrimination against African Americans and Mexican Americans. He had hoped to learn skills leading to a vocation in civilian life; he learned none so returned to migrant labor when discharged in 1946.

In 1948 Chávez married Helen Fabela. They both continued to labor in the fields, then tried sharecropping, and eventually moved to Crescent City in northern California where César worked in the woods. His family did not like northern California weather and moved to San Jose, where Chávez found a job in a lumber mill and in fruit orchards. The unfocused César Chávez would soon find his life's cause and work.[24]

In 1952 Chávez was living in a barrio in San Jose called *Sal Si Puedes* (get out if you can), a section of the city "dirtier and uglier than the others."[25] Later, he would change this negative image into a positive one for his workers' movement, *"Si, se puede"* (Yes, we can). During the eventful year of 1952 he met two men who dramatically and forever determined his life's direction: Father Donald McDonnell and Fred Ross. Father McDonnell, a Roman Catholic priest stationed at a local mission, became acquainted with Chávez while visiting in Sal Si Puedes. He soon began teaching Chávez about social justice and labor movements among farm workers, sharing the ideas of *Rerum Novarum*, Pope Leo XIII's encyclical outlining the church's support for workers who protest oppressive conditions. Through McDonnell, Chávez encountered ideas that would work their way into the center of his own personal philosophy, and with the priest's help he met a group of activists for social justice who would inspire his own crusade for farm workers. Chávez described McDonnell's place in his journey toward labor leader:

> [He] sat with me past midnight telling me about social justice and the Church's stand on farm labor and reading from the encyclicals of Pope Leo XIII in which he upheld labor unions. I would do anything to get the Father to tell me more about labor history. I began going to the bracero camps with him to help with Mass, to the city jail with him to talk to prison-

ers, anything to be with him so that he could tell me more about the farm labor movement.[26]

While Father McDonnell gave Chávez an intellectual and moral basis for organizing workers, Fred Ross taught him how to be an effective organizer. Ross was a seasoned grassroots organizer for the CSO, a self-help group for Mexican Americans that was sponsored by Saul Alinsky's Industrial Areas Foundation (IAF). Hearing that Chávez had promise as an organizer, he sought a meeting with the young Mexican American. After initially rejecting a meeting with still one more Anglo outsider whose motives he suspected, Chávez met and listened to Ross. He later recalled Ross's effect on his life: "Fred became sort of my hero. I saw him organize, and I wanted to learn. Right away, I began to see that organizing was difficult. It wasn't a party. . . . I wanted to do it just as he did; so I began to learn. It was a beautiful part of my life. And eventually, like him, I became an organizer."[27] Ross was equally impressed with Chávez: "I kept a diary in those days. And the first night I met César, I wrote in it, 'I think I found the guy I'm looking for.' It was obvious even then."[28]

Chávez started as an unpaid organizer for the CSO. One of his first projects signed up four thousand Mexican American voters and helped Mexican Americans gain citizenship papers. After some early successes, he became a full-time CSO organizer, working initially in Oakland and then in the San Joaquin Valley. He quickly improved his skills, developing successful techniques for making contacts with people, convincing them to become active in the CSO, and then keeping them energized once they had committed to the organization. He especially sought those who could work independently. Organizing demanded hard work and follow-through, he discovered, for "if you go around preaching, telling people that things can be done, they begin to deposit their problems with you and expect you to do something for them."[29]

Chávez set out an ambitious scheme to improve his skills as an organizer. A major part of his program included reading. To learn from the lives of great leaders in history, he read books on a wide variety of subjects including St. Thomas Aquinas, St. Paul, and Mexican American history, as well as biographies of labor leaders like John L. Lewis, Eugene V. Debs, and the leaders of the Knights of Labor. He was particularly drawn to the writings of Mohandas Gandhi and to his tactics of nonviolence. The image of the poor and frail Gandhi taking on and defeating the rich and powerful British must have been inspiring to a young Mexican American who dreamed of challenging entrenched agricultural interests in the United

States. His literary tour provided him with insights as well as tactics for ideas and topics that would surface in his discourse throughout his career.

A second major element in his self-improvement plan required Chávez to develop his understanding of and skills in public address. Realizing early that he could not achieve his goals unless he spoke effectively, Chávez painstakingly analyzed and improved his manner, methods, and style of public speaking. In "The Organizer's Tale" he discussed his experiences as an organizer in Oakland in the 1950s, recalling how after each house meeting and presentation he would "lie awake going over the whole thing, playing the [mental] tape back, trying to see why people laughed at one point, or why they were for one thing and against another."[30]

Shortly after Chávez began addressing farm workers, he discovered essential elements of an effective approach. "When you're trying to recruit a farm worker," he learned, "you have to paint a little picture, and then you color the picture in."[31] In a letter to his mentor in organizing, Fred Ross, Chávez discussed a speech he gave to a group of workers in Oxnard, California, in 1958. The workers were receptive to his message but asked him difficult questions afterward. He confided, "But you know how it is a lotta times, Fred, when you're up there in front of 'em: knowing you gotta produce sorta makes you bear down and strain the ideas out of you—ideas that wouldn't come out on their own."[32]

In an interview in 1981 Chávez made it clear that he did not enjoy performing in public. "I don't like public speaking. Not at all," and he admitted: "I still get butterflies in my stomach. It's terrible." But like most of us, he felt better when the speech was finished: "Once it's over I say 'Oh, thank God, it's over. I can rest now.' I'm still like that, and I've done a million of them."[33]

Chávez's careful efforts slowly bore fruit. Dolores Huerta, who worked with Chávez in the CSO and would later become his best known coworker in the United Farm Workers, initially found Chávez shy and not memorable. Yet she also noticed that he somehow inevitably made things happen. Later she "heard him speak one time at a board meeting and . . . was really impressed."[34] Among the lessons he had learned were not to confront opponents until he understood them and had the means to defeat them, and to provide services to people as a means of building support among them.

As Chávez rose to high leadership positions in the CSO, he gained vital experience coordinating voter registration drives, helping people obtain citizenship papers and old-age pensions, and fighting for improved services and for an end to police violence in barrios. His strongest desire, however, was to organize farm workers into a union. In 1958 efforts by the United Packinghouse Workers of America (UPWA) in Oxnard provided that opportunity. There he succeeded in mobilizing a group of workers, but after he left they lost power and disbanded. Although the effort failed, Chávez had acquired vital skills in organizing.[35] And, as he said, "I began to see the potential of organizing the Union."[36]

CSO leaders resisted Chávez's desire to organize unions. In frustration, he resigned in 1962. "More than anything else I wanted to help farm workers," he said in justification of his departure; "I was a farm worker when I joined the CSO ten years before, and I thought the organization could help us. . . . I began to realize that a farm workers' union was needed to end the exploitation of the workers in the fields, if we were to strike at the roots of their suffering and poverty."[37]

From his early life and CSO years Chávez took not only a set of attitudes, experiences, and skills that would be indispensable to his later career, he formed a worldview that would direct him to the rhetorical elements characterizing his discourse and would motivate him to speak and write incessantly. To understand the discourse of the man, we must first understand his view of the world.

CHÁVEZ'S WORLDVIEW: RHETORIC, RELIGION, AND REFORM

Chávez's public address reflected his interrelated perceptions of God, reform, and rhetoric. A devout Roman Catholic, he described the church as a "powerful moral and spiritual force" in the world;[38] God controls the earth's events and people, seeing to it that good causes triumph. As a labor leader Chávez developed an optimistic interpretation of history and the future based on his beliefs in God, the injustices suffered by the poor, the need to organize workers, and the power of public address to achieve that end.

In his broad scheme of things, the United Farm Workers was more than a union; it was a movement to change the conditions of life for workers. His convictions that the union's cause was just, that "history is a story of social revolution, and that the poor shall inherit the land," led him to announce, "We will win, we are winning, because ours is a revolution of mind and heart, not of economics."[39]

Chávez identified himself and other farm-worker orators as essential agents in God's design to eliminate injustice toward the poor and minorities. Once the public understood a good cause, in Chávez's case the UFW's cause, it would carry out God's will to end injustice. Thus to provide the education necessary for the public to end injustice, and to recruit other farm workers to the movement as rhetor/organizers, Chávez believed that he had only to present a clear message of pertinent facts and moral considerations. Notwithstanding awesome challenges and temporary set-backs, then, Chávez felt that he could be divinely guaranteed of eventual success if he persisted in presenting his righteous case. If he could clearly and understandably present his message to enough people, the farm workers would inevitably win. As he stated, "I contend that not only the American public but people throughout the world will respond to a cause that involves injustice."[40]

In Chávez's rhetorical world, any single address served as but one strand in a web of messages that informed audiences. "You can't really change people with one speech," he claimed; "rather, you can reinforce what had been previously done and said by others." In his view, "you're really trying to strengthen. There's a base you're trying to build on." To the fund of information and ideas existing in the audience, rhetors must add new facts and ideas. As Chávez put it: "The people came to hear what I was going to say and they need to take something with them and they take something that's not trite . . . or something that people are tired of, something a little different."[41]

CHÁVEZ'S RHETORICAL PROFILE

Chávez's rhetorical profile—his characteristic elements, strategies, and techniques—was a direct result of his worldview featuring rhetoric and reform. Always striving to educate, he crafted messages whose emphasis on informing was uncharacteristic of charismatic rhetors. Thus he consistently relied heavily on statistics and examples to explain his ideas and to prove his arguments, on concrete stories to illustrate his points, and on a clear style notable for its simple language and syntax and frequent restatement of facts and ideas. His speeches were unusually well organized, with ample use of signpost and transition sentences and of rhetorical questions and previews to direct listeners to his points. He ordinarily stressed moral issues and treated his opponents generously and usually adapted his topics to immediate audiences and pressing issues. His calm delivery focused attention on the message, not on himself, befitting a leader whose success rested on informing audiences rather than aggrandizing himself. In speaking to Mexican Americans he displayed patterns, forms, and appeals common in that culture: dichos or maxims, anecdotes or stories (cuentos), Spanish formality, graciousness and respect, and familial and religious themes and images. When appealing to Anglo idealists he again was an ideal spokesman, whose case rested on abundant facts and high moral principles.

Although the sheer importance of public address to his career motivated him to prepare carefully developed standard texts that he would present many times, he also often gave speeches "off the cuff." "Once in a while I can prepare," he confessed; "I have like a lecture [a standard speech]. The speech is a lot better when I can prepare. I mean they're more thought out."[42] When he lacked time to prepare, he sought out a briefing on the audience, occasion, and local issues and then adapted himself and his ideas to those elements in his rhetorical situation.

Thoroughly prepared or not, Chávez throughout his career indefatigably carried his message to audiences and steadfastly retained his faith in his righteous rhetoric. Such faith continuously motivated his rhetorical campaign but did not ensure the success of any single address. "Sometimes I'm inspired and some times I'm not," he confessed, "Sometimes it's flat." He talked about an extensive tour in 1969 where he delivered "an average of eight speeches a day. For three months. Every single day." During that tour, he never asked anyone how he did. "I looked at the people," he recalled. "I was nursing a bad back, so a nurse was struggling to keep me together. . . . I'd go speak and I'd come back and I looked mostly at her, or some of the other people, and I knew if I had done good. If I had done bad, they'd just talk about other things. And if it was good, 'that's a great speech.'"[43]

It would be wrong to conclude that Chávez was often unprepared for his speeches. A more accurate conclusion is that he was sometimes tired or did not prepare as much as he would have wished. Our extensive analysis of his addresses shows that he developed standard themes, arguments, explanations, evidence, forms of organization, metaphorical figures of speech, and syntatic measures like anaphora, that these standard components of his speeches surfaced time and again, that they grew directly out of the principles for effective communication he had slowly developed through many years of studying his speaking and audiences, and that these components flowed directly from his worldview. Thus the rhetorically savvy and meticulous Chávez always carried with him the basis for a speech on the pressing topics of the day. It is true, however, that he was rarely bound to a narrow outline and almost never read directly from his speech notes. These were intentional tactics, for Chávez believed that reading from a prepared text insulted the workers who comprised his primary audiences and would likely fray lines of identification with all audiences.[44]

Though he spoke to literally thousands of audiences, he believed that his speaking had not changed during the course of his career. "My goal has always been very simple," he explained; "Don't preach to people, try to involve people, and get serious." He identified one fundamental principle he had learned: "When I do public speaking, I want to make it simple, just very simple. And whatever I do, not long, not long at all because that's the worst thing. If you can't say in ten minutes what you have to say, then you shouldn't say it." He often talked about how he tried to keep his speeches brief.[45]

Chávez frequently addressed audiences comprised of English-speaking or Spanish-speaking members or both. He sometimes prepared linguistically mixed audiences for his choice of language in this manner: "I say, 'Look, if I go too much in English, too much in Spanish, forgive me.' And then I set the crowd so they'll accept. If I do a lot of Spanish, they'll accept—if I do a lot of English, they'll accept it. I get permission from them. I condition them really by using a little joke—an analogy."[46] Chávez's speeches were usually translated into Spanish. He knew that many of his listeners did not speak English, so such translations added to their understanding and created a sense of identification with them.[47]

The only detailed rhetorical analysis published on any of Chávez's oratory, other than the analysis in our *Rhetorical Career of César Chávez* and other writings, was by Winthrop Yinger. Yinger thoroughly critiqued the speech Chávez gave ending his first fast in 1968 and commented briefly on a number of others. He found that Chávez relied upon everyday illustrations and directives and used personal pronouns, a simple style, clear allusions, and appeals to humanity (especially through nonviolence). The labor leader's manner was "conversational, nonoratorical," allowing him to identify with his farm-worker audiences, to become the "ordinary farm worker's spokesman." "Chávez's unique style," Yinger observed, "stands in stark contrast to other contemporary Mexican American spokesmen who do employ flamboyance and fiery oratory, the two principal examples in the Southwest being Rodolfo 'Corky' Gonzales and Reies [López] Tijerina."[48] After hearing the soft-spoken Chávez speak "three or four dozen times," Yinger reported that the quiet persuader "has spoken so often and to so many that the words veritably spill and tumble out like a torrent. His manner is consistent, however: he is reticent, shy. He still blends into crowds and often goes unnoticed by many."[49]

In a recent scholarly study of Chávez, historians Griswold del Castillo and Garcia also noticed his consistency across time and place:

> Chávez's speaking has changed very little from his CSO days. He was not an emotional speaker. He convinced students to support the union through

his sincerity, humility, and command of the facts about the struggle between the farm workers and the grower. His low-key approach was disarming
in an age of radical and flamboyant rhetoric.[50]

CHÁVEZ'S RHETORICAL TRANSFORMATION OF AUDIENCES

By understanding Chávez's worldview and well-developed plan of
public communication, we understand better his motivation for his un-
ending rhetorical campaign and why he fashioned his message as he did.
To understand his stunning effects on many audiences, however, requires
an explanation of deeper dynamics through which Chávez influenced audiences. In our prior book on Chávez and in articles in the *Southern Communication Journal* (1994 and 1999), *Communication Monographs* (1998),
and the *Howard Journal of Communications* (2000), we have together and
singly laid out a critical approach suitable for discourse that aims to
change an audience's character rather than only to shift opinions or attitudes on issues. Chávez sought, he once noted, to "create a new man"; and
he realized early in his campaign that he must instill a new identity in
many listeners in order for them to act out his demanding agenda.

For farm workers and others to join his cause exposed them to danger,
deprivation, frustration, and long periods of little progress and stinging defeats. This involved nothing less than a new self-definition for many listeners, an identity that featured bravery, perseverance, self-sacrifice, and a
willingness to work tirelessly for justice regardless of physical discomfort
or a lack of material rewards. The new identity sought for Chávez's audiences, a result of reordering personal qualities through which listeners defined themselves, can occur when a rhetor merges first persona (the communicated picture of oneself), second persona (the picture communicated
of the listener or reader, the implied auditor), and substantive message
(themes, argument, explanations). These three components can combine
to facilitate a powerful, synergistic, and deep identification between rhetor
and audience, a connection that clearly occurred between Chávez and his
audiences. The theoretical basis for this transforming process, a basis that
reflects Kenneth Burke's concept of identification rather than the Neo-
Aristotelian notion of persuasion, is laid out in our other writings.

Chávez embodied his message in many ways in his first persona by expressing his ideas in a form, style, and manner fitting for the ideas he ad-
vocated, for his discourse subtly and overtly depicted him as a teacher of
truth, even as he called for listeners and readers to become organizers
whose message must be presented clearly in an effort to carry out God's

will. Thus such common stylistic techniques as clear transitions, signpost sentences, simple forecasts, and abundant repetition, restatement, and rhetorical questions added importantly, albeit subtly, to Chávez's incarnation of his substantive themes, arguments, and appeals. Moreover, Chávez's life and appearance contributed to a persona appropriate for his ideas. Chávez, as labor historian Cletus E. Daniel put it, "more than any other labor leader of his time, and perhaps in the whole history of American labor, . . . leads a union that is an extension of his own values, experience, and personality."[51] Adding to the synergy unleashed by the merger of man and message, his second persona created a mold into which audiences could easily fit if they identified with Chávez. As we concluded in *The Rhetorical Career of César Chávez,*

> Chávez redefined often-fearful farm workers so that they could act out their courage, dignity, idealism, dedication, and willingness to work hard and sacrifice for their cause without expectation of appreciation or material gain. In turn, these reconstituted farm workers would themselves become rhetors who embodied their message as they educated, persuaded, and at times reconstituted audiences. Chávez lifted the character of audiences and others to sacrifice for and serve in a just cause as they became unpaid organizers and workers in his movement. And he liberated in the general public its nascent generosity of spirit, belief in ideals, and commitment to justice, motivating in it allegiance to his boycott and support in various other ways.[52]

The stage was now set for the consuming drama of César Chávez's life. He settled in Delano in 1962 to begin organizing farm workers, knowing that all earlier attempts had been soundly defeated by agribusiness. Most observers would have rated his chances for success somewhere between zero and nearly impossible. He himself had witnessed the failures firsthand during his years as a migrant. Multiplying his problems, farm workers lacked money, often spoke little or no English, and were illiterate. As migrants, they moved about frequently and thus were not easily mobilized. Yet, Chávez also understood that Mexican Americans had a history of joining unions like the United Auto Workers (UAW); he reasoned that if they could join the UAW they would join his union.

On the surface it appeared that the shy and soft-spoken Chávez was the wrong person, in the wrong place, at the wrong time against the wrong opponent. As we demonstrated in *The Rhetorical Career of César Chávez* and in the foregoing pages, however, a search beneath the surface reveals a far different picture. Chávez was an experienced and skilled organizer well prepared for his daunting task. He understood firsthand the world and life of his primary audience and would relate well to these listeners and readers; and he possessed an ideal worldview that would provide necessary motivation to sustain and energize him in the discouraging times sure to follow, that would direct him to the perfect set of rhetorical strategies and elements for reaching his interrelated rhetorical and career goals. Moreover, he had identified the deep rhetorical processes that produced the changes in audiences that his goals required, and he had developed a rhetorical profile necessary to tap into these processes. He would need all of this preparation and each of his qualities on the treacherous road ahead, for as he confessed, "What I didn't know was that we would go through hell because it was all but an impossible task."[53]

As you read Chávez's texts that we have compiled in this book, consider not only their content, important though that content is to the history of the man, movement, and period. Remember that César Chávez's striking successes as a leader rested largely on his ability to reach and move his audiences; his extraordinarily demanding and extensive lifelong rhetorical campaign documents his own commitment to rhetorical discourse as the primary means to his lofty, seemingly "impossible," goals. Thus, we invite you to study the surface and deeper interlocking elements of Chávez's rhetorical profile, a profile he consciously constructed to create rhetorically the "new men and women" whom he saw as indispensable to the UFW's success. These coworkers would identify with Chávez, absorbing many of his characteristics that were necessary for enacting his cause. In your reading, then, you might note how Chávez's abundant use, even apparent overuse, of such everyday rhetorical devices as restatement, rhetorical question, forecast, and concrete evidence took on vital importance by helping Chávez to embody his substantive themes and arguments. He was a teacher whose righteous case he believed to be divinely ordained to triumph if presented clearly, widely, and convincingly, and that is what he told audiences. To ensure ultimate victory regardless of obstacles, farm workers and their supporters had only to keep and act out their faith in an almighty God and in clearly presented ideas and well-supported arguments. Through his embodiment of his substantive message, fused synergistically with his second persona, he strove for an identification that could reformulate the identity of many of his audiences. In the pages to follow, we invite you to become rhetorical analysts and communication critics, to share a bit of César Chávez's own deep commitment to things rhetorical.

THE WORDS OF CÉSAR CHÁVEZ

▰▰▰▰▰▰

CHAPTER 1

Finding the Message and Creating the Union, 1962–70

In 1962, when César Chávez resigned from his position with the Community Services Organization (CSO) and moved his family to Delano, he undertook the enormous task of organizing a seemingly powerless group of migrant workers into a union strong enough to match the power of growers. Through his extensive, incessant, and exhausting rhetorical campaign he would convince farm workers and potential union supporters that an effective organization could be created and sustained—but only if they joined his crusade, if they gave of themselves even as he so obviously was giving of himself. He chose Delano largely because he had relatives in the area who could provide necessary support and because many workers lived in that region year-round doing the labor required to tend grapes. Chávez sought to transform this contingent of resident workers into the core membership of the union. Once that core was created, he could turn to recruiting migrant farm workers and to building economic, political, and moral support among crucial segments of the general public.

One of Chávez's primary goals in this first phase of his campaign was to teach audiences about the history of agriculture and farm worker unions in California. Once they learned of past failures, he could explain the need for unions in the present. He thus had to educate workers on the value of unions, show members of other unions the plight of farm workers and ask for their help in organizing the United Farm Workers union, and inform the general public about the importance of farm worker unions while appealing for financial and moral assistance in building and maintaining his labor organization. Because farm workers were often unseen or ignored, he would make them visible—to place them in the public's attention and keep them there. In these early years he alternated his time between working in the fields, speaking in local workers' homes and meetings, and traveling the country to spread his message and find friends for his fledgling labor organization.

Chávez's rhetorical campaign featured speeches, writings, personal conversations, and other forms of expression such as pickets, marches, and fasts.[1] In the beginning he was the sole voice; eventually he recruited other effective organizers, many of whom had worked in the CSO and some of whom, like Dolores Huerta and Gilbert Padilla, would become leaders in his new union.

His first step in organizing was to learn the physical makeup of the region and begin talking with workers. Soon after locating in Delano, he recalled: "I drew a map of all of the towns between Arvin and Stockton—eighty-six of them, including farming camps—and decided to hit them all to get a small nucleus of people working in each. For six months I traveled around, planting an idea."[2] When he saw workers in the fields, he approached them to assess their interest in joining a union. Meanwhile, with the help of his wife and others he passed out eighty thousand questionnaires to potential union members. The answers helped him to understand the needs of workers, to formulate goals for the union, to gather facts and ideas useful in rhetorically identifying with workers, and to invent potent appeals in his rhetorical discourse.

The heart of his early organizing consisted mainly of one-to-one discussions and meetings in the homes of workers, tactics learned in the CSO. In these presentations he did not talk about a union but about a vaguely defined organization of like-minded individuals. It was premature to discuss unions, for local farm workers knew well the long history of defeats—often violent defeats—attached to all prior efforts to unionize local farm workers.

Chávez quickly convinced enough followers to form an official union. In September of 1962, 232 people met in Fresno to establish the National Farm Workers Association (NFWA). The group would change its name several times, finally settling on the United Farm Workers (UFW). Chávez was named president, Gil Padilla and Dolores Huerta vice presidents. Drawing upon insights gained in the CSO, the young president knew the importance of offering services for members. The union would establish a credit union, cooperative food store, drugstore and service station, burial insurance, and a newspaper, and it provided its members with legal counseling and grievance committees.

From the onset Chávez realized the value of outside help. Once in Delano he met with leaders of religious groups and quickly gained support from members of the California Migrant Ministry, a mainly Protestant group. He was puzzled that the Catholic Church had no programs to assist the mainly Catholic workers. Eventually, the church did assign priests to work with the UFW. During this period his entreaties to the Catholic Church constituted a standard appeal in his public discourse.

Convinced that prior unions had failed by calling strikes before acquiring sufficient power, Chávez sought to avoid strikes until his organization had sufficient members and influence. Although he would have preferred to wait longer, a propitious set of circumstances among the rose workers in McFarland, California, in May of 1965 compelled Chávez to lead his maiden strike. The rose workers successfully won a pay increase but returned to work without a union contract. Chávez subsequently directed a series of small strikes to perfect the union's tactics in preparation for later and larger strikes.

Unexpected events interrupted Chávez's timetable for his first major effort. It all began in Delano on September 8, 1965, when two thousand Filipino members of the Agricultural Workers Organizing Committee (AWOC) left their jobs in protest over receiving lower salaries than braceros, the temporary workers from Mexico. The head of AWOC, Larry Itiong, asked Chávez and the UFW to join the strike against grape growers, and Chávez agreed. On December 2, 1965, Chávez announced a boycott against the grapes produced by Schenley industries. The boycott broadened the following year to include all grape producers and continued until the end of the strike. In 1966 the two unions combined into one, the United Farm Workers, and affiliated with the AFL-CIO. The grape strike would last for five years and be one of the longest and most bitter in American labor history. It featured UFW marches and boycotts, a twenty-five-day fast by Chávez, and a host of innovative tactics introduced by Chávez, including mobile picket lines and the persuasive performances of El Teatro Campesino, a UFW theater group.

The union appeared hopelessly overmatched by its foe. In the beginning, the growers' response was typical of corporate organizations under attack: they denied that there was a strike, claiming that their farm workers were happy with their jobs and pay and they belittled Chávez and his union, calling them outsiders, troublemakers, and Communists. It is easy to see why the growers had crushed all prior strikes. They had powerful allies in the courts, the press, the churches, and even the local police forces who harassed the strikers. Large professional organizations that represented the growers united against the strikers, contributing huge financial resources and providing, among other things, slick, professional public relations. In addition other pro-grower groups in the farming communities joined the fray. In contrast, Chávez and the workers found few allies, the California Migrant Ministry being a rare exception. Most of their support came from individuals not affiliated with farming—college students, liberals in urban areas, and workers in industrial unions like the United Auto Workers.

Like everyone else, the growers underestimated Chávez's rhetorical capabilities to sustain and even intensify the energy and solidarity of the strike. In addition to his own indefatigable speaking, and to a lesser extent his writing and other communication, he originated a set of innovative and effective tactics for spreading his message: roving pickets to communicate with workers in the fields, new and effective slogans and chants, and the mobilization of artists, including the union's theater group, El Teatro Campesino.

Across the many forms and formats of his discourse, Chávez employed symbols of the Catholic Church and Mexican American culture. At the suggestion of some women strikers, for example, he and his brother built a small alter in the back of a station wagon. They parked the vehicle outside the entrance to a ranch where they were having a particularly difficult time gaining access to workers. The union announced on a Spanish-language radio station that an around-the-clock vigil would be held followed by a mass. Many workers left the ranch to attend the mass; they were then recruited by Chávez and the strikers.

Chávez also appropriated Catholic traditions from Mexico in the UFW's twenty-one day, 250-mile protest march from Delano to Sacramento in 1966. Judith Dunbar described Chávez's speaking during that march:

> At speech time, many cried out for "César"; the zealot in many of us wanted a king. César Chávez took the platform—shyly, briefly, but with authority. No long speeches; no demagoguery. No hero's uniform. Here was a worker. He refused to be lionized. His strength was in simplicity, his power in humility, and his spirit rang true.[3]

At the end of the march, the workers entered Sacramento. Dunbar compared Chávez's actions to Christ's actions in the Bible:

> It echoed the spirit of another king, at another entry into a capital full of factions, in what we now call Eastertime. Here was an authentic, not a destructive meeting of religious and political: each gave both critique and life to the other. This march put protest in the context of pilgrimage, the struggle for justice in the context of penitence.[4]

The march took the form of a pilgrimage, a powerful tradition in the Spanish-speaking world. The image of farm workers marching through the central valley illustrated the union's lack of fear of the growers. It issued an open challenge to the groups in power and brought many workers and potential followers into the union while intensifying the commitment of participants in the march. Chávez's Catholic beliefs were also frequently manifested in religious pictures and statues and in the paintings hung on the wall of his UFW office. Of particular importance was the Virgin of Guadalupe, a symbol present at virtually every meeting, procession, or march.

Chávez attracted widespread attention in 1968 through his twenty-five day fast to express his concern about potential violence in the union. He consciously employed fasts as part of his rhetorical campaign as well as for spiritual reasons. Daily masses accompanied fasts, stimulating tremendous public interest and uniting union members. (See chapter 5 for a full discussion of the fast.) A short speech written by the weakened Chávez and read by Jim Drake was part of the widely and internationally reported celebration ending the fast.

During the grape strike, Chávez created his most enduring tactic, the boycott. In 1965, believing that the union could influence growers through economic pressure, he directed his first boycott. Grapes produced by Schenley Industries were the target. After achieving a victory over Schenley he announced a second boycott, this one against the DiGiorgio Corporation. When other grape producers supported DiGiorgio, the boycott was expanded to all producers of grapes.

To broaden the boycott, Chávez sent volunteers to cities throughout the United States. With few resources other than an argument designed to solicit support, many volunteers nevertheless successfully prodded supermarkets into removing grapes from their stores. This initial boycott was successful, demonstrating the power of a tactic that Chávez would use throughout his career.

By 1970 the union had won most of its demands and signed contracts with major grape growers. What had seemed inconceivable and in need of nothing short of a miracle had become reality. The UFW was a certified, legitimate, and growing union of farm workers, and the unlikely persuader who led it had gained national stature and a reputation for charismatic effects on audiences. Both the man and his cause had been assisted by a national social climate marked by concern over injustice to minority groups and by widespread and noisy protests.

In this chapter we include representative texts that contain signature rhetorical elements of Chávez's campaign to educate, inform, persuade, and in some cases reformulate his audiences during this initial period of his lifelong crusade.

Chávez speaking at Bruce Church in September 1970. *Photo by Cris Sanchez. Courtesy Walter P. Reuther Library, Wayne State University*

Early in the grape strike Chávez took his message directly to the public. In December of 1965, for example, at a meeting of the Student Nonviolent Coordinating Committee (SNCC) in Fresno, he outlined the early history of the United Farm Workers and laid out his views on community and labor organizing. A community organizer goes into a local community with the goal of discovering issues of importance to people in the community and attempts to identify leaders. The organizing is done in settings such as churches or community centers that already have identifiable communities of people. The organizer does not impose issues on the community but allows them to emerge. The goal is to form organizations that function independently of the organizer. Labor organizing, in contrast, has specific goals that deal with union contracts, wages, and working conditions. The organizer has those goals in mind from the outset and is successful when these goals have been met.[5]

This speech delivered in Fresno yields insights into Chávez's thoughts and ideas at the point where the union gambled its future on a single strike (the initial grape stike). It also illustrates the rhetorical elements used to teach the lessons he had learned about organizing, and it shows many elements of the rhetorical profile through which he persuaded and reconstituted listeners who would then energetically and doggedly support his agenda.

In 1966 Chávez organized the famous march from Delano to Sacramento. It began on March 17 and ended on April 10, Easter Sunday, with a rally outside the state capitol. Before the march Chávez issued the "Sacramento March Letter" to teach the meaning of the march to the public as well as to workers. During the march helpers read and distributed his famous Plan of Delano and distributed written copies in English and Spanish. The Plan, an adaptation of a well-known form of discourse traditionally used in Mexico, borrowed from the Plan of Ayala issued by Emiliano Zapata in Mexico in 1911. At each stop on the march the plan was read aloud at an evening rally; it would be presented orally or in print in many other locations, at many other times, to many other audiences. Few rhetorical documents have been more powerful for Mexican Americans.[6]

During the years covered in this chapter Chávez spoke often to members of other unions and to religious groups. Both kinds of organizations, in his view, were essential for his campaign, both containing audiences to inform, persuade, and reconstitute. In April of 1967 he addressed members of the United Auto Workers (UAW), chronicling the history of farm labor in California, the first attempts to organize unions among farm laborers, the early history of the UFW, and the relationship between the UFW and the UAW. In 1968 at an interfaith luncheon in New York City he outlined the history of labor in California, the place of religious organizations in helping farm workers, and the demands the workers were making during the strike.

By 1969 the grape strike had lasted for four years. The polarized sides had found little upon which they could agree. Chávez attempted to overcome the gap by reaching out to growers in his "Good Friday Letter," an invitation for understanding the plight of farm workers. The letter, which appeared in both the *Christian Century* and *National Catholic Reporter,* captured the essence of Chávez's quest to prick the country's moral conscience.[7] Although his entreaty was rejected, the fundamental message and rhetorical profile that surfaced in the letter would remain consistent and win him many victories.

On April 16, 1969, he testified about the deadly effects of pesticides on farm workers. He graphically described the numbers of workers being injured and the long-term harm of the poisoning. This concern about pesticides would be a common theme throughout the years that Chávez led his union.

These speeches and writings reflect Chávez's thinking and actions during the early years of the union. In their pages lies the fundamental rhetorical profile that would bring him so many successes through his career. Many of his ideas, themes, and rhetorical qualities would remain virtually unchanged in the more than thirty years that he led the union; others would evolve as he faced new circumstances and challenges and matured as a rhetor.

César Chávez Talks About Organizing and About the History of the NFWA, December 1965

This is a transcription of an impromptu speech delivered to a statewide meeting of the California Students Nonviolent Coordinating Committee (SNCC) in Fresno in November of 1965. The text was printed in SNCC's journal, *Movement*, December 1965, 3–6 and reprinted as "César Chávez: Grass-Roots Organizer," in *Aztecas Del Norte: The Chicanos of Aztlán,* edited by Jack D. Forbes (Greenwhich, Conn.: Fawcett, 1973).

I have been asked to discuss some of my thoughts on community organizing. Labor organizing, as I know it, has a lot of community organizing in it. When you read of labor organizing in this country you can say there is a point where labor "is organized." But in community organizing there never is a point where you can say "it is organized."

In community organizing you need a continuous program that meets the needs of the people in the organization. I have seen many groups attempt community organization and many have failed. The biggest reason for this is that there is a big emphasis on meetings and discussion and writing up programs and not on working with the people. Many organizers get lost in the shuffle of going to meetings, and somehow those who are being organized are lost. Too often we see as a remedy to this, people suggesting that you should have a survey or a study made.

Anyone who has done any community organizing would agree with me that you can't have a program until you have the people organized. I don't mean you have to wait until you're fully organized, but how can you write a program without the participation of those you are trying to organize?

Community organization is very difficult. You can't put it in the freezer for a couple of years and then thaw it out and you're in business again. Or even a month. Community organization can disintegrate right from under you. This is why we see so many other kinds of groups—church and labor—and so few community organizations formed.

There are a lot of different ideas of what community organization is. When I think of a community, I think not of Fresno, but of Negroes or Mexican Americans or poor workers.

BUILDING POWER

Anyone who thinks they can organize a community and then join with the power structure is in for an awful surprise. And a disappointment because things don't happen that way. When you speak of community organization you are also speaking, really, of power. If you haven't the power to do things you're not going to do anything. Some organizers I know say, "All I need is a good public relations man." This is a lot of nonsense. The only PR the opposition knows is power, and having the power to strike him where it hurts him, political and economic. You're building power based not on the prestige of your group, but on how many actual bodies you have with you and how many bodies can be united and directed. In many cases community organizations have been started just because there was money available to have them started. This is another real problem in getting something permanent.

MONEY

I was in CSO for many years. In some ways we were successful, but in one of the most important aspects we were a complete failure, and this was in getting the group to generate its own finances so it becomes permanent. I remember many times stopping organizing so we could go organize another part of the community to raise money. In most cases when you get money, though this varies in degree, you have some strings attached. We got a lot of money for CSO and we made very clear to the donors that there could be no strings attached.

But there's always one string attached—that is when people give money, they expect miracles. Then your staff or Executive Board starts compromising between a well-thought-out long-range program and something that will show immediate progress.

WHAT IS AN ORGANIZER?

When there's another problem, people say, "I'm just an organizer." An organizer is an outsider in many cases—there's nothing wrong in that. But then he assumes a sort of special position in that program. If you organize a good group, pretty soon you find yourself hoping, "I wish I had a vote in this outfit."

If you're going to do community organizing, you'll find out in the course of doing your job, some of the good people and some of the bad people invariably get hurt.

Another problem is respectability. If a minority group does "nice" things, like taking a petition to the Mayor, or having tea parties with the PTA, it's going to become respectable. And once you become a respectable group, you're not going to fight anymore. I've had a lot of experience in that. So if your group is going to City Hall or the Police Department and fight with the Police Chief, and someone on your Executive Board is friends with him, you're going to think twice before attacking him.

If an organizer comes looking for appreciation he might as well stay home. He's not going to get any, especially out of a group that's never been organized or had any power before.

In the Association, to get 100 members, we had a heck of a time. When we were over that, some joined. It wasn't because an organizer or an officer told him to join, but because another worker was right beside him in the fields telling him about it. So if you get a small group, they become the organizers. The only way I know is to spend an awful lot of time with each individual—hours and hours— until he understands and you've got him going.

HOW NFWA BEGAN

It was a major decision for me to leave Los Angeles and the CSO. CSO was the only organization I had ever known; it was my whole world. So it was difficult to quit and go out on my own. To go a little further back:

I was working in the fields when CSO came to San Jose. I was in the orchards, apricots and peaches. I talked to their organizer, Fred Ross, and the first thing I asked him was "How is the CSO going to help the farmworker?" And he told me— if we get strong enough, we're going to build a union. And I said, "That's for me." And of course I had a lot of hatred for the cops and that was one of the main issues of CSO in LA.

And so it was just perfect for me; I was learning a lot of things. But after a while, it was growing too fast, and it was making a name for itself, and it was attracting a lot of people who were not farm workers, but who were semiprofessional and professional Mexican Americans. It developed a verbal commitment to farm workers, but no action, just legislation.

BEST MOTEL IN TOWN

There were other problems. It was unheard of that CSO would meet in a room like this (a meeting room in a low-rent housing project). It had to meet in the best motel in town, very expensive, and it cut off all the farm workers who couldn't afford to be there. The reason given was—we have to build prestige. The politicians have to know who we are; we can't take them to a dump. We have to take them to the best place in town and then we can relate to them about farm workers. I was naive about farm workers. I was naive enough in the beginning to buy that.

So we ended up just with farm workers who had gone to school or who weren't farm workers anymore. They just thought that going to school gave them the right to be leaders—which incidentally isn't the case; I'll debate that with anyone.

OUT OF TOUCH

Pretty soon we developed conflict between the people with problems in the cities, whether to help them or the farm workers. Then somehow we got messed up with programs that meant little or nothing to the worker. For example—legislation. Too remote. The farm worker isn't trained to understand the processes of government, so having a big fight for unemployment insurance or a minimum wage [he or she] had no idea how laws were made.

We'd constantly get into situations where we'd explain about legislation and a guy would get up in the back and say, "I've been a farm worker all my life. This is a lot of nonsense. Let's go directly to the President." Or—"The Governor should issue a statement saying we should get paid more." And we'd have to explain that the Governor couldn't do that; and we lost him.

Or, when the officers of CSO were semiprofessional or professional it became a problem of communicating with the workers. In most cases the leadership had more to lose than the workers; they'd say, "We should fight, but we should be moderate."

SPLIT

We couldn't get them to organize a union—they felt that farm workers were outside the jurisdiction of CSO—it was a "labor" problem. Some of us in the movement felt the only way to get it was to force the issue and if we lost move out and create a group that would serve only farm workers. We felt if we had nothing but farm workers in their own group a lot of ills we had known in CSO would not be present.

So in April 1962 I moved out of LA and came down to Delano. A lot of people have asked me—why Delano, and the answer is simple, I had no money. My wife's family lived there, and I have a brother [in Delano]. And I thought if things go very bad we can always go and have a meal there. Any place in the Valley would have made no difference.

I had some ideas of what should be done. No great plans; just that it would take an awful lot of work and also that it was a gamble. If I can't organize them to a point where they can carry on their own group then I'm finished, I can't do it, I'd move on and do something else.

I went around for about eleven months, and I went to about eighty-seven communities and labor camps and in each place I'd find a few people who were committed to doing something; something had happened in their lives and they were ready for it. So we went around to the towns, played the percentages, and came off with a group.

FIRST MEETING

We had a convention here in Fresno, the first membership meeting, to set up a union—about 230 people from as many as 65 places. We knew the hardest thing would be to put across a program that would make them want to pay the $3.50 (monthly dues), because we were dependent on that. I felt that organizing couldn't be done on outside money.

We had signed up about 1,100 people. The first month 211 paid. At the end of three months we had 10 people paying. Talk about being scared! But we went back and kept at it. By this time Dolores (Huerta) was helping me up in the northern part of the Valley, and I was getting help from Gilbert Padilla, both of whom are Vice Presidents now. Gradually the membership was increasing.

At the end of six months we were up to about two hundred members. Instead of going all over the Valley as I did at first, I started staying in one place long enough for them to get in touch with me if they wanted to. We put a lot of emphasis on the people getting members.

HOUSE MEETINGS

We had hundreds of house meetings. Sometimes two or three would come, sometimes none. Sometimes even the family that called the house meeting would not be there.

I wasn't trying to prove anything to a board or a grant. I don't think it would have worked. In the first place, I had to get the dues in order to eat. I suspect some of the members were paying dues because they felt sorry for me.

A guy who's paid his dues for a year or three years has a stake in the Association. In CSO if I was making a report, and there were five people in the room and I mentioned four of them, the fifth would take off—very sensitive. We never got any arguments, any debate in CSO. Here there are a lot of questions about how the money is spent. It should be that way.

At the beginning of the strike we had $85 in the treasury. We had the problem of people going out on strike and having no way to support them. So we had a big drive to get workers to go outside the area to work so they wouldn't be strike-breakers.

ROLE OF ORGANIZER

The organizer has to work more than anyone else in that group. Almost no one in a group is totally committed. And in the initial part of the movement there's the fear that when the organizer leaves, the movement will collapse. So you have to be able to say, I'm not going to be here a year, or six months, but an awful long time—until when they get rid of me they'll have leaders to do it themselves.

Sacramento March Letter, March 1966

This letter was reprinted in Winthrop Yinger, *César Chávez: The Rhetoric of Nonviolence* (Hicksville, N.Y.: Exposition, 1975), 106–107.

In the "March from Delano to Sacramento" there is a meeting of cultures and traditions; the centuries-old religious tradition of Spanish culture conjoins with the very contemporary cultural syndromes of "demonstration" springing from the spontaneity of the poor, the downtrodden, the rejected, the discriminated-against baring visibly their need and demand for equality and freedom.

In every religious orientated culture "the pilgrimage" has had a place, a trip made with sacrifice and hardship as an expression of penance and of commitment—and often involving a petition to the patron of the pilgrimage for some sincerely sought benefit of body or soul. Pilgrimage has not passed from Mexican culture. Daily at any of the major shrines of the country, and in particular at the Basilica of the Lady of Guadalupe there arrive pilgrims from all points— some of whom may have long since walked-out the pieces of rubber tire that once served them as soles, and many of whom will walk on their knees the last mile or so of the pilgrimage. Many of the "pilgrims" of Delano will have walked such pilgrimages themselves in their lives—perhaps as very small children even; and cling to the memory of the day-long, marches, the camps at night, streams forded, hills climbed, the sacral aura of the sanctuary and the "fiesta" that followed.

But throughout the Spanish speaking world there is another tradition that touches the present march, that of the Lenten penitential processions, where the penitentes would march through the streets, often in sack cloth and ashes, some even carrying crosses as a sign of penance for their sins, and as a plea for the mercy of God. The penitential procession is also in the blood of the Mexican American, and the Delano march will therefore be one of penance—public penance for the sins of the strikers, their own personal sins as well as their yielding perhaps to feelings of hatred and revenge in the strike itself. They hope by the march to set themselves at peace with the Lord, so that the justice of their cause will be purified of all lesser motivation.

These two great traditions of a great people meet in the Mexican American with the belief that Delano is his "cause," his great demand for justice, freedom, and respect from a predominantly foreign cultural community in a land where he was first. The revolutions of Mexico were primarily uprisings of the poor, fighting for bread and for dignity. The Mexican American is also a child of the revolution.

Pilgrimage, penance and revolution. The pilgrimage from Delano to Sacramento has strong religio-cultural overtones. But it is also the pilgrimage of a cultural minority who have suffered from a hostile environment, and a minority who means business.

CÉSAR CHÁVEZ
GENERAL DIRECTOR, NFWA
MARCH, 1966

The Plan of Delano

The Plan of Delano was published in the union's newspaper, *El Malcriado,* March 17, 1966, 11–14. It was reprinted in *The Chicanos,* edited by Gilberto López y Rivas (New York: Monthly Review Press, 1974, 107–10).

PLAN for the liberation of the Farm Workers associated with the Delano Grape Strike in the State of California, seeking social justice in farm labor with those reforms that they believe necessary for their well-being as workers in these United States.

We the undersigned, gathered in Pilgrimage to the capital of the State in Sacramento in penance for all the failings of Farm Workers, as free and sovereign men, do solemnly declare before the civilized world which judges our actions, and before the nation to which we belong, the propositions we have formulated to end the injustice that oppresses us.

We are conscious of the historical significance of our Pilgrimage. It is clearly evident that our path travels through a valley well known to all Mexican farm workers. We know all of these towns of Delano, Madera, Fresno, Modesto, Stockton and Sacramento, because along this very same road, in this very same valley, the Mexican race has sacrificed itself for the last hundred years. Our sweat and our blood have fallen on this land to make other men rich. This Pilgrimage is a witness to the suffering we have seen for generations.

The Penance we accept symbolizes the suffering we shall have in order to bring justice to these same towns, to this same valley. The Pilgrimage we make symbolizes the long historical road we have traveled in this valley alone, and the long road we have yet to travel, with much penance, in order to bring about the Revolution we need, and for which we present the propositions in the following PLAN:

> **1.** This is the beginning of a social movement in fact and not in pronouncements. We seek our basic, God-given rights as human beings. Because we have suffered—and are not afraid to suffer—in order to survive. We are ready to give up everything, even our lives in our fight for social justice. We shall do it without violence because that is our destiny. To the ranchers, and to all those who oppose us, we say, in the words of Benito Juarez, "EL RESPETO AL DERECHO AJENO ES LA PAZ."

2. We seek the support of all political groups and protection of the government, which is also our government, in our struggle. For too many years we have been treated like the lowest of the low. Our wages and working conditions have been determined from above, because irresponsible legislators who could have helped us, have supported the rancher's argument that the plight of the Farm Worker was a "special case." They saw the obvious effects of an unjust system, starvation wages, contractors, day hauls, forced migration, sickness, illiteracy, camps and sub-human living conditions, and acted is if they were irremediable causes. The farm worker has been abandoned to his own fate—without representation, without power—subject to mercy and caprice of the rancher. We are tired of words, of betrayals, of indifference. To the politicians we say that the years are gone when the farm worker said nothing and did nothing to help himself. From this movement shall spring leaders who shall understand us, lead us, be faithful to us, and we shall elect them to represent us. WE SHALL BE HEARD.

3. We seek, and have, the support of the Church in what we do. At the head of the Pilgrimage we carry LA VIRGEN DE LA GUADALUPE (the Virgin of Guadalupe) because she is ours, all ours, Patroness of the Mexican people. We also carry the Sacred Cross and the Star of David because we are not sectarians, and because we ask the help and prayers of all religions. All men are brothers—sons of the same God; that is why we say to all men of good will, in the words of Pope Leo XIII, "Everyone's first duty is to protect the workers from the greed of speculators who use human beings as instruments to provide themselves with money. It is neither just nor human to oppress men with excessive work to the point where their minds become enfeebled and their bodies worn out." GOD SHALL NOT ABANDON US.

4. We are suffering. We have suffered, and we are not afraid to suffer in order to win our cause. We have suffered unnumbered ills and crimes in the name of the law of the land. Our men, women, and children have suffered not only the basic brutality of stoop labor, and the most obvious injustices of the system; they have also suffered the desperation of knowing that that system caters to the greed of callous men and not to our needs. Now we will suffer for the purpose of ending the poverty, the misery, and the injustice, with the hope that our children will not be exploited as we have been. They have imposed hungers on us, and now we hunger for justice. We draw our strength from the very despair in which we have been forced to live. WE SHALL ENDURE.

5. We shall unite. We have learned the meaning of UNITY. We know why these United States are just that—united. The strength of the poor is also in union. We know that the poverty of the Mexican or Filipino worker in California is the same as that of all farm workers across the country, the Negroes and poor whites, the Puerto Ricans, Japanese, and Arabians; in short, all of the races that comprise the oppressed minorities of the United States. The majority of the people on our Pilgrimage are of Mexican descent, but the triumph of our race depends on a national association of all farm workers. The ranchers want to keep us divided in order to keep us weak. Many of us have signed individual "work contracts" with the ranchers or contractors, contracts in which they had all the power. These contracts were farces, one more cynical joke at our impotence. That is why we must get together and bargain collectively. We must use the only strength that we have, the force of our numbers. The ranchers are few; we are many. UNITED WE SHALL STAND.

6. We will strike. We shall pursue the REVOLUTION we have proposed. We are sons of the Mexican Revolution, a revolution of the poor seeking bread and justice. Our revolution will not be armed, but we want the existing social order to dissolve; we want a new social order. We are poor, we are humble, and our only choice is to strike in those ranches where we are not treated with the respect we deserve as working men, where our rights as free and sovereign men are not recognized. We do not want the paternalism of the rancher, we do not want the contractor; we do not want charity at the price of our dignity. We want to be equal with all the working men in the nation; we want a just wage, better working conditions, a decent future for our children. To those who oppose us, be they ranchers, police, politicians, or speculators, we say that we are going to continue fighting until we die, or we win. WE SHALL OVERCOME.

Across the San Joaquin Valley, across California, across the entire Southwest of the United States, wherever there are Mexican people, wherever there are farm workers, our movement is spreading like flames across a dry plain. Our PilGRIM-AGE is the MATCH that will light our cause for all farm workers to see what is happening here, so that they may do as we have done. The time has come for the liberation of the poor farm workers.

History is on our side.

MAY THE STRIKE GO ON! VIVA LA CAUSA!

El Plan De Delano: "Peregrinación, Penitencia, Revolución"

PLAN libertador de los hijos campesinos del Estado de California, afiliados a la Huelga de la Uva en Delano que defiende el cumplimiento de la justicia social en el trabajo del campo, con las reformas que han creído convenientemente aumentar en benficio de ellos como trabajadores en los Estados Unidos.

Los que suscribimos, constituidos en Peregrinación a la capital del Estado en Sacramento para hacer Penitencia por todas las faltas de los campesinos como hombres libres y soberanos declaramos solemnemente ante todo el mundo civilizado que nos juzga y ante la Nación a que pertenecemos, los propósitos que hemos formulado para acabar con las injusticias que nos oprimen. También estamos concientes del sentido histórico de nuesta Peregrinación. Se puede ver claramente que el camino de la marcha incluye un valle bien conocido por todos nosotros los mexicanos, y que conocemos todos estos pueblos de Delano, Madera, Fresno, Modesto, Stockton y Sacramento, porque por todo este camino, por todo este valle la raza mexicana se ha sacrificado, ya por casi los cien años. Entonces que nuestro sudor y nuestra sangre han caído en esta tierra para hacer ricos a otros hombres; entonces que esta Peregrinación también es un testigo al sufrimiento que hemos visto ya por varias generaciones, y que la Penitencia que aceptamos también simboliza el sufrimiento que vamos a tener para realizar la justicia en estos mismos pueblos, en este mismo valle; entonces que la Peregrinación representa el largo camino histórico que hemos caminado nomas en este valle, y el largo camino histórico que aún tenemos que caminar con mucha Penitencia para cumplir con esa Revolución que es necésaria, por la cual se quedan determinados los propositos en el siguiente Plan:

1. Este es el comienzo de un movimiento social de hechos y no de pronunciamientos. Luchamos por nuestros derechos humanos, como criaturas de Dios. Porque hemos sufrido—y estamos dispuestos hasta morir por nuesta causa que es la justicia social. Lo vamos hacer sin violencia porque ese es nuestro destino. A los rancheros, y a aquellos que se nos oponen, les decimos como dijo Benito Juárez, "EL RESPETO AL DERECHO AJENO ES LA PAZ."

2. Pedimos el apoyo de todos los grupos políticos, y la protección del gobierno, que es también nuestro gobierno, en nuestra justa causa. Por demasiados años se nos ha tratado de lo más bajo. Nuestros sueldos y condiciónes de trabajo han sido determinados desde arriba porque demasiados legisladores irresponsables, quienes pudieran habernos ayudado, han apoyado a los rancheros en su argumento de que la miseria del campesino es un "caso especial." Las injusticias mas patentes del sistema, los sueldos de hambre, los contratistas, los trabajos migratorios, los campos y viviendas miserables, las enfermedades, la ignorancia, etc., fueron tratados como causas irreparables. El campesino ha sido abandonado a su suerte—sin representación y sin poder—a la merced y capricho del ranchero. Estamos cansados de palabras, de traiciones, de indiferencia. A los políticos les decimos que ya se acabaron los años cuando el campesino no decía ni nada para levantarse. De este movimiento brotarán los líderes que nos comprenden, nos guien, nos sean

fieles, y a los cuales eligiremos a los puestos políticos de la nación. NOS ES-
CUCHARÁN!

3. Pedimos y tenemos el apoyo de la Iglesia en lo que hacemos. En frente
de la Peregrinación llevamos a la Virgen de Guadalupe porque ella es nuestra, toda nuestra, REINA DE LOS MEXICANOS. También llevamos la Santa
Cruz y la Estrella de David porque no somos sectarios, y porque pedimos la
ayuda y las oraciones de todas las religiones. Todos los hombres son hermanos, hijos del mismo Dios, por eso les decimos a todos los hombres de
buena voluntad, en las palabras del Papa Leo XIII, "El primer deber de todos
es el de proteger a los trabajadores de las avaricias de los especuladores,
quienes usan a los seres humanos como simples instrumentos para hacer
dinero. No es ni justo pero ni humano oprimir a los hombres con trabajo ex-
cesivo a tal grado que sus mentes se embrutezcan y sus cuerpos se gasten."
DIOS NO NOS HA DE ABANDONAR!

4. Estamos sufriendo, hemos sufrido y no nos da miedo sufrir aún mas
para ganar nuestra CAUSA. Hemos sufrido males e injusticias en el nombre
de la ley. Nuestros hombres, mujeres y niños, han sufrido no solo las brutali-
dades del trabajo en los files y las injusticias mas patentes del sistema, sino
también la desesperación de saber que el sistema benefica la avaricia de
hombres sin conciencia y no a nosotros. Se nos hace que ahora sufriremos
con el próposito de acabar con la pobreza, la miseria, la injusticia, con la es-
peranza de que nuestros hijos no sean explotados como hemos sido. Nos han
impuesto el hambre, ahora sentimos el hambre por la justicia. Nuestra
fuerza brota de la misma desesperación en que vivimos. BASTA!

5. Nos uniremos. Hemos aprendido el sentido de la UNIDAD, sabemos el
porqué de la unidad de los Estados Unidos—la fuerza de los pobres también
está en la unión. Ya sabemos que la pobreza del trabajador mexicano o filipino en California es igual a la de todos los otros campesinos en la Nación,
hay blancos y negros, portoriqueños, japoneses, y árabes, en fin, todas las
razas que forman la minorias oprimidas en los Estados Unidos. La mayor
parte de nosotros en esta Peregrinación somos mexicanos, pero el triunfo de
nuestra raza depende en la asociación de todos los campesinos de la Nación.
Los rancheros nos quieren divididos para tenernos débiles. Muchos de
nosotros hemos firmado contratos de trabajo individuales con los rancheros
o los contratistas, en los cuales ellos tenían todo el poder. Estos contratos
eran farsas, una burla mas a nuestra impotencia. Por eso nos tenemos que
juntar en convenios colectivos para realizar la única fuerza que tenemos, la
fuerza do los numeros; los rancheros son pocos, nosotros somos muchos.
UNIDOS NOS LEVANTAMOS!

6. Tendremos Huelgas. Cumpliremos nuestro proposito de hacer una REV-
OLUCIóN. Somos hijos de la Revolución Mexicana, que fuera una revolución

de los pobres buscando pan y justicia. Nuestra revolución no será armada, pero queremos que el orden que hoy existe se deshaga y que venga un neuvo orden social. Somos pobres, somos humildes, nuestro único recurso es salirnos en huelga de todos los ranchos donde no se nos trata con el respeto que merecemos como hombres trabajadores y no se reconocen nuestros derechos como hombres libres y soberanos. No queremos el paternalismo del patroncito, no queremos el contratista, no queremos caridades a costo de nuestra dignidad. Queremos igualdad con todos los trabajadores de la Nación, queremos sueldos justos, mejores condiciones de trabajo, un porvenir decente para nuestros hijos. A los que se nos oponen, sean rancheros, contratistas, policias, políticos, o interesados, les decimos que vamos a seguir hasta morir o vencer. NOSTROS VENCEREMOS.

Ahora por todo el Valle de San Joaquín, por todo California, por todo el Suroeste de los E.U., por dondequiera que haya raza, por dondequiera que hayan campesinos, nuestro movimiento se va extendiendo como llamas atraves de un llano seco. Nuestra PEREGRINACIóN es la MECHA, para que nuestra causa prenda, para que todos los campresinos vean su luz, vean lo que estamos haciendo aqui y sepan que ellos también lo pueden hacer. Ha llegado la hora de la liberación del pobre campesino.

Así lo dispone la historia. QUE SIGA LA HUELGA!

Chávez Speech at Solidarity House, April 1, 1967

This impromptu speech was delivered at Solidarity House in Lansing, Michigan. An audio tape and transcript are in the United Farm Workers Papers in the Archives of Labor and Urban Affairs, Wayne State University, Detroit, Michigan.

Brother [Walter] Reuther and Friends. I am very happy to be here with you this evening. I'd like to take what time I have to bring to you, at least in part, the story of the strikers in the Delano Area. There is one difficulty in getting up to speak before groups. On one hand, I've had not too much experience and on the other hand I've had some bad experiences with instruments. I've been in jail three times recently as a consequence of the strike and each time I've been in jail because I've been using microphones to talk to scabs in the fields. So every time I get to speak before people and I see these things in front of me, I get somewhat uneasy.

The workers in Delano asked me to be very sure to tell all the members of the U.A.W., Brother Reuther, all of the leadership, how much they sincerely appreciate all of the help that has been given in our efforts to organize in California and Texas. And a little while later I will tell you of some of the specific things that they have done for us. So much help and so many things that I can't begin to tell you everything that has been done for our struggle by the U.A.W. But there are some important things, in my opinion, that should be shared with you.

Have you ever considered land—a lot of land—a lot of free water and a lot of cheap labor. Have you ever considered what this combination can do and is doing in the West? Because of the combination of these three elements, there are growers in California and the western part of this country that are not only rich but are very powerful. These are the growers, these are the people that control and have a say in what legislation is going to be enacted or not going to be enacted especially when it deals with agriculture and with farm labor. And they have been doing this for years. And this is, I suppose, one of the biggest difficulties in organizing workers. It all started seventy or eighty years ago. And it was probably quite by accident that it started this way.

Soon after the railroads had been built, according to history, and there were a lot of Chinese workers that had been laid off the railroads and had gone into the cities of San Francisco and Stockton and Sacramento and other cities waiting for some work, the growers began to develop and use the system which even up to this day they follow. And this is the system of the farm labor contractor. Among the Chinese there were those who were looking ahead and began to recruit workers in San Francisco and bring them into the Valley. We have the same thing even today. But this was the early beginning. Soon after the Chinese had gone to work in the fields and they understood that there was no real future for them, they moved into the cities and began to go into small businesses—restaurants and laundries and so forth.

The growers realizing full well that this was a very good arrangement that they had with the Chinese and wanting to keep that, they went to Japan and made the same arrangement with the Japanese. And after a few years of working, the Japanese began to develop the slow-down, attempts to organize, but they did something else. They went out and bought their own land and they became small growers. And then the growers sent to India for the Indians, but that didn't work out too well. Then they got the Filipino and they worked out very well. And lastly they got the Mexican. The Negro they didn't have to import. He had already been imported many years before. And with the Mexican, we see with the beginning of the Mexican Revolution when thousands of families were fleeing from the conflict there; they came to the States and also were put to work in the fields. And when a lot of people in this group were moving out of agriculture, then they went and devised somehow the infamous bracero program. And here they were able, first of all because of the manpower shortages during the Second World War, they were able to keep this program until up to just a few years ago. The exploitation that these workers suffered is something that is very difficult to understand and quite difficult to explain. But while all of these things were taking place there were attempts to organize workers.

And while we sometimes are not fully satisfied with the American labor movement in their attempts to organize workers, we realize that they have made some very valiant attempts. Back in 1913 in Wheatland, California, the hub of the cotton belt, the pickers had a strike.[8] And as we read history, depending on who writes the history, if it is someone who is partial to labor it is usually called a great and glorious strike that failed, that was called by the I.W.W. [Industrial Workers of the World]. On the other hand, if the history was written by someone who was not so partial to labor, then it was a great and a big and nasty riot. And through the years during the first part of the century these attempts persisted and every time the Union would start in, every time that workers wanted to organize those attempts were broken and they were never able to succeed.

And we in the union, even before we started to organize, wanted to know really everything that was written and talk to everyone available that had been involved in past strikes and to find out why they had failed so often. No victories. We came up with some parallels as we talked to people, as we read what had been written about the strikes and so forth. We saw some parallels. First of all, that the unions in organizing were trying to do two jobs at once. They were trying to organize on the one hand and they were trying to strike at the very same time. And as you know it's a very big job.

Now it is only so because as farm workers we are excluded from protection of the National Labor Relations Act. We can't go to the employer and say we got 30 percent or 50 percent or 100 percent of the workers signed up and we want you to recognize our union. Or we couldn't go to the Board and ask for an election. We can't do either one. We may have a thousand percent signed but and they won't give us that protection. And so while they were trying to strike and organize at the same time, it seemed to us that they were losing that valuable time that must be spent by the organizer to be able to do a real job of developing an understanding, the brotherhood, the solidarity of the workers to be able to stick together. And best of all to be able to understand what the opposition is.

Then, the other problem was that in all the attempts to organize, the ones that we could see, there was the International Union, the C.I.O. [Congress of Industrial Organizations], the A.F.L [American Federation of Labor], and the AFL-CIO[9]—[all] came in with great expectations and with some money. And organizing farm workers takes quite a bit of money—thousands and thousands of dollars. And after they had spent the money, they saw that things were not really going any place, The International Unions had to pull out because they had spent more than what they had intended to spend in the first place. On the attempts of the AFL as we see in some attempts back in the mid-30s, and the CIO had a very large attempt which also failed.

We also saw in examining the failures that in most cases the unions were going out to the fields to organize workers after the workers had revolted. The workers were out on strike—on one of those suicide strikes, and they couldn't put the thing together to hold it, to give it permanence. And we also saw then in most of the reports that the people felt that the union had sold them out and the leaders felt that the people didn't really want a union. And so we had just a number of failures to contend with and we wanted to change that around.

First of all, we were convinced that because of the exclusion from the law and not having that protection, we wanted to convince ourselves that workers really wanted a union this time. They had to show us that they wanted a union, and we had to help them to do that, by their paying for the initial organizing drive. So we began on April 10, 1962, a very small operation called the National Farm Workers Association (NFWA). There was no reference to a union in the name and we were a scab[10] outfit. The AWOC [Agricultural Workers Organizing Committee], under the AFL-CIO, didn't like us at all. We knew that sooner or later we would have to get together with them, but we also knew that we wanted time to try out some ideas we had, basic attempts to see if they would work, and sure enough, as it turned out, now both groups are one and the same. But during those first few years it was a very difficult thing to organize on the one hand and then have to be confronted every time you met someone from the other union and be called a scab. And we saw that workers if they were told what the whole idea was and they were permitted to participate and they were told that the only way that it could be done was that they had to pay for it. When we met, they voted for a dues of $3.50 a month without collective bargaining agreements, without really anything. It was just the idea.

We went out to try to implement the $3.50 a month dues and it was a very difficult thing to do, but we gradually succeeded. And I think if any one thing is said about any success that we've had, the fact that we got people to put up their own money, however little it was, to do the initial organizing was what got them together. Because, you see, they had an investment now. They were coming to the meetings, if for nothing else, but to see what was happening with their money that they were paying. And while they were there, we were taking advantage of educating them.

But it seems to me that one other reason that it was difficult to organize was that for some time back and more so today, people tend to romanticize the poor people. Or romanticize the Negro or the Mexican or anybody who was discriminated against. And we say that to help someone help themselves we have to look at him as a human being. And we cannot romanticize his race or his poverty if we are really going to deal with the problem and to help him as a human being.

So we went along for almost four years and we came to September 1965 when the AWOC called a strike in Delano. Eight days later we called our membership together, we took a vote, and we struck for the same things. We wanted recognition and we wanted a wage increase and a written contract. The growers were paying then from $1.10 to $1.15 an hour. We were demanding $1.40, recognition and a written contract. Most of us in the NFWA had no idea of what a written contract was but my experience in organizing had been strictly, at that point, in community organizing.

In trying to put the union together, when the other union was organizing workers, we felt that they were approaching the organization of farm workers just on those issues that the workers were confronting with their employers and that they weren't doing anything on the community part of it. We wanted to do both things. We wanted to have a community union. We didn't have that name for it at the time, but we wanted first of all to deal with the community problems, get the people together, show them that there is some power in numbers, win some small personal victories, pull all those things together, begin some programs and gradually move that into a union setting, striking and really confronting the employer. And all these four and a half years we had a lot of time to do this. Only once did the press find out what we were doing. Only once did it get through—but for four and a half years no one knew what we were doing except our most immediate friends. And we kept building and building until that September. When we took the vote on September 26, 1965, it was a unanimous vote to strike. We wanted to strike Schenley and the workers said—No, let's strike them all at once. And we struck forty.

We had also read in the many attempts to organize workers that violence had played a large part in suppression of the union. We knew that the moment we struck that justice was going to be about 20 percent for us and 80 percent for the opposition. And we know that because of the violence of which strikers had been accused and convicted, for things that they had never committed. So I asked the workers to take a vote to consider that this strike be a nonviolent strike. And many of them didn't know what a nonviolent strike meant. But many of them did know that there was another group in the country that had been making a lot of progress for human rights and that was also committed to nonviolence, and this was the civil rights movement.

And so we went out that first day to the picket lines, and the moment we hit the picket lines at 5:30 in the morning we began to have reaction from the growers. They had guns and they took shots at us on two or three occasions. They were poor shots and didn't hit us. And in a period of seven days we had fourteen incidents where they actually fired a gun at the strikers. And not even in one case were we able to get the District Attorney to take that case. They wouldn't take it.

When we went on strike there were some very great miscalculations. First of all, we thought we were striking the growers. The strike was only against the growers, and we were convinced that the other forces in the community, at the worst, would probably tend to say that they were neutral or to say that they didn't like the strike but we can't do anything about it. As it turned out we were dead wrong. Within twenty-four hours from the moment that we had hit the picket lines, the City Council had passed a resolution condemning the Red ties. The High School Board and the Elementary School Board had done the same thing. And the Chamber of Commerce did it also with the exception that their statement was a lot more wordy. And three days later when everything seemed to be against us the Church had not yet acted. And we thought, this is the group that is going to be the conciliator. And for the first time as I know it, the first time in the history of Delano, the [Protestant] Ministerial Association agreed to meet with the three priests in the town. They got together and passed a resolution condemning the strike. At that point we were cut off completely. We had no friends in Delano except the workers. We had no money. Our union was so poor that we had only $70.00 in the treasury when the strike started. And we had no way of getting labor support because we were a scab group. We had no way of getting anyone to give us money except some friends that we had in the Church. Immediately when the strike started, I called on the Migrant Ministry. It is a group that had been around California for about forty-years trying to do something for workers, and it was that group that gave us the first $500.00 to use for the strike. And things went very badly for us during the first two or three months. We were having difficulty in letting the rest of the country know about our strike difficulty—raising money—all sorts of difficulties. We were not getting together with the other Union although we stood for the same things. Things looked very bad for us.

At this time the AFL-CIO was having its convention in San Francisco and we were hoping that someone from that convention would come and talk to us, at least be present with us for a short while to show that the great American labor movement was behind us. We didn't know how but we thought if someone would come that we would be able to get some help. Maybe it would scare the growers into signing a contract. On December 15, there were rumors that Walter Reuther was coming to Delano. The City Council thought it was going to be a demonstration so they passed a resolution prohibiting demonstrations and marching on the street. And we had a copy of the resolution delivered by the Chief of Police to my office saying that "this was just passed today and we mean to enforce it."

And so on December 17 Walter Reuther did come to Delano. He arrived at the local airport and there were a lot of people from all over. It seemed that all the farm workers in the Valley had come down to greet him. And we got into our cars and marched over to the local picket line. We were picketing the local railroad yard. We didn't know anything about secondary boycotts and injunctions—we were picketing. And it sounded very strange to us that AWOC wouldn't join us in the picketing, and when they did they would carry our NFWA signs and not their own. And they wouldn't carry their own signs. And we couldn't understand these things.

Well anyway, Walter Reuther came and he got off at the picket line. It was December and it was cold. And he said, "Does this picket line ever march?" And the people said, "No. Yes." And he said, "Well, let's march." And before I could say that we had a regulation against it, he started marching and we followed. And everybody started marching. And the Chief of Police who saw all these people couldn't do anything except to direct traffic for us as we're marching through the streets. That same evening we had one of the largest meetings we had in Delano since the strike had begun and Brother Reuther spoke. People were very happy that he was there and we felt that now that we had some backing, that we were going to do things.

The Mayor of the town, who was also a dentist and who was very much against the strike, came to the hall to hear Walter Reuther, and then he invited him to meet with some of the growers at their homes. But while he was talking, Walter was explaining to us what your Union, those of you who are in the UAW, had gone through. And I began to think that really this wasn't something very different, that if we kept insisting and working and striking that we too might get there. But there was something else very important to us. We were a scab union even then. When he pledged his help, Walter Reuther didn't say that you were going to help the AFL-CIO Union and that we were going to get a little bit or nothing because you happen not to be in the family of labor. He said we are going to give you money and we are going to cut it right down the middle. Now to us this was great recognition and, of course, a lot of help because we needed the money very badly. And from that time a lot of things began to happen.

First of all we had to go down to the other Union office because the money was coming there and we had to go there to pick up our share. And so soon we began to talk to them and became friendly. And we began to see that they were people just like us. They were on strike and wanted to win just as badly as we did. And to make a very long story short, we did merge in August of 1966.

I would like to point out some of the other things because we don't have too much time. You haven't eaten and I haven't eaten. There are some things that I would like to leave with you to give you an idea of what we are going through.

For the first nine days of the strike things were very quiet from the police side. They weren't really harassing us. They were calling us Mr. Chávez and Mr. Garcia and so forth. The first day of the strike seventeen Deputy Sheriffs came to Delano. And the Sergeant, I shall never forget his name, Sergeant Dodd, came and told me that the Sheriff of the County had sent this group of deputies to protect the strikers. I had never been in a strike before and I thought this was really great. And I thanked him kindly. Two days later he called me to an emergency conference. So I went to his office in the morning. Sergeant Dodd was sitting there with three other officers and two police dogs. Sergeant Dodd said, "I want to ask a very special favor of you." And I asked, "What is it?" And he said, "Well, we want to keep our relationship. We want to have a nice clean strike. Would you do me a favor?" And I said, "Yes." "Well, the poor people working in the fields." And I said, "Well, they are strike breakers and we call them worse than that some-time." He said, "Well, I've had a lot of complaints that you are shouting HUELGA (strike) at them and its annoying a lot of them. And if you stop doing this I think it would be a lot of help to all of us."

I called a membership meeting that evening and I asked for permission to do that and for their approval. And the members weren't too happy about it, but they took a vote after our discussion and it was decided that the next day instructions would be given not to shout HUELGA at the people in the fields.

So two or three days later, Sergeant Dodd called me to his office again. He wasn't satisfied because although we had stopped shouting HUELGA we were still calling out "Huelga" in a normal tone of voice to the strikebreakers and they ob-jected to that. By this time I said, "Well, what is your objection to the word. It is only a word." And he said, "Well, first of all, we live in America and English is the official language and we want you to use the English language." And I said, "I un-derstand that." And even then I wasn't aware of what he was trying to do. And I continued, "Yes, but most of the people who are breaking the strike come from Mexico. They are green-carders and they don't understand English. We want them to understand us so we say Huelga." Sergeant Dodd said, "Well, you can't do that. Also, there are rumors here that the only reason that you are using HUELGA is because you want to be best understood by the Communist Party in Latin America." This was just too much for me and I began to argue with him. And after a big argument with him about how I was a citizen and although I wasn't blond I was still an American, and about my rights and the Constitution, the Supreme Court decisions and so forth, he said to me, "You can't convince me. All of the arguments that you have for your work and all the arguments that we have against it: I have an additional argument. That word sounds downright nasty."

So I called the workers and that evening we had another meeting and a great debate, and I asked them not to use *Huelga,* and perhaps coin another word. Let's do something else, because we have a strike to win. The members told me to go back to the picket line.

The next day we went out, forty-four workers including my wife and six or seven ministers. They went out, spaced themselves fifty feet apart and shouted HUELGA at the top of their lungs and sure enough, Sergeant Dodd kept his promise. They arrested every one of them. I got the call in the office that forty-four people were in jail—at the County Jail in Bakersfield and for me to come quickly. I didn't have the money and I didn't quite know what to do. I got in the car and instead of going south where the strikers were I traveled about 300 miles to Berkeley to the campus. I spoke to the students at noon and I said, "Look, what I want is your money—your lunch money because we have forty-four people in jail and we don't have any money to bail them out."

The students gave us $6,600 that afternoon and we went to Bakersfield and bailed the strikers out of jail. We got an attorney. Every single case was dismissed but we spent about $10,000 on that case.

We've had over 150 arrests (some of the strikers have been arrested five times), and we have had only one conviction.

Then the winter came and there was very little activity in Delano. We wanted to keep the movement moving and so we decided to have a pilgrimage from Delano to Sacramento. It was during this pilgrimage, on April 6, that we arrived in Stockton, California, and a telephone call came from a man claiming to be an attorney for Schenley saying that they wanted to settle. It was so unexpected that I thought it was another crank trying to pull my leg so I hung up the phone and started to walk out. The phone rang again and I picked it up. It was the same man. He identified himself. The next day we met in Los Angeles and Schenley gave us a recognition agreement. It was just a very simple document about two-thirds of a letter-sized paper saying that they recognized us and were prepared to give the workers a thirty-five cent an hour across-the-board wage increase. It was some weeks later that I showed this to Paul Schrade of the UAW in Los Angeles, and he told me that in the history of the UAW that they had gotten less than that. They just got a recognition agreement and no wage increase when they won their first battle.

We then moved into the DiGiorgio conflict. And this was open war. By this time we had another union which had come in and was, with the aid of the Company, trying to form a company union. We were having great difficulties and we had just ended the Schenley Boycott and we had people all over the country and we didn't have any money to bring them back. Some were proposing to hitch-hike—others were thinking of U-Drive cars that you can rent.

And it was in San Francisco at this time that I again met Walter Reuther. I told him we were having problems. He asked me what kinds of problems. I told him that we had to get our organizers who were all over the country back to Delano to organize and beat DiGiorgio. Also we don't have any automobiles. We need money to bring our people back and we need automobiles. And the response to that, although I expected something, didn't quite come up to what he said. He said, "Anything you need." Now I've had a lot of friends in my life who have said, "If there's anything you need, César, just call on me." Walter turned to Jack Conway and said, "Jack, work out with him the arrangements." And sure enough, two days later we had seven cars in Delano and in less than twenty-four hours later we had all of our people right back in Delano working on the strike.

This is the kind of support . . . you know that somehow if you persist and if you continue the support that we are going to move forward and build a union.

I have one grave concern about the American Labor Movement, and it comes to me mostly because I don't quite understand it yet. I'm very new in it yet. But it seems to me that the capitalists are at least twenty-five years ahead of most of the unions in this country. Coming from a background of not knowing anything about injunctions and Taft-Hartley and so forth, it seems to me very difficult to understand. For instance, if I am on strike here, how come my brother who belongs to this other union cannot do something in direct action to help me or vice versa. I couldn't understand this. And we went to some of the other unions that were supplying DiGiorgio with materials that were needed for packing, transportation and so forth. And they said they couldn't help us. And we said, if we place our pickets here would you help, and they said they couldn't because they would get in trouble. And it seems to me that by legislation, by agreement, and I guess just by laxity more than anything else that we are permitting the public, all of us, to let the labor movement be divided in such a way that we can't understand it. For instance, why do we have so many laws to control the activities of unions. For instance, if you have a railroader you have one kind of law; if you are industrial workers, you have another kind of law; if you are a public employee, another kind of law; if you are a farm worker, no law at all.

While money is a very important help during a strike as all of us know and other technical advice and help, I don't think we will ever see in America again a general strike. And I know that some real great battles have been won when the workers say that although I am not on strike I'm going to support my brothers. And I don't know where we are going to go. But I'm just frightened that more laws, more restrictions are being placed that the situation will be such that although the workers would really want to help that they wouldn't be able to do it.

We're in a bit of trouble, you know, for not believing that things are as they are. We started picketing the chain of Mayfair Stores in California—three hundred stores. And we picketed for five weeks, and they couldn't remove the Perelli-Minetti Liquors. We told the people, "Don't buy at Mayfair. We don't care about secondary boycotts. We don't want you to buy at Mayfair." And today I received the news that the Board is prepared to get an injunction against us. And what is so very difficult to understand is that, on the one hand, they will enjoin us. They will use the law to enjoin us but, on the other hand, we petitioned the Board three times for an election on the Perelli-Minetti dispute, and they said they couldn't handle it because it is out of their jurisdiction. On the other hand, they are going to enjoin us. It is very difficult to understand.

I am very happy to be with you. We have many fond memories of the UAW. Many fine memories of that fine convention in Long Beach, and we have come to understand that when the UAW says that they are going to help, they mean it.

César Chávez Talks in New York, 1968

This impromptu speech was given to an interfaith lunch for clergy and labor people at Calvary Episcopal Church in Manhattan. The text was published in *Catholic Worker,* June 1968, 3. There is a copy of the transcript in the San Joaquin Valley Farm Workers Collection, Fresno State University Library, Fresno, California.

We are not in the age of miracles, and yet it is surprising that we can attract, and keep, and increase the type of support that is needed to keep our economic struggle going for thirty-three months. It is a struggle in which the poorest of the poor and weakest of the weak are pitted against the strongest of the strong. We are fighting not against the family farm, not against agriculture, but against agribusiness.

When we think of powerful interests, we think of General Motors and other great corporations. But we must turn our minds to the power of the land. It is hard to think that agribusiness could have such tremendous power as it has in California—it is worth $5 billion in our state alone. We must see it as it is, a similar situation to Latin America. The interests can control not only the land but everything that moves, everyone that walks in the land. They control even the actions of the Congress of the United States, even some church groups. Right up to today, some groups in the churches think we are a bunch of Communists. I can take the credit for one of the first ecumenical actions of the churches in the Delano area. Some ministers and priests got together to make a statement denouncing us as outside agitators.

You must have some of the background of agriculture in California to understand what we have been doing. The three basic elements people, poor people, to provide the cheap labor.

We know how the land was acquired. The railroads, the Union Pacific and the Southern Pacific, got large tracts of land, and so did the Bank of America. Who would think that the Bank of America is a grower, but it is.

When the land was reclaimed, water had to be brought in from great distances, even six-hundred to seven-hundred miles. Your taxes are paying for this water supply today. Ours are not, right now, because we are on strike. Back in the early part of this century, legislators began to see that the family farm should be helped. So water was to be supplied to 160-acre farms. This was never enforced. The water went to the larger tracts.

One thing was necessary to the success of the exploitation of California land: workers. The whole cry to get poor people to do the work of the land is a story in itself. When the Southern Pacific and Union Pacific railroads were completed, the Chinese were left without work to do. They went to the cities. The growers who needed workers dealt with contractors who supplied the Chinese. The contractors, who were Chinese themselves, began to sell their brothers for profit.

When the Chinese wanted to own their own land, we had the Chinese Exclusion Act. The Chinese land workers could not own land nor could they marry Caucasian women, so they left agriculture for the cities.

The growers went to Congress for special legislation. Tailor-made immigration laws made it possible for them to recruit labor from Japan. When the Japanese used the slow-down (they had no unions and could not strike) to get better conditions, the growers began to get rid of them. The Japanese could not own land either but began to rent it. In time they began to exploit the laborers.

The growers even went to India for labor, and in the early twenties they were recruiting in the Philippines. When they saw that many Mexicans were leaving their country because of the Revolution, they saw an opportunity. One grower explained that Mexicans were good for California land work because they were short and close to the ground. The growers went further than they ever went before. During World War II, our own government became the recruiter for laborers, "braceros." Even today, as I stand here talking to you, we cannot choke off production on the great farms for one simple reason. The regulations on immigration are not being enforced. Our own government is the biggest strikebreaker against the union. The biggest weapon in the hands of the growers is the "green card" commuter.

You can live in Mexico and come in to work for a season and then go back home. This is not like the regulations covering immigrants from Europe. Hundreds of thousands of people are recruited and put into employers' camps. We cannot reach them there. They are like concentration camps. If the laws were enforced, we would not have to boycott. Employers are not supposed to recruit workers while labor disputes are in progress.

We have to play the game without any rules or procedures. In New York, the rights of unions are enforced, but in our case 95 percent of the workers were signed up with the union, but the producer of table grapes, Giumarra, refused to sit down with us for representation procedures. We were willing to abide by the results of the election. The employers would not talk to us. The only approach left to us is the strike and the boycott.

Now that the growers are hurting, they want an election. Their strikebreakers are inside. Who can win an election this way? This is the predicament we are in. We say to Giumarra, you are not going to get two bites at the same apple. You will have to sign an agreement under pressure. With Edison, we called off the strike and the boycott and we had a contract. Then the land was sold to another grower and we are out of a contract. The day the contract is concluded with Giumarra, that day we take off the pressure.

Even if you have an election—without rules or procedures or protection—what do you have but the law of the jungle? The Board says we have no protection, but when we institute a boycott, the growers go the Board and get protection.

People raise the question: Is this a strike or is it a civil-rights fight?

In California, in Texas, or in the South, any time you strike, it becomes a civil-rights movement. It becomes a civil-rights fight.

The local courts say we have no right to use an amplifier to reach strikebreakers who are a quarter of a mile away. In every case, the growers get an injunction against us immediately. Then we go up to the Appellate Court and up to the Supreme Court. Justice is very expensive sometimes.

We go further. We take advantage of modern technology. I even went up in a plane with two priests to broadcast to the strikebreakers from seven hundred feet up. As soon as we came down, the growers were there to protest.

We have had priests with us before, during and after the strike. The priests of the California Migrant Ministry, Chris Hartmeier and Jim Drake, have been with us from the beginning. They took losses in their church because of the Migrant Ministry and the suffering they accepted was for the migrants and for justice. It was from them that we learned the importance of the support of the church in our struggle. The church is the one group that gives help and never qualifies it or asks for favors.

The priests and ministers do everything from sweeping floors to giving out leaflets. They developed a true worker-priest movement. In the field and in the center, a minister and a worker joined together. The importance of Christian teachings to the worker and to his struggle for dignity becomes clear. Now we have a Franciscan priest working full time with us.

The three most important issues at this time are these.

First, union recognition by the employers. We have certain rights as human beings. Every law is for this recognition—except when it comes to farm workers. Recognizing the union is recognizing us as human beings. Second, an increase in wages is important. Third, in my opinion and in the opinion of the workers, is safety. The whole question of pesticides and insecticides must be met. The men who work to apply these poisons should have protection. Two or three weeks after working with pesticides a man begins to have trouble with his sight. In some cases, he begins to lose his finger-nails. It does not happen immediately. Someday our government will have to undertake real research to determine the effects of these poisons, not only on the workers who are in direct contact with them, but on the consumers. Millions of dollars are spent in the research on the effectiveness of the poisons in destroying pests and insects on plants. This is from the business angle. Millions must also be spent on the effects of the same poisons on human beings.

There is a fine dust that nature puts on grapes. It is called bloom. The contamination from the insecticides remains in this fine dust.

I don't eat grapes because I know about these pesticides. You can stop eating grapes for your safety as well as for the boycott. Even our strongest supporters are afraid of the boycott of table grapes. The key to the success of this boycott is right here in New York. Action is necessary. If you don't do anything, you are permitting the evil. I would suggest that labor take a page in the largest newspaper and make the issue clear to all, and I would suggest that the clergy also take a page. The message of the clergy should be different, bringing out the morality of our struggle, the struggle of good people who are migrants, and therefore the poorest of the poor and the weakest of the weak.

Good Friday Letter, 1969

This letter to E. L. Barr, Jr., President of the California Grape and Tree Fruit League, was originally published in *Christian Century,* April 23, 1969, 539–40. It was reprinted in *Pain and Promise: The Chicano Today,* edited by Edward Simmen (New York: Mentor, 1972), 29–32, and in Winthrop Yinger, *César Chávez: The Rhetoric of Nonviolence* (Hicksville, N.Y.: Exposition, 1975), 106–107.

Dear Mr. Barr:

I am sad to hear about your accusations in the press that our union movement and table grape boycott have been successful because we have used violence and terror tactics. If what you say is true, I have been a failure and should withdraw from the struggle. But you are left with the awesome moral responsibility, before God and man, to come forward with whatever information you have so that corrective action can begin at once.

If for any reason you fail to come forth to substantiate your charges then you must be held responsible for committing violence against us, albeit violence of the tongue. I am convinced that you as a human being did not mean what you said but rather acted hastily under pressure from the public relations firm that has been hired to try to counteract the tremendous moral force of our movement. How many times we ourselves have felt the need to lash out in anger and bitterness.

Today on Good Friday 1969 we remember the life and the sacrifice of Martin Luther King, Jr., who gave himself totally to the non-violent struggle for peace and justice. In his Letter from Birmingham Jail, Dr. King describes better than I could our hopes for the strike and boycott: "Injustice must be exposed, with all the tension its exposure creates, to the light of human conscience and the air of national opinion before it can be cured." For our part I admit that we have seized upon every tactic and strategy consistent with the morality of our cause to expose that injustice and thus to heighten the sensitivity of the American conscience so that farm workers will have without bloodshed their own union and the dignity of bargaining with their agribusiness employers.

By lying about the nature of our movement, Mr. Barr, you are working against non-violent social change. Unwittingly perhaps, you may unleash that other force that our union by discipline and deed, censure and education has fought to avoid; that panacean short cut: that senseless violence that honors no color, class, or neighborhood.

You must understand—I must make you understand—that our membership and the hopes and aspiration of the hundreds of thousands of the poor and dispossessed that have been raised on our account, are above all, human beings, no better no worse than any other cross section of human society; we are not saints because we are poor but by the same measure neither are we immoral. We are men and women who have suffered and endured much and not only because of our abject poverty but because we have been kept poor. The color of our skins, the languages of our cultural and native origins, the lack of formal education, the exclusion from the democratic process, the numbers of our slain in recent wars—all these burdens generation after generation have sought to demoralize us, to break our human spirit. But God knows that we are not beasts of burden, we are not agricultural implements or rented slaves, we are men. And mark this well, Mr. Barr, we are men locked in a death struggle against man's inhumanity to man in the industry that you represent. And this struggle itself gives meaning to our life and ennobles our dying.

As your industry has experienced, our strikers here in Delano and those who represent us throughout the world are well trained for this struggle. They have been under the gun, they have been kicked and beaten and herded by dogs, they have been cursed and ridiculed, they have been stripped and chained and jailed, they have been sprayed with the poisons used in the vineyards. They have been taught not to lie down and die or to flee in shame, but to resist with every ounce of human endurance and spirit. To resist not with retaliation in kind but to overcome with love and compassion, with ingenuity and creativity, with hard work, and longer hours, with stamina and patient tenacity, with truth and public appeal, with friends and allies, with mobility and discipline, with politics and law, and with prayer and fasting. They were not trained in a month or even a year; after all, this new harvest season will mark our fourth full year of strike and even now we continue to plan and prepare for the years to come. Time accomplishes for the poor what money does for the rich.

This is not to pretend that we have everywhere been successful enough or that we have not made mistakes. And while we do not belittle or underestimate our adversaries, for they are the rich and the powerful and possess the land, we are not afraid nor do we cringe from the confrontation. We welcome it! We have planned for it. We know that our cause is just, that history is a story of social revolutions, and that the poor shall inherit the land.

Once again, I appeal to you as the representative of your industry and as a man. I ask you to recognize and bargain with our union before the economic pressure of the boycott and strike takes an irrevocable toll; but if not, I ask you to at least sit down with us to discuss the safeguards necessary to keep our historical struggle free of violence. I make this appeal because as one of the leaders of our nonviolent movement, I know and accept my responsibility for preventing, if possible, the destruction of human life and property. For these reasons and knowing of Gandhi's admonition that fasting is the last resort in place of the sword, during a most critical time in our movement last February 1968 I undertook a 25-day fast. I repeat to you the principle enunciated to the membership at the start of the fast; if to build our union required the deliberate taking of life, either the life of a grower or his child, or the life of a farm worker or his child, then I choose not to see the union built.

Mr. Barr, let me be painfully honest with you. You must understand these things. We advocate militant nonviolence as our means for social revolution and to achieve justice for our people, but we are not blind or deaf to the desperate and moody winds of human frustration, impatience and rage that blow among us. Gandhi himself admitted that if his only choices were cowardice or violence, he would choose violence. Men are not angels and the time and tides wait for no man. Precisely because of these powerful human emotions, we have tried to involve masses of people in their own struggle. Participation and self-determination remain the best experience of freedom; and free men instinctively prefer democratic change and even protect the rights guaranteed to seek it. Only the enslaved in despair have need of violent overthrow.

This letter does not express all that is in my heart, Mr. Barr. But if it says nothing else it says that we do not hate you or rejoice to see your industry destroyed; we hate the agribusiness system that seeks to keep us enslaved and we shall overcome and change it not by retaliation or bloodshed but by a determined non-violent struggle carried on by those masses of farm workers who intend to be free and human.

SINCERELY YOURS,

CÉSAR E. CHÁVEZ

Testimony before the Subcommittee of Labor of the Senate Committee on Labor and Public Welfare, April 16, 1969

This testimony was delivered to a congressional subcommittee. Chávez read the speech from a text. The text is in San Joaquin Valley Farm Workers Collection, Special Collections Department, Fresno State University Library, Fresno, California.

My name is César E. Chávez. I am Director of the United Farm Workers Organizing Committee, AFL-CIO, a labor organization whose office is Post Office Box 130, Delano, California 93215

It is indeed a privilege to address this body, so many of whose members have distinguished themselves over the years by their genuine concern for the welfare of farm workers. For this we are grateful. What has impressed us most is your open mindedness, your desire to explore our problems in depth. Unwilling to believe what you have heard or read about the farm worker, some of you have even come to our valley to see for yourselves and experience at first hand our deprivation, our frustration and our struggle for social justice.

We welcome the decision of this subcommittee to hold hearings on S.8 in order to explore still further the question of whether and in what way farm workers should be covered by the National Labor Relations Act, as amended. The fact that so many Senators have joined in co-sponsoring S.8—and that so many members of the other House have co-sponsored a somewhat similar measure—demonstrates at least that much. No one any longer seriously argues that the issue of labor relations legislation for agriculture can be resolved simply by striking the exclusion of "agricultural laborer" from the definition of "employee" in section 2 (3) of the act.

Perhaps because of certain similarities between our employment situation and that of the building trades, some have been led in their search for the right answer to experiment with the construction industry exemptions of section 8(f). We do resemble the building trades in certain characteristics of our employment, though not in others—a matter I shall return to later.

First, let me say that we too have been learning. In the no-nonsense school of adversity, which we did not choose for ourselves, we are learning how to operate a labor union. The difficulty of our struggle, together with the growing possibility of labor relations legislation for agriculture, has led us to challenge again and again the assumption that coverage under the NLRA would prove the ultimate salvation of the farm worker.

This much at least is certain. His salvation will not be found in sloganeering.

Through long hours of discussion and debate, officers of our union have tried to envision just what real trade union life would be like under various provisions of the NLRA. At times we have wondered whatever led our friends to say we had been denied the "protections" of that act.

Our conclusion is that we do support coverage under the NLRA, but with certain amendments, for not every kind of amendment will really benefit the farm worker.

The need is for amendments that will make strong, effective labor unions realistically possible in agriculture.

I say "make realistically possible" because laws cannot deliver a good union any more than laws can bring an end to poverty. Only people can do that through hard work, sacrifice and dedicated effort.

The end to be achieved, and therefore the starting point of the debate, is the elimination of rural poverty in America. How can the nation, how can the Congress help the farm worker close the yawning gap between his own social and economic condition and that of other wage earners, even those of comparable skill in other industries such as manufacturing and construction?

Answer? Through strong, effective, well-run unions. The road to social justice for the farm worker is the road to unionization. Our cause, our strike against table grapes and our international boycott are all founded upon our deep conviction that the form of collective self-help which is unionization holds far more hope for the farm worker than any other approach, whether public or private. This conviction is what brings spirit, high hope and optimism to everything we do.

No one has said it better than President George Meany of the AFL-CIO: "The United Farm Workers Organizing Committee already has awakened the nation's conscience. Even more important, it has demonstrated to farm workers across the country that they can obtain first class membership through self-organization."

Repressive legislation is not the answer to strikes during harvest time and boycotts of farm products. The farm worker has learned that his sub-human existence is not inevitable. He has awakened to the realization that something better is possible for himself and his family. Laws are not going to stop strikes and boycotts so long as his honest, law-abiding efforts to improve his condition are met with massive, hostile grower resistance. Such resistance will only feed the fires of his own burning frustration. The best insurance against strikes and boycotts lies not in repressive legislation, but in strong unions that will satisfy the farm worker's hunger for decency and dignity and self-respect.

Unionization cannot make progress in the face of hostile employee attitudes unless it receives effective governmental support. Despite a resigned acceptance by some farm employers that collective bargaining under law is inevitable, grower attitude on the whole remains exceedingly hostile. If farm unionism is to make progress, we need sufficient economic power under law to be able to wrench signed agreements from unwilling hands of growers who still refuse to admit that unionization and collective bargaining have a rightful place to take in agriculture for the genuine long-run benefit of all concerned. Coverage under the present NLRA would not give us the needed economic power, and it would take away what little we have.

As Senators well know, there are times when legislative proposals become part of the strategy of calculated retreat. We urge a hard, questioning look at any farm labor proposal designed to make union recognition easier than ever while keeping all the economic power where it has always been—in the hands of the grower.

Under the complex and time-consuming procedures of the National Labor Relations Board, growers can litigate us to death; forced at last by court order to bargain with us in good faith, they can bargain in good faith—around the calendar if need be—unless we are allowed to apply sufficient economic power to make it worth their while to sign.

We want to be recognized, yes, but not with a glowing epitaph on our tombstone. Union recognition is of value only in terms of what it leads on to. At the end of the trail we seek

> —not recognition, but signed contracts;
> —not recognition, but good wages;
> —not recognition, but a strong union.

And these things are not primarily a matter of elections and representation procedures, or even of court orders, but of economic power.

To equalize the inequality of bargaining power—this was the high legislative purpose of both Wagner and Taft-Hartley, was it not? The more basic reason why we oppose coverage under the present Taft-Hartley, without more, is that it would not correct the inequality of bargaining power between growers and ourselves.

In the last Congress, the House Special Subcommittee on Labor chaired by Rep. Frank Thompson of New Jersey, which will also hold hearings soon on this subject, published a report entitled "National Labor Relations Act Remedies: The Unfulfilled Promise."

The report quotes Mr. William L. Kircher, Director of Organization of the AFL-CIO, as saying: "It is very natural for workers to unionize because unionism and the collective bargaining process enable them to increase their wages and obtain that dignity and self-respect which comes with job security."

Mr. Kircher testified that when there is no employer opposition to the desire for unionization, the union almost always wins the election. In 29 representation elections held over a 13-month period, unions won 28 and tied the other. In all but seven cases the margin of victory was in excess of 2 to 1.

The burden of the report, however, was that "in campaign after campaign in the southeastern, southwestern and midwestern parts of the United States" the union encounters all-out organized opposition not only from the employer, but also from the police, the local courts, and the business and political leadership of the community.

What the report said about the trials of the textile, retail clerks and other unions could have been written as well about our own experience with the table grape industry in California. Anyone who thinks coverage under the present NLRA would be a tremendous favor to farm workers should study the Thompson Report and ponder its contents as well.

How then did it happen that so many people for so long a time made so much of NLRA "protections" for farm workers?

To better understand this, I think we must go back 34 years in time to 1935, when Congress passed the original NLRA, the Wagner Act. We almost made it that time, but not quite, and people concerned about the plight of the farm worker began to say we had been denied the protections of the act. They said it for 12 years when it could fairly be called a pro-labor act. They kept on saying it after the Taft Hartley revision of 1947 and the Landrum-Griffin amendments of 1959 converted into an anti-labor act.

The policy of the original Wagner Act and its administration for the succeeding 12 years was to promote unionization of the unskilled and semi-skilled workers in mass production industry. Its aim was to quiet widespread industrial unrest and to meet the social and economic challenges of the Great Depression.

Senators will recall that when the 80th Congress passed the Taft-Hartley Act over President Truman's veto, labor leaders called it a "slave labor act." They were ridiculed by their enemies at the time, and they were ridiculed later when their unions survived. But what survived? Large, well-established unions which had on-going collective bargaining relationships with employers who were by that time accustomed to dealing with labor unions. That's what survived.

Taft-Hartley did, however, accomplish the purpose of its sponsors in that it effectively decelerated the pace of union organizing as annual union membership statistics will show. History will record that Taft-Hartley and Landrum-Griffin, together with continuing business community determination to oppose unions at nearly every turn, succeeded in checking the progress of labor organization in America before it had accomplished half its job.

Even today, some of the most striking gains in union membership are occurring among teachers and other public employees who, like us, must operate without benefit of labor relations law. Public employee unions were greatly helped, it is true, by the executive order of the late President John F. Kennedy and by similar policies adopted by certain state and local governments.

Where would the large industrial unions be today in Congress had "protected" them from the beginning, not with the Wagner Act, but with the Taft-Hartley Act in its present form?

We too need our decent period of time to develop and grow strong under the life-giving sun of a favorable public policy which affirmatively favors the growth of farm unionism.

Of utmost importance is an exemption for a time from the Taft-Hartley and Landrum-Griffin restrictions on traditional union activity. The bans on recognition and organizational picketing and on the so-called secondary boycott would be particularly harmful, and the mandatory injunction in both cases makes them truly disastrous.

How does it happen that the law provides no mandatory injunctions against employer unfair labor practices, such as discharges for union activity or promotion of company unions?

As to the secondary boycott, it is shameful that the richest nation on earth, confronted with the moral challenge of farm worker deprivation, should create a legal fiction of "innocent neutrality" for those who reap a monetary profit from the sale of scab grapes. Union security is most essential in an industry like agriculture which is marked by seasonal and casual employment and where a work force can build up from a few hundred to several thousand in a few short days and just as quickly disappear.

While the nation is busy fighting poverty in all its forms, let us not create new situations where nonunion farm worker poverty in "right to work" Texas or Arizona will become a threat to the small measure of union farm worker prosperity in California.[11]

We therefore urge that farm workers and their unions be exempted from section 14(b) which makes misnamed state "right to work" laws operative in interstate commerce.

All of labor ought to be liberated from section 14(b), but this much at least. It makes no sense for Congress to labor hard at making collective bargaining possible for farm workers if it leaves untouched that major obstacle which is 14(b). Railroad employees are not subject to "right to work" laws and we see no reason why we should be.

Regarding section 14(c), we are opposed to any exemption of small growers whether legislative or administrative.

It is a matter of principle with us that the single employee of a small grower is as entitled to his union as anyone else, and if a union cannot represent him under a regulatory law, then it will have to proceed as we do at the present, without benefit of a specific law.

It is perhaps but natural that small growers should see the coming of unionism only in terms of wage cost. We think that the problem is much more complex than that.

If Congress passes a bad law, making us worse off than we are at present, but exempts small growers from coverage, then we might have to concentrate most of our organizing effort for a time on small growers and let the big agribusiness corporations go until we can get the law changed.

If on the other hand Congress passes a law which really makes it possible to get contracts with the big growers, but which exempts the small ones, something else is apt to happen. We would certainly begin by going after the big growers. Then I suspect that internal union politics would have the tendency to force a concentration on getting higher and higher wages from the big corporations while ignoring both the small growers and their employees completely.

This might be a welcome prospect to the small grower who thinks he can find competent, efficient workmen at nonunion wage rates and so continue to compete effectively. We think such a view highly unrealistic if one considers what is going on in the world of agriculture—the mass exodus of small farmers to the cities, the increasing concentration of more and more farm land in fewer and fewer hands. This is taking place without the presence of labor unions in any significant sector of agriculture, and without any consideration of union vs. nonunion farm wages. What will happen if unions are permitted to organize big corporate agribusiness but not small growers is this: Big agribusiness will get the benefit of better workers attracted by higher union wages, of higher union worker productivity, and of whatever benefit derives from political alliance with the union when there is a question of union employers against nonunion employers. This could affect such issues as support payments and other forms of federal subsidy, federal money for retraining employees to operate new farm machines, and so on.

Let me say right here that all of this is a prospect which the leadership of our union does not relish at all. Our natural sympathy is to favor the small grower and to help him in every way we can to remain in business and to prosper. We do not want to be forced into a political and economic alliance with large growers against small growers. We are, however, trade unionists and our first obligation is to our members. Our cooperation must be reserved for those employers who believe in unions, or who are at least willing to tolerate unions, and who sign fair union contracts.

We urge small growers to give the matter a great deal of thought before pressing for an exemption from NLRA coverage.

If we could have our own way, what we would really like to see is a family living wage for every farm worker, a family living income for every family-sized farm owner, and a fair return on investment for every grower, whether he is an employer or not.

To this end we urge Congress to give favorable consideration to the proposed National Agricultural Bargaining Act of 1969, or whatever legislative assistance may be needed so that all agricultural producers can obtain a fair price for their produce in the various commodity markets.

Concerning section 302, our only objection is to the requirement of subsection (c)(5)(B) that employers have equal representation with employers in administration of the funds. These monies are for the benefit of the workers, who have elected to take part of their negotiated pay increase in the form of pension or health-welfare or other benefits. We believe that the trust agreement offers sufficient protection for these funds and that unilateral administration by employee representatives should be legally possible under the act.

Some unions, notably the building trades, derived little benefit from the original Wagner Act, but all of them in some way had something else going for them. The skilled trades, together with the professions, enjoy first of all a natural limitation on labor supply in that their members possess some kind of skill or formal training. In addition, they have been permitted by public policy to restrict freedom of entry to the occupation, or freedom of access to the needed training.

Where would they be today if they had to contend with the same economic forces that we do?

The seasonal farm worker does not possess extensive skills. While experience accounts on the farm as well as anywhere, he is scarcely called upon to do anything that cannot be learned passably well in half a day.

Our potential competition appears almost unlimited as thousands upon thousands of green carders pour across the border during peak harvest seasons. There are people who, though lawfully admitted to the United States for permanent residence, have not now, and probably never have had, any bona fide intention of making the United States of America their permanent home. They come here to earn American dollars to spend in Mexico where the cost of living is lower. They are natural economic rivals of those who become American citizens or who otherwise decide to stake out their future in this country.

In abolishing the bracero program,[12] Congress has but scotched the snake, not killed it. The program lives on in the annual parade of thousands of illegals and green carders[13] across the United States-Mexico border to work in our fields.

To achieve law and order in any phase of human activity, legislators must apply heed to other laws not made by man, one of which is the economic law of supply and demand. We are asking Congress to pay heed to this law in the light of some hard facts about farm labor supply along our southern border. Otherwise, extension of NLRA coverage to farm workers in that part of the country will not produce much law and order.

What we ask is some way to keep the illegals and green carders from breaking our strikes—some civil remedy against growers who employ behind our picket lines those who have entered the United States illegally, and, likewise those green carders who have not permanently moved their residence and domicile to the United States.

An especially serious problem in agricultural employment is the concerted refusal of growers even to discuss their use of economic poisons or pesticides. There are signs that several members of Congress are becoming increasingly aware of the dangers posed by economic poisons to human life and to wildlife, to the air we breathe and the water we drink. Senator Gaylord Nelson of Wisconsin is to be congratulated for proposing a federal ban on DDT.

For us the problem is before all else one of worker health and safety. It is aggravated in California by the refusal of county agricultural commissioners to disclose their records of pesticide application and by state court injunctions against such public disclosure.

The economic poison threat is a major reason why we need strong unions and collective bargaining in agriculture. Growers who try to pass our complaints off as a cheap smear campaign for consumer benefit reveal thereby that they are not very well acquainted with the daily anxieties and sufferings of their field workers.

Some there may be who dread the adjustments they think may be required by the coming of unionism to ranch and farm. Our leadership has given much thought to this matter.

Perhaps Congress could create a temporary Joint Committee on Family Living Farm Income, along the lines of the Joint Committee on Labor Management Relations set in 1947 by the old Taft-Hartley Title IV. The new committee would have such time as Congress deems expedient to study and report on such subjects as these: methods for improving employer-employee relations in agriculture; conditions necessary to produce a family living wage for farm workers and a family living income for farm owner; requisites for a national policy of enabling and encouraging farm workers to become self-sustaining family-sized farm owners; requisite sizes for various kinds of self-sustaining family-sized farms; structural changes needed to enhance the bargaining power of agricultural producers in the various commodity markets; suitable methods for expanding agricultural production to meet the challenge of hunger at home and abroad; training programs needed to equip unemployed and underemployed persons, both urban and rural, to fill the new jobs created by such expanded production; methods for reversing the current trend toward concentration of more and more agricultural land in fewer and fewer hands.

As one looks at the millions of acres in this country that have been taken out of agricultural production; and at the millions of additional acres that have never been cultivated; and at the millions of people who have moved off the farm to rot and decay in the ghettoes of our big cities; and at all the millions of hungry people at home and abroad; does it not seem that all these people and things were somehow made to come together and serve one another? If we could bring them together, we could stem the mass exodus of rural poor to the big city ghettoes and start it going back the other way; teach them how to operate new farm equipment; and put them back to work on those now uncultivated acres to raise food for the hungry. If a way could be found to do this, there would be not only room but positive need for still more machinery and still more productivity increase. There would be enough employment, wages, profits, food and fiber for everybody. If we have any time left over after doing our basic union job, we would like to devote it to such purposes as these.

Walter P. Reuther, President of the United Automobile Workers, described the right order of priorities for us in these words:

"The journey of farm workers and their families into the mainstream of American life has begun with a struggle to build their own community unions and through them to reach out for the elementary rights so long denied them."

Eventually, we will reach out for the rights denied us, such as full and equal coverage under minimum wage laws and the various forms of social insurance. But first things first. Today we ask the American people and the Congress to help us build our union with some special help in the face of some especially stubborn opposition of long standing. Give us that and the rest will come in due time.

Thirty-four years ago a nation groping its uncharted course through the seas of the Great Depression faced the threatening storms of social and economic revolution.

The late President Franklin D. Roosevelt met the challenge with the Wagner Act and with other New Deal measures, then considered quite revolutionary such as Social Security, unemployment insurance and the Fair Labor Standards Act.

While these measures modified the existing capitalistic system somewhat, they also saved the nation for free enterprise.

They did not save the farm worker. He was left out of every one of them. The social revolution of the New Deal passed him by. To make our union possible with its larger hope that the farm worker will have his day at last, there was required a new social revolution.

The relief we seek from Congress today, however, is neither new nor very revolutionary. It has proved beneficial to the nation in the past when unions were weak and industry strong. We need and favor NLRA amendments along the lines of the original Wagner Act, but we oppose for this period in history the restrictions of Taft-Hartley and Landrum-Griffin.

■

CHAPTER 2

Years of Triumph: 1970–75

The first half of the 1970s was as tumultuous for Chávez and the UFW as it was for a nation racked by the violent protests that marked the end of a period of intense activism. As other militant activists one after another disappeared into the footnotes of history, however, Chávez became ever more visible on the public scene. He further developed his rhetorical means to appeal to workers, taking what he had years before learned in the CSO and adapting it to the needs and exigencies of his union and cause. In so doing, he devoted much of his time to addressing a wide variety of audiences, ranging from students on campuses to religious groups to members of established labor unions to readers of various magazines and newspapers. His broad rhetorical net also brought to him uncommitted and uninvolved audiences of potential supporters among the general public.

For each audience, in each setting, Chávez almost always took on the role of a teacher. He sought to convince listeners and readers that a successful union could be built, to recruit members and then persuade them to unite into a well-functioning organization, and to remake the self-identification of those most-ardent followers who would take on many of Chávez's own qualities and, in some cases, become effective organizers and rhetors themselves. The rhetorically induced reordering of audiences' personal qualities required him to fuse synergistically his depiction of himself (first persona), his implicit and explicit depiction of his audience (second persona), and his substantive message of themes, arguments, explanations, and evidence.

The UFW's victory over the grape growers changed Chávez's place in the movement and redirected the aim of his public discourse. He faced mounting pressure to shift from an agitator leading a movement to an administrator overseeing a union. He had become a public figure, one who worked in state and national political arenas in an attempt to defeat political proposals damaging to his union, to pass legislation helpful to the union, and to promote the national civil rights agenda. Yet he had also devoted considerable time touring the country to raise funds and to reinforce support among his allies, as well as to convert audiences into union activists or into more-indirect supporters who boycotted grapes or gave other valuable aid from a distance. Chávez's successes brought him national stature and veneration beyond mere respect. As historian Ignacio M. Garcia said, Chávez became "the hero needed to give the struggle a national appeal. He became the first and most famous Chicano leader of the twentieth century. He was the Mexican American version of Dr. Martin Luther King."[1]

The unlikely hero found precious little time to celebrate his victories or to enjoy his fame. Just when the union's leaders began to implement the terms of their contract with the grape growers, a dangerous challenge arose from an unexpected source. The Teamsters Union had previously agreed to organize drivers and warehouse workers and leave the field workers to the UFW. In violation of that agreement, Teamsters began to organize workers in the lettuce, strawberry, and vegetable fields in the Salinas Valley. Seeking to block the UFW from the fertile valley and to reverse its burgeoning power, growers collaborated with the Teamsters against Chávez's union.[2]

The fight with the Teamsters forced the UFW and Chávez to redirect material and rhetorical resources from rebuilding its boycott network, and "it distracted Chávez and his most competent aides" at the time the union was transforming itself "from an organization expert in agitation into one equipped to administer contracts covering thousands of workers in the grape industry."[3] For example, the union's leadership could not effectively establish a badly needed hiring hall and a grievance committee because so many of its resources were spent fighting the Teamsters.[4] Once the battle lines were drawn, Chávez immediately set up a UFW office in Salinas in the center of the valley. He openly challenged the Teamsters, announcing: "They can't get away with this. . . . They're going to have a big fight on their hands. . . . They're not going to sign up our people."[5]

On August 2, 1970, in his speech in Salinas to a massive rally of farm workers, Chávez alternated between English and Spanish when accusing the Teamsters and growers of attempting to intimidate workers and of ignoring the historical reality that times had changed. "It's tragic that these men have not yet come to understand that we are in a new age, a new era," he proclaimed. "No longer can a couple of white men sit together and write the destinies of all the Chicanos and Filipino workers in this valley."[6] The UFW workers then devised a plan to defeat both the Teamsters and the growers.

While Chávez was busy fighting the Teamsters, Chicano activists called for a moratorium and march against the Vietnam War on August 29, 1970. Although Chávez could not attend the Los Angeles protest, he sent an antiwar message in which he reiterated his beliefs in nonviolence in all aspects of life:

> It is now clear to me that the war in Vietnam is gutting the soul of our nation. Of course we know the war to be wrong and unjustifiable, but today we see it has destroyed the moral fiber of the people.
>
> Our resistance to this, and all wars, stems from a deep faith in nonviolence. We have to acknowledge that violent warfare between opposing groups—be it over issues of labor or race—is not justifiable. Violence is like acid—it corrodes the movement's dedication to justice.[7]

Fortunate in having a corps of trained organizers from the grape battles, Chávez quickly organized a boycott augmenting the picketing in the Salinas area. He initially focused the boycott on lettuce and eventually expanded it to grapes and Gallo wines. Employing another standard means, he began a fast for hope and thanksgiving that lasted for six days and attracted intense attention to the cause. Although the U.S. Catholic Bishops' Committee on Farm Labor agreed to mediate between the Teamsters and UFW, the strike and ensuing violence only escalated. The Teamsters brought in hired guards to harass and frighten UFW pickets. Amidst growing violence on both sides, Chávez rejected union violence: "If we mean nonviolence," he told members in a meeting, "we have to say, 'Damn it, we mean it, and it's not going to happen.'"[8]

Chávez soon suffered from health problems and retreated to San Juan Bautista, a mission town a half hour from Salinas. He remained active in the strike by communicating with the union's organizers by phone.[9] The tide eventually turned in Chávez's favor, partially as a result of a major mistake by the growers and their allies. In December of 1970 Chávez was jailed for refusing an order to stop boycotting Bud Antle lettuce. His jailing created enormous media attention, reenergized the workers, and brought a friendly and well-publicized visit by Ethel Kennedy, the widow of Robert Kennedy.[10] Eventually the union won a series of contracts with growers and by 1971 had forged still another agreement with the Teamsters. Chávez seemed to have achieved labor peace in the fields.

In 1971 the UFW moved its headquarters from Delano to La Paz, a former tuberculosis sanatorium in the Tehachapi Mountains south of Bakersfield. Union offices in Delano remained open, including the hiring hall, the credit union, and the medical clinic. The ever more revered Chávez claimed that he moved to La Paz "because I wanted to remove my presence

Chávez speaking at a rally in Sacramento in July 1971. *Photo by Cris Sanchez.*
Courtesy Walter P. Reuther Library, Wayne State University

from Delano, so they could develop their own leadership, because if I am there, they wouldn't make the decisions themselves. They'd come to me."[11] Although physically out of Delano, he continued to make most of the union's decisions. La Paz's isolated location allowed Chávez to escape from the news media and rest between his many trips.

During 1971 and 1972 Chávez participated actively in several legislative battles. He and his followers convinced the governor of Oregon to veto an antiunion bill; in Arizona they unsuccessfully attempted to recall the governor for signing an antiunion bill but successfully helped to register one hundred thousand new voters who were part of a political shift that led to the election of more minority leaders in the state. In California he and the union's supporters helped defeat Proposition 22, which would have outlawed the boycott and other union tactics.[12]

Peace between the UFW and Teamsters again dissolved when many growers in 1973 signed highly favorable contracts with the Teamsters rather than extending their contracts with the UFW. Chávez's renewed campaign against the Teamsters and growers unleashed violence against UFW farm workers that far exceeded what had occurred in 1971. The Reverend Howard Matson chronicled the frustration of that time by describing a rally at a park in Coachella in 1973. It had been a day of confrontation with the Teamsters, "an ugly day on the picket line. People had been beaten up, cars fired upon, organizers knocked unconscious." The workers were worried that the next day might be even worse. A group of people spoke and as often happened, Chávez closed the meeting. He "looked clean and rested as though he had spent a leisurely day at home instead of a grueling one in the fields at 110 [degrees] . . . subject to personal abuse and physical danger." At the end of his talk he asked a series of questions:

> "Will you return to the picket lines tomorrow?"
> "Yes!" everyone shouted.
> César continued, "Are you not afraid?"
> "No!" everyone cried.
> "Not even a little?"

The tension broke. Everyone laughed. Of course they were afraid. Who would not be? When morning came there they were all at their stations including César Chávez.[13]

The new violence attracted increased media attention and only increased Chávez's resolve. "This might be the ultimate confrontation," he declared. "If we win, they'll leave us alone. Systems die a slow death, and the farmworker feudal system will take a long time to die."[14] But Chávez

United Farm Workers, including Chávez, march in Douglas, Arizona, in July 1972.
Photo by Glen Pearcy. Courtesy Walter P. Reuther Library, Wayne State University

underestimated the viciousness and resolve of his opponents. After many workers were beaten and two picketers, Nagi Daifullah and Juan de la Cruz, were killed, Chávez called off all picketing "until federal law enforcement agencies guarantee our right to picket and see that our lives are safe and our civil rights are not trampled on."[15]

Recognizing the need to change tactics, Chávez moved to the political arena to promote legislation that would afford his union a better chance in its fight with the growers. His timing was perfect. His longtime enemy Ronald Reagan had left the governor's office, replaced by UFW supporter Jerry Brown. To demonstrate their continued political power, UFW workers returned to a well-tested tactic: the march. The walking began in San Francisco, where Chávez knew it would generate maximum media coverage, and ended at the office of Gallo wines in Modesto. By the time the activists reached Modesto, more than twenty thousand had joined the long line of trekking unionists.

The march encouraged Brown and other politicians to support the California Agricultural Relations Act (ALRA), which granted migrant workers rights in union elections and gave union members the secret ballot in elections, control over the timing of elections, and the right to boycott.

ALRA also created a mechanism for conflict resolution between unions and growers and established the Agricultural Labor Relations Board (ALRB) to supervise union elections.

In June of 1975, soon after the passage of the law, Chávez embarked on another pilgrimage, an ambitious one-thousand-mile, fifty-nine day march through California's agricultural valleys in order to explain the bill's implications and its potential effects on the UFW and its workers. Each day ended with a rally where Chávez would speak about the new law and its effects on workers. The march drew widespread media coverage and added solidarity within the UFW.

During 1975 it became apparent that the boycotts were effective, as stores throughout the nation quit carrying the targeted products. By 1976 a number of large agricultural companies, like Giumarra, had signed with the UFW. While Chávez's union seemed on its way back to power, its opponents were not defeated. They simply bided their time, waiting for an opening to attack once again.

Chávez's public addresses from this period reflect his struggle with the Teamsters. On February 6, 1971, in Austin, Texas, Chávez spoke initially in English and then in Spanish to a crowd of about five thousand, including a group of strikers. In the first part of the speech he discussed the desire of workers at the Economy Furniture plant to join a union, the power of the boycott, and the value of nonviolence. In Spanish he spoke of the power of unity among workers, his hope that Mexican Americans would continue to support one another in time of need, and the significance of education for training future leaders, the children. As you read this text, notice that Chávez heavily employed cuentos, dichos, and other elements common to Mexican rhetorical traditions, and that stories dominate his Spanish section.

In May of 1971 Chávez spoke out against the war in Vietnam at a major rally in Exposition Park in Los Angeles. Linking his audience and the occasion to his cause, he compared the violence of the war to that commonly practiced by growers against workers and illustrated how violence was common in families in the United States. He nevertheless appealed for nonviolence as a tool against the union's opponents and pleaded for training programs through which young people would reject violence in their own lives and refuse to use violence against those in other lands. Broadening his scope from union to society, he argued that an acceptance of nonviolence could usher in a dramatic change in American society.

Through his manifest themes and explicit goals but also in such rhetorical resources as his persona, his careful organization, and his use of language, evidence, argument, and delivery, Chávez embodied the qualities of a teacher throughout this period—as he would throughout his career. In an address to a religious group at a retreat in La Paz, for example, he taught his listeners about the long history of farm workers' attempts to unionize, the early days of the UFW, and the possibilities for the union's future.

In a speech that showcases his standard rhetorical qualities, delivered at the University of Santa Clara in 1972, he began by acknowledging a current labor problem between the university and Chicano students. Identifying himself and his cause with the local issues, he compared the fight on campus to the battle between growers and union members. Proposition 22, he pointed out, served as a ready example of tactics the growers used against the union. He carefully outlined changes proposed by the proposition and their effects on the UFW and concluded by championing nonviolence as a way to defeat dangerous proposals like Proposition 22. His reliance on facts and clarity in this speech, as in many of his addresses, stands out along with his customary humility and relative lack of personal criticism or bitterness aimed at his opponents.

During these years of intense Teamster attacks on the UFW, Chávez often spoke on the values of labor solidarity. In 1973 he talked to workers in Coachella about the powerful need for a union, the many ways they could improve their lives through membership in the UFW, the good reasons for preventing outsiders from destroying their organization, and the dreams that came with the UFW. Notice especially how he adapted this address to his audience of workers.

In Los Angeles the following year, at a convention of the United Auto Workers, he thanked the union members for their help in the past and asked them to support the current boycott against lettuce and Gallo wines. He again assumed the role of teacher, educating listeners about which lettuce to boycott and about other issues. He spun out a standard anecdote he repeatedly used during this period about Gallo wines and President Nixon's favoritism toward Gallo's interests. After he related an ample set of facts to the ongoing battle between the Teamsters and the UFW and to the relationship between the Teamsters and the Nixon administration, he presented a standard story that made fun of the Teamsters. Turning to more sober matters, he identified how growers translated their power over local political and legal systems into anti-UFW tactics in the communities where farm workers lived. In a signature characteristic, Chávez told unionized workers who they were and ought to be—his second persona—by discussing in detail the UFW workers' desire for a strong union and their commitment to struggle against any odds until they succeeded.

In this text, as in others in this book, Chávez depicted listeners in his own image, melding explicitly and implicitly his first and second personae. The personal persona he constructed and communicated relied on the content and manner of his discourse but also on widely known details about his self-sacrifice, extraordinary dedication, exhaustive speaking campaigns, and spiritual belief that God would ensure the victory of a right cause by moving the public—once sufficiently informed of the pertinent facts and reasons—to support justice. This persona carried the personal qualities necessary to enact Chávez's commitment to a well-reasoned and clearly presented case where facts and ideas had their best chance to be understood easily. Thus Chávez's personae and substantive message synergistically merged, with the personae an extension of his substantive themes, and the themes dependent on the person for their implementation. Together his personae and themes created multiple and overlapped layers of identification that possessed rhetorical power to reconstitute character in some audiences while informing and persuading others.

Chávez's public discourse now reflected the UFW's growing strength and its leader's increased stature. As a public figure and hero he was able to rivet public focus on his cause, enlarging his audience and claiming more and more attention in the public arena. Although he faced the twin problems of building solidarity in the union and fighting the growers and Teamsters, his discourse maintained its essential nature even as it adapted its subthemes, evidence, and specific arguments to the specific issues and circumstances of the day. The following texts reveal both the enduring and changing nature of his rhetorical campaign.

Chávez at Austin, Texas, February 6, 1971

The text of this impromptu speech in Spanish and English appears in Robert Tice, "The Rhetoric of La Raza," an unpublished manuscript housed in the Chicano Studies Collection, Hayden Library, Arizona State University, Tempe, Arizona. The transcript and translation were done by Robert Tice.

Muchísimas gracias, Senador Bernal, hermanas y hermanos. De repente es necesario hablar en dos idiomas y se me hace que ahora es una ocasión de estas. De manera que lo voy a tener que hacer es . . . si cuando hablaban del inglés y español preguntaba un señor que si cual era la diferencia. Y le digo que la diferencia era simple; que el idioma inglés es para los negocios, es para hacer negocios. Y el idioma español es el idioma de los ángeles y también se usa para enamorar. Les voy a reseñar los negocios primero y luego termino con lo, con lo más bueno. (Thank you, Senator Bernal [Texas Senator Joe Bernal of San Antonio who introduced Chávez], sisters and brothers. Suddenly it is necessary to speak in two languages, and it appears that now is such an occasion. So we must use both languages—English and Spanish. A man was asking what difference there was between them and I said, "English is the language of business; Spanish is the language for angels and people in love." I'll start with business and end with the better part.)

Friends, sisters and brothers, honored guests. I'm extremely pleased to be here in Austin and in Texas. I've heard so much of the warm Texas hospitality, and let me tell you that I really know what you mean when you say, when we hear in California about the Texas hospitality. I think that everyone that I've come in contact with in this day and a half has been extremely gracious and courteous and friendly. The only thing that I heard—there's a newspaper in Dallas that didn't like the idea of my coming here or being honored [by the Texas legislature], but that's only one against millions since I've been here.

We're here to visit with you and we're here to share with you. But we're here mainly because there's a job to be done. We're here because we want to see Lencho Hernandez, Pancho Ramirez, compañero [comrade] "Cowboy" Salcedo—all the strikers in Economy Furniture—to get a contract. And we're here to plan . . . and we're going to do our share in the boycott. We're now boycotting in sixty-five cities across the land, and when I get back to Delano I'm going to ask our boycotters to also include in their list all of the Economy Furniture labels so they won't be bought at the Montgomery Ward stores.

And I'm asking you to do a couple of things: First of all, don't buy at Montgomery Wards until they give up that scab furniture. And secondly, don't eat tacos. But if you need tacos, don't eat lettuce. But if you can't give up the lettuce in the tacos, then don't eat tacos and enchiladas for the duration!

We think it's high time that these men and women who've been suffering now for two and a half years have a union. It's outright disgraceful that this employer, one employer, is able to give, to hold people back from having their rightful place in society by having a union. It's high time that not only in Texas but California—everywhere across this land—that workers should not be made to suffer for two and a half years for the right that was given them, not by the employer, not by any legislation—by inherent right. They were born with the right to be able to join unions or union of their choice. And in this case, the people at Economy Furniture have been waiting for two and a half years. And I ask all of you, sisters and brothers, that from now on begin doing the job on Montgomery Ward and the other stores that sell the furniture. Tell them you're not going to buy ni siquiera un carreto de hilo [even a spool of thread] until they give up the furniture.

Anyway, we know things that the owners of Economy Furniture don't know. We know that they've lost! We know that they've lost; it's just a matter of signing the contract. See, they don't realize that because the boycott is so powerful. The boycott is one of the most powerful weapons that poor people and people who struggle for justice have in this world. It's so powerful because it's really nothing more than the extension of love from one human being to the other. It makes it possible for people in the east coast and in California and in other places, in Texas, in Austin, and all over the world to help one another in a very direct way— and in the case of Economy Furniture by not buying at Montgomery Ward, by not buying that scab furniture; in the case of the lettuce workers, of course, by giving up the lettuce. You see, once you get that, once you get the idea of a boycott in motion, on track, and it begins to function on its own, nothing in this good earth will stop it—except a signed contract.

I visited with Lencho and Pancho and Cowboy and the other leaders in the strike. I visited with them. I went to the picket line. I went to their office. I went to the picket shack and I went to their homes. And, you know, it reminds me so much of Delano. So much—the office, their office that they have—so much like Delano. And you see really why you might speak with envy because people that have been fighting for two and a half years must have a same kind of spirit. And they, they can destroy, and they can, and they can harass and they can imprison and they can do all sorts of things. But the spirit they will never destroy. And it's the spirit of our people that's speaking loudly today.

There's so many good people that must be thanked: the resolutions that were passed in the house and the senate; the resolution that was passed at the county, by the county commissioners [Bexar County, Texas]; all of you good people here and last night at the airport.

And I think that we're getting together really because we accept that we've had it. Ya Basta [That's enough!]. From this day on we're going to make progress. We're going to be dealt with as human beings. We're going to have our place under the sun—the Texas sun. And we're going to be counted—as equals. With no offense to the present governors of the various southwestern states, I'm making a prediction that before the decade of the seventies is over we're going to have a Chicano in one of those governors' seats. And when that day comes we're not going to stop there. We'll want to go on to Washington too.

I'd like to mention a friend of yours and a friend of ours and a friend of our movement. This man who served us so faithfully and well, and that's one of the reasons, I guess, he lost. We met him in Washington, in Delano, and we met him in Coachella [Coachella Valley, California]. He was marching with us in 120-degree weather. A great, a great man. Senator Yarborough is here (Former U.S. Senator Ralph Yarborough of Texas, who received a standing ovation). He's a good man and a kind man. You know, I don't feel as secure now since he had to leave Washington. If you don't want him in Texas, let us have him in California. We'll do something with him over there.

You know, the development of the power of the boycott is so garbled because it is the extension of love from one individual to the other, and it creates a chain reaction that has tremendous consequences—good. It reminds me of a couple of stories:

As the progress of the boycott in the grape went on, you know, for almost five years some very beautiful things happened. I could stand here and tell you for a whole day of many of the stories, but I'd like to tell you two short stories to illustrate to you what it means. Remember during the boycotting of grapes in Washington, D.C., there's a family there who's been very partial to our movement, a lady and a man with young children who used to speak of the grape boycott and the campesino movement in California almost daily at the dinner table. And one day the mother was out in the store shopping with one of her children, a four-year-old girl. And they were pushing a cart down the aisle and they came upon this huge display of table grapes. And the little girl stopped as the mother was going by. And the little girl stopped, pulled her mother's dress, and she said, "Mommy can I have some boycotts."

And the other one . . . I was in New York not long ago, and I was asked to speak at the large cathedral in New York. And I was coming into the lobby to go into the cathedral. And we met this young couple with young kids. And he told me a little story that had taken place that morning. He got the kids up and said, "Look, we have to go to the cathedral and we're going to have to go hear César Chávez speak." He asked the six-year-old kid, "Do you know who César Chávez is? "and the little boy said, "Sure, who wouldn't. He invented grapes."

You know, one of the things that we have to be very careful [about] ourselves is that we struggle for our own *raza* (people) and as we do our thing to protect ourselves, we have to constantly think that there are also other people, not necessarily Chicanos, who are in our same condition or even worse. And many immigrant groups have come to this country and have pulled themselves [up] by their own bootstraps and have forgotten about the next guy that was behind them. And so nothing really big was accomplished. But if we can turn that around a little bit and bring ourselves up by our own bootstraps and then turn around and give our hand to our brother—whether it be black or Chinese or Japanese or Filipino, it doesn't really matter. If we can do that, then I think that we're going to be the lasting glory of our own race and of our own country.

A while ago, while I was having another meeting at Lencho's house, I talked to a black fellow who came to talk to me. And he was saying that was there anything we could do to create a coalition to help one another? He said roughly there are 20 or 30 percent black and 20 or 30 percent Chicanos. And then we need, what? 10 percent more, and we can get them from the students, so we'll have a majority. So, of course, I thought it was a great idea. It's easier to fight with the majority on your side than to be a minority; you know how it is to be a minority anyway.

I want to tell you one, one more thing. The International Upholsterer's Union is a good union. It's a clean union. It's a union that's been here with Lencho and the other strikers for two and a half years. Very few unions want to take on a losing fight, or at least what seems to be losing in the beginning. But it's also their contribution and their understanding that the fight to organize Economy Furniture is not really a fight to organize a single union in one locality, but it goes beyond that. You let those people at Economy Furniture get their contract and all of the organized plants in the area are going to get contracts. And it's going to be the beginning of a big drive among the Chicanos to get themselves organized into their own union.

Friends, let me close by just saying that we know that when human beings are concerned for one another, that the thing that all of us want when we're concerned for one another is to build and not to destroy. And we're concerned really for the dignity of man. We're saying that we're concerned not only for the guy that makes the headlines or the guy that has the money or the guy that has the good word. But we're concerned for the least of our own brothers. And we're concerned for human dignity. We're concerned for everyone and particularly concerned for the poor. And it's at this point then that I think that we realize that [we have] to struggle and to struggle very hard and to want to change things so we can get justice and dignity for our people.

I think it means also we're concerned about the whole question of how we do it. Either we want a total victory or we want a half-baked victory. And I think all of us want a lasting, total victory. And I think the only way to get it is by working hard, understanding what we're doing. Con capricho [with firmness]. Never give up. And I think doing it nonviolently is going to really, really make the difference.

So you see, the power structure loves nothing better than to put you behind the eight ball, nothing better than to have you defending yourself instead of defending your people. And we have an agreement in our own movement that the movement should be big enough so that it's never going to be defending things that are not right, even though it may be someone in the leadership position of the movement. And secondly, [it] should be small enough to take care of the smallest of the smallest problems that the least member might have. And I think these are guidelines that one has to set for himself. If not, then it becomes a mass movement that tends to look just above peoples' heads and tends to count social security numbers instead of names, instead of living and breathing human beings.

One of our biggest problems today in America is that as organizations get big they get immobile because they stop being individually oriented groups and they become mass-oriented. And mass orientation sometimes tends to take away the very important, very important ingredient—you've got to be with people if you're going to win.

I want to thank you very much for being here, and I want to say a few words in Spanish.

Todos sabemos, todos sabemos y reconocemos la necesidad de unirnos porque en la unión está la fuerza, como dice un dicho mexicano. No hay, ustedes imaginanse en el mundo, somos, aquí estamos seres humanos, reconocemos la necesidad de organizarnos. Hay que . . . la necesidad de organización es tan reconocible que hasta las hormiguetas nunca andan solas, siempre andan en "bonche" ¿verdad?

Dejenme platicarles un cuento que dice tambien la necesidad de organización. Me platican que por allá en Mexico había unos señores que eran arrieros y que día iban dos amigos uno, dos arrieros caminando por una vereda ¿entienden español? Caminando por una vereda y uno de ellos era muy listo con el azote. El azote es un "whip" ¿verdad? Y allí en esos contornos, en esos pueblitos era reconocido como el más bueno azotero en esos pueblitos. Era tanta la fama que todas las gentes que lo miraban lo adoraban porque era muy bueno para el azote. Iban caminando él y otro muchacho y este muchacho que iba con él iba tratando de sacar a ver de que tamaño era, lo iba "testeando" como decimos nosotros acá con mitad español . . . y cuando pasaron así por un nopal allí donde iban por una lomita, le dice el muchacho al senor éste le dice, mire señor, usted que es muy bueno para el azote? Porqué no corta esta tuna? Esta sacó el azote y cuando se arrima a la tuna, le pegó con el azote a la tuna y la cortó como si hubiera sido con un cuchillo. Y luego la tuna así en la vereda, así la levantó. Y para esto el señor que iba con el pués se quedó viendo pues se quedó bien sorprendido, se quedó muy admirado.

Caminaron por poco y llegaron a un árbol que estaba una rama así enfrente y al pasar les iba a tumbar el sombrero. Dice, mire señor, usted que es tan bueno para el azote? porqué no corta esta rama? Pues sacó el señor, cuando se iba arrimando allí, sacó el azote y tumbó la rama, la cortó con el azote y pues ya pasaron ¿verdad? Pues esto le causó gran admiración al señor; ya no hallaba que hacer. Iban caminando y ahí paso así una mosca así volando, y dice ¡mire aquí una mosca! El señor sacó el azote y le cortó la cabeza y para esto ya se quedó el hombre que no sabía ni que decir; se quedó tan sorprendido que ya no podía ni hablar.

Siguieron andando un rato, y para esto pasó una avispa. Y dice, mira ahí va una avispa péguele. Y el señor sacó el azote y se encaminó a pegarle a la avispa y luego se detuvo. Dice, mira, a esas no, dice porque ellas están organizadas si le pega una se me echan todas encima. Y entonces así debe de ser con nosotros. Un mal en contra de uno de los nuestros es un mal en contra de todos nosotros.

Yo me acuerdo no hace mucho tiempo en California cuando trabajábamos como migratorios, se quebraba el carro—eran carros viejitos en aquel entonces estabamos mucho mas jóvenes que hoy. Y se quebraba el carro a la orilla del camino y no pasaban ni diez minutos y el primer carro de mexicanos que pasaba se paraba, y ni tenían ni un mexicano en esos lugares. Y ahora hermanos, entre más grande se hacen, los carros y mas grande las carreteras mas aprisa corren los mexicanos en los carros y menos atención ponen a sus hermanos.

Tenemos que empezar a cambiar; si deveras creemos por nuestra raza; él que es buen juez comienza por su casa empieza. Si deveras creemos en nuestra raza, entonces comenzar a hacer tales cuales. Como quién pensaba que anos? quién pensaria veinte anos atrás que hoy en la moderna íbamos a mandar a mi papá y a mi mamá a una "rest home" porque ya están viejitos. ¡Nunca! Era una verguenza hacerlo. Nos quedábamos con ellos porque es parte de la familia, es parte de la unidad, de la seguridad de la familia mexicana y más y más la gente, como dice, no mira, todavía tiene sesenta anos—setenta y cinco—hay que mandarlo a un "old men's home" a este hombre. Una persona que me dice que quiera a su raza pero desprecia a su padre no me puede convencer que deveras quiere a su raza.

Porque una persona que no puede ni llevar a su mamá cuando todo es porque tiene que ir a trabajar porque si no trabaja no gana dinero y si no gana dinero pierde la televisión de color y el carro y el "vote." No me pueden decir que, que tienen mucho cariño por su raza. Porqué es la unidad básica y si no tenemos tiempo para nuestra madre, entonces? como vamos a tener tiempo para los demás?

Son los ideales que comienzan a cambiar. Y mientras no cambiemos y no paremos y examinemos? porqué esos ideales cambian? No porque nosotros estemos cambiando sino porque la presión sobre nosotros. Si lo que sucede aquí es de que hay lo que nombramos la presión en este pais es tremenda del . . . nos tienen que hacer super consumidores para poder vivir. Si vamos a una tienda a comprar una cajetilla de cigarros, llevamos cinco dólares mal, mal, mal que tengamos que salir, vamos a gastar tres o cuatro dólares. No teníamos que gastar pero lo gastamos. Porque ahí tienen los dulces allí abajo con muchas luces; todo lo que venden con luces y colores. aunque no necesite uno, va y lo compra porque en la mente le están poniendo a uno que lo tiene que comprar aunque no quiera. Si tiene uno un carro del "1970" ya quiere uno; viejo, compreme uno "71" porque mi comadre ya compró uno del "71."

De manera que cuantas presiones comienzan a tener impacto en nuestros ideales y en nuestros valores. Mientras no cambiemos eso vamos a ser víctimas de lo que criticamos. Ya para terminar, a mí se me hace que uno de los mejores trabajos que se esta haciendo es con la juventud. Los jovenes están llenos de idealismo, llenos de fuerza; pueden trabajar día y noche y no están decepcionados si son ellos los que van a comenzar a guiar. Son ellos los que tenemos que darles el apoyo pa' que nos puedan guiar. Y de todos lados nos llegan recordatorios ¿verdad? Yo tengo un niño que tiene doce años y trae el pelo, a mí se me hace que está muy largo; y pues les dije pues cortate el pelo; y me dice, no yo no me lo quiero cortar. Y le dije, pues yo no le hablaba así a mí papá ¿verdad? Y entonces comencé a tratar de buscarle manera y entonces dijo mire? como le gustaría si comiera lechuga? Y allí se acabó la cosa.

La necesidad por la educación es una necesidad básica y por tanto si no entonces nos atascamos como un grupo. De manera que el pleito para componer a todo el sistema que existe que está contrario a nuestro . . . a nuestros costumbres, que está contrario a lo que nos han enseñado y a lo que pensamos ser; el asunto de como nos educan y las discriminaciones y muchas veces los problemas que pasamos como niños, a pasan nuestros niños porque asunto de educación no está adecuada, no está hecha a tal manera que vaya a tratar con nuestros propios problemas de antecedencia, de raza y en fin hay que cambiarlos. Si no los cambiamos va a pasar lo que pasó en México una, un chiste que me platican. Allá en, durante la época del Presidente Cárdenas se hizo una campaña tremeda para educar a todo mundo. Todo niño que es taba analfabeto se iba a educar y comenzó el gobierno a organizar escuelas por todos lugares de México. Pero un lugar, allá un pueblecito en la sierra que se les olvidó. Y cuando los residentes allí en las campillas miraron que, pos, que el gobierno los habia olvidado, ellos se pusieron a hacer una escuelita de adobe. Y luego buscaron a ver quien iba a ser la profesora y había una niña de catorce años que había ido al dos años de escuela "so" la pusieron de profesora. Ya tenía como pos ya como unos seis meses con los niños, cuando el gobierno en México, en la capital, se dio cuenta de que estaba esa escuelita allí, y mandó a un, a un inspector federal de educación que fuera a ver que estaba pasando en la escuelita. Cuando llegó el inspector federal a la escuelita esa entró y dijo, señorita, yo soy inspector federal de educación y como hay costumbre allá salga se para afuera porque quiero hacerle un examen a los niños a ver que han aprendido. Pues la señorita se salió para afuera y dice el profesor este, este inspector, les dice a los niños, miren, voy a hacerles un examen sobre la histórica de México a ver que han aprendido. Había como unos treinta niños alli donde dice miren ¿quién de ustedes me puede decir quién fue el que le quemó los pies a Cuauhtemoc? Y todos . . . todos se quedó serio, nadie respondió. Dijo bueno diganme ¿quién le quemó los pies a Cuauhtemoc? Y se miraron uno al otro y nadie respondía. Al fin un, un niño allí más atrevido se paró y dice, mire, Señor inspector, yo le quiero asegurar a usted que aquí somos muy pobres pero somos muy honrados así es de que nadie de nosotros le quemamos los pies a Cuauhtemoc. Y entonces para la educación nuestra no queremos que pase esto. Tenemos que saber quien le quemó los pies a Cuauhtemoc.

Muchisimas gracias. ¡Que Dios los bendiga!

[We all know and recognize the need for unity. And as a Mexican saying goes, "In unity there is strength." We recognize the need for organizing ourselves. Even little red ants are never alone, always in a bunch.

Let me relate a Mexican anecdote about two cowboys walking on a path. And one was recognized in the surrounding towns as being very good with a whip. The man with him was testing him. As they passed a cactus plant, he challenged the other to use his whip to cut off the fruit (called tuna) of the cactus. He did so as though he were using a knife. The companion was impressed. As they passed a tree the companion challenged the man to cut off a branch with his whip; the man did a clean job of it. And this caused a great reaction in the other cowboy. They walked some more and a fly passed by. Being challenged again, the man cut off the fly's head. The companion—left speechless—really didn't know what to do any longer, when a bee came and he said, "There, get that bee!" The whip handler thought a minute and said, "No, they're very organized; if I harm it I'll have thousands of its kind on me soon." So then that is how we ought to think: a wrong doing against any one of us is a wrong doing against all of us.

I remember back in California, working as migrants; we were young then. Our car would give out, and we waited on the roadside. If a car with Mexicans came they would stop immediately and help us poor Mexicans. But now with cars so new and big the Mexicans will rush by, not noticing their brothers in trouble.

We must change, really begin to look out for our raza. Charity begins at home. For instance, who'd ever have dreamed that one would even consider sending Mama or Papa to a nursing home because they're old? Never! Shameful! Because we have family unity and love as Mexicans. A person who claims love for his raza but does not love his father can't convince me he loves his people. A woman who can't take in and take care of her mother because she has to work because she wants a color TV or a new car can't tell me she'll be able to love her raza. Because if we have no love for our mother how can we love anyone else?

Those ideals are changing. And that's not because we are changing but because the pressure's on us. The pressures in this country are tremendous; it is seeking to make super-consumers of us in order to live. The rat race. My wife wants to change her 1970 model car because my godmother has a 1971 car. All those pressures are having an impact on our ideals and values. As long as we let it, we'll be victims of what we criticize.

Now that I'm going to finish, I must say that one of the best jobs being done is by youth. They are strong and can work day and night. They're not disappointed in knowing they are tomorrow's leaders. They need our encouragement and support. We get reminders from all over: My twelve-year-old son has his hair too long, I thought. He said he didn't want to cut it. I said I didn't speak that way to my father. When I just could not get to him, he asked, "How would you like it if I ate lettuce?" The discussion ended.

Education is a basic and important need. If we have no education we are stuck—spinning our wheels—as a group. All this existing system that is contrary to our traditions and customs—that is contrary to what or how we think of being—can be fought only with education. The way we are educated, the discrimination, the problems we have as children is because our education is not adequate. Our education is not enough to deal with our problems of ancestry and raza. If we don't learn to educate ourselves something may happen like what took place in Mexico during President Cárdenas' term.

It's a joke they tell me about—there was a tremendous campaign to educate the people. Every child of age was to be educated; schools were organized. But they forgot a small place up in the mountains. And when the authorities found out there was no school, they built one out of adobe. They found a fourteen-year-old girl, who had two years of schooling, for the teacher. When the governmental authorities heard of this they sent out an inspector to the little place in the mountains. When he arrived he identified himself and asked the teacher to leave the classroom so he might examine the pupils as to their learning. The federal man told the nearly thirty children that he was going to test them on Mexican history: "Who can tell me who burned Cuauhtemoc's feet?" No one answered. Upon the inspector's insistence one boy stood up and said, "Listen, Mr. Inspector, we are very poor but we are very honest. I guarantee you none of us burned Cuauhtemoc's feet!" We must know everything; we must know who burned Cuauhtomec's feet!

Thank you. May God bless you.]

Speech at Exposition Park, May 2, 1971

A transcript of this impromptu speech is in the United Farm Workers Papers, Wayne State University.

Thank you for inviting me to participate in this meeting. It is hard for me because we in the farm workers movement have been so absorbed in our own struggle that we have not participated actively in the battle against the war.

In thinking about the memorial service I keep thinking about the women in Washington, D.C., who participated in the veterans' protest against the war. The *L.A. Times* reported it as follows:

Anna Pine of Trenton, NJ, wanted to discard her dead son Fred's Air Medal & Bronze Star and Purple Heart and a half-dozen other awards for heroism. But she had already turned away crying when the first former soldier announced hands trembling, "And so we cast away these symbols of dishonor, shame and inhumanity."

"My son would be here," Mrs. Pine said. "He would throw these things away. But where do I throw them," she wondered, peering through tears about the crowd that had edged her away from the veterans. An hour passed, the crowd dispersed, Mrs. Pine approached the fence. Digging into a big plastic bag, she grabbed a handful of medals and threw them against the statue.

I have eight children. It is almost impossible to imagine the pain of seeing your own child die for a cause that neither of you believe in—especially when there are so many needs in the world and so many specific ways to work for change.

What causes our children to take up guns to fight their brothers in lands far away?

In our case thousands and thousands of poor, brown, and black farm workers go off to war to kill other poor farm workers in Southeast Asia. Why does it happen? Perhaps they are afraid or perhaps they have come to believe that in order to be fully men, to gain respect from other men and to have their way in the world they must take up the gun and use brute force against other men.

They have had plenty of examples: In Delano and Salinas and Coachella all the growers carry gun racks and guns in their trucks. The police all carry guns and use them to get their way. The security guards (rent-a-cops) carry guns and nightsticks. The stores sell guns of all shapes and sizes.

It would be easy to put all the blame on the generals and the police and the growers and the other bosses. Or on violence in TV or the movies or war toys.

But we are also responsible. Some husbands prove to their children that might makes right by the way they beat on their own wives. Most of us honor violence in one way or another, in sports if not at home. We insist on our own way, grab for security and trample on other people in the process.

But we are responsible in another, more basic way. We have not shown our children how to sacrifice for justice. Say all that you will about the army but in time of crises the army and the navy demand hard work, discipline and sacrifice. And so too often our sons go off to war grasping for their manhood at the end of a gun and trained to work and to sacrifice for war.

For the poor it is a terrible irony that they should rise out of their misery to do battle against other poor people when the same sacrifices could be turned against the causes of their poverty. But what have we done to demonstrate another way? Talk is cheap and our young people know it best of all. It is the way we organize and use our lives every day that tells what we believe in.

Farm workers are at last struggling out of their poverty and powerlessness. They are saying no to an agricultural system that has condemned them to a life of economic slavery.

At the same time they are making a new way of life for themselves and their children. They are turning their sacrifices and their suffering into a powerful campaign for dignity and for justice.

Their nonviolent struggle is not soft or easy. It requires hard work and discipline more than anything else. It means giving up on economic security. It requires patience and determination. Farm workers are working to build a nonviolent army trained and ready to sacrifice in order to change conditions for all of our brothers in the fields.

Our opponents are at work every day to crush us or to get us off target or to out-maneuver us with the American public. There is no way to defeat them unless we also are at work every day—week after week, month after month, and year after year if necessary, outlasting the opposition and defeating them with time if necessary.

That is what it takes to bring change in America today. Nothing less than organized, disciplined nonviolent action that goes on every day will challenge the power of the corporations and the generals.

The problem is that people have to decide to do it. Individuals have to decide to give their lives over to the struggle for specific and meaningful social change. And as they do that others will join them, and the young will join too.

If we provide alternatives for our young out of the way we use the energies and resources of our own lives, perhaps fewer and fewer of them will seek their manhood in affluence and war. Perhaps we can bring the day when children will learn from their earliest days that being fully man and fully woman means to give one's life to the liberation of the brother who suffers. It is up to each one of us. It won't happen unless we decide to use our own lives to show the way.

César Chávez on Money and Organizing, October 4, 1971

This impromptu speech was delivered to a group of church people at La Paz, California. A transcript of the speech is in the United Farm Workers Papers, Wayne State University.

"When we are really honest with ourselves we must admit that our lives are all that really belong to us. So it is how we use our lives that determines what kind of men we are. It is my deepest belief that only by giving our lives do we find life. I am convinced that the truest act of courage, the strongest act of manliness is to sacrifice ourselves for others in a totally non-violent struggle for justice. To be a man is to suffer for others. God help us to be men!"[16]

What I'm going to say may not make much sense to you. On the other hand, it may make an awful lot of sense. This depends on where you are in terms of organizing and what your ideas are about that elusive and difficult task of getting people together—to act together and to produce something.

Labor unions today have a heck of a time organizing workers. The church has a heck of a time organizing people. The government has a heck of a time organizing people. The Republican Party has a very difficult problem. So does the Democrat Party. So does almost any institution have a heck of a time organizing people. Why is it difficult? First of all, if these institutions hadn't been successful, they wouldn't exist. There were churches that were successful. There were unions that were successful. There were government departments that were successful. Someone had the right idea. But that's in the past. Talking about those successes is like getting up and telling workers about the great and joyous campaigns in the 30s to organize workers. And they say, "So what? What about us today?"

Organizing is difficult because in our capitalist society we believe the only way things get done is with money. Let's examine this assumption by using the farm worker struggle as an example. Since about 1898, there have been many efforts to organize farm workers in California and other states. Almost invariably, at the end of each struggle someone would report, "The workers weren't ready for it. They didn't want the union. They didn't do their share to get organized." But every report of organizing attempts also included a more honest statement: "We had to stop the organizing drive, or we had to temporarily disband, because we ran out of money." It's a shame.

There isn't enough money to organize poor people. There never is enough money to organize anyone. If you put it on the basis of money, you're not going to succeed. So when we started organizing our union, we knew we had to depend on something other than money. As soon as we announced that we were leaving the Community Service Organization (CSO), the group that I worked with so many years, to organize field workers, there were people who wanted to give us money. In fact one lady offered us $50,000 to organize workers. When I said, "No," she was very hurt. I told her, "If I take the money now that would be the worst thing I could do. I don't want the money. Some other time I will, but not now." Fifty thousand dollars wasn't enough. The AFL-CIO had just spent a million and a half dollars and they failed. So why did we think we could do it with $50,000?

We started with two principles: First, since there wasn't any money and the job had to be done, there would have to be a lot of sacrificing. Second, no matter how poor the people, they had a responsibility to help the union. If they had $2.00 for food, they had to give $1.00 to the union. Otherwise, they would never get out of the trap of poverty. They would never have a union because they couldn't afford to sacrifice a little bit more on top of their misery. The statement "They're so poor they can't afford to contribute to the group" is a great cop-out. You don't organize people by being afraid of them—you never have; you never will. You can be afraid of them in a variety of ways. But one of the main ways is to patronize them. You know the attitude: Blacks or browns or farm workers are so poor that they can't afford to have their own group. They hardly have enough money to eat. This makes it very easy for the organizer. He can always rational-ize, "I haven't failed. They can't come up with the money, so we were not able to organize them."

We decided that workers wanted to be organized and could be organized. So the responsibility had to be upon ourselves, the organizers. Organizing is one place where you can easily get away with a failure. If you send a man to dig a ditch three feet by ten feet, you'll know if he did it or not. Or it you get someone to write a letter, you'll know if he wrote it. In most areas of endeavor, you can see the re-sults. In organizing, it's different. You can see results years later, but you can't see them right away. That's why we have so many failures. So many organizers that should never be organizers go in and muddy the waters. Then good organiz-ers have to come in, and it's twice as hard for them to organize.

We knew we didn't have the money. We knew farm workers could be organized and we were going to do it. We weren't going to accept failure. But we were going to make sure that workers contributed to the doing of this organizing job. That has never been done in the history of this country.

We started out by telling workers, "We are trying to organize a union. We don't have money, but if you work together it can be done." Ninety-five percent of the workers we talked to were very kind. They smiled at us. Five percent asked us questions, and maybe 1 percent had the spirit and really wanted to do some-thing.

We didn't have any money for gas and food. Many days we left the house with no money at all. Sometimes we had enough gas to get there but not enough to come back. We were determined to go to the workers. In fact at the very begin-ning of the organizing drive, we looked for the worst homes in the barrios where there were a lot of dogs and kids outside. And we went in and asked for a hand-out. Inevitably, they gave us food. Then they made a collection and gave us money for gas. They opened their homes and gave us their hearts. And today they are the nucleus of the union's leadership. We forced ourselves to do this. We kept telling ourselves, "If these workers don't get organized, if we fail, it's our fault not theirs."

Then the question came up, how would we survive? My wife was working in the fields. We used to take the whole family out on Sundays and earn a few dol-lars to be able to survive the following week. We knew we couldn't continue that way. And we knew that the money had to come not from the outside but from the workers. And the only way to get the money was to have people pay dues.

So we began the drive to get workers to pay dues so we could live, so we could just survive. We were very frank, very open. At a farm worker's convention, we told them we had nothing to give them except the dream that it might happen. But we couldn't continue unless they were willing to make a sacrifice. At that meeting everyone wanted to pay $5.00 or $8.00 a month. We balked and said "No, no. Just $3.50. That's all we need." There were about 280 people there, and 212 signed up and paid the $3.50 in the first month.

Ninety days from that day, there were twelve people paying $3.50. By that time we had a small community. There were six of us—four of us working full time. There were a lot of questions being asked. Some said, "They're very poor and can't afford it. That's why they're not paying." And a few of us said, "We're poor too. We're poorer than they are, and we can afford to sacrifice our families and our time. They have to pay."

I remember many incidents when I went to collect dues. Let me tell you just one. I'd been working twelve years with the mentality that people were very poor and shouldn't be forced to pay dues. Keep that in mind because that comes in handy in understanding what you go through when you're not really convinced that this is the way it should be.

I went to a worker's home in McFarland, seven miles south of Delano. It was in the evening. It was raining and it was winter. And there was no work. I knew it. And everyone knew it. As I knocked on the door, the guy in the little two-room house was going to the store with a $5.00 bill to get groceries. And there I was. He owed $7.00 because he was one full month behind plus the current one. So I'd come for $7.00. But all he had was $5.00. I had to make a decision. Should I take $3.50 or shouldn't I? It was very difficult. Up to this time I had been saying, "They should be paying. And if they don't pay they'll never have a union." Three-fifty worth of food wasn't really going to change his life one way or the other that much. So I told him, "You have to pay at least $3.50 right now or I'll have to put you out of the union." He gave me the $5.00. We went to the store and changed the $5.00 bill. I got the $3.50 and gave him the $1.50. I stayed with him. He bought $1.50 worth of groceries and went home.

That experience hurt me, but it also strengthened my determination. If this man was willing to give me $3.50 on a dream, when we were really taking the money out of his own food, then why shouldn't we be able to have a union, however difficult. There had never been a successful union for farm workers. Every unionizing attempt had been defeated. People were killed. They ran into every obstacle you can think of. The whole agricultural industry along with government and business joined forces to break the unions and keep them from organizing. But with the kind of faith this farm worker had, why couldn't we have a union?

So we set out to develop exactly that kind of faith. And by the time the strike came, we had that kind of resolution among members. Only a small percentage of the workers were paying dues. But it was ingrained in them that they were going to have a union come hell or high water. That's the kind of spirit that kept us going and infected other farm workers—this little core of people who were willing to stop talking and sacrifice to get it done.

That was seven or eight years ago. We had different problems in the Union then than we have today. But the kind of problems we had then were problems like not having enough money to pay rent. We told the workers, "If you're buying a house, leave it. Better get a smaller house where you pay little rent because we can't pay much rent." It was a lot of sacrifice and they did it. And we won the strike.

A few months ago, a local union from San Francisco came to ask us to help organize people from a couple of factories that are moving from the Bay Area to the San Joaquin Valley and running away from their contracts—runaway shops. They offered us money. We told them we didn't need money. All we needed was a telephone and a little money for gas and for food to eat on the picket line. We got that. But we said we needed someone from their union to direct us because we couldn't direct the drive. We wouldn't want to commit mistakes. It wouldn't be fair for us to do all the work for their union. But we told them we'd do everything if they provided the director. You know what? We assigned ten people to that drive. How much does it cost to be on the picket line? The way we eat? Nothing, you know. We've come from the struggle. And how much gas? A dollar and a half per car each day. Four cars at a dollar and a half a day. You know what? They couldn't put an organizer in the field for that job. You know why? Because they didn't have the money. It's too expensive to do it. It's too damned expensive for a guy earning about $22,000 a year including fringes. We told them, "Look. Bring him anyway—not knowing, you know. We'll get him a place to sleep with the workers. And we'll find a home that will feed him." And they said, "Our organizers won't do that. They have to have a motel and all those things." I said, "You won't have a union then." And they said, "That's right." In that union those two or three plants represented about 25 percent of their membership. They won't increase their membership anymore. They can't organize because they depend on money.

When we had that big fight with the Teamsters in Delano, we beat them with the numbers game. Every time they brought in an organizer, I think they get $35,000 a year in some cases, we got ten workers and told them, "Your job is to keep that guy from gaining any ground with the workers." The Teamsters brought in a lot of organizers but after a while it was too expensive. All we needed was just enough to eat and a little gas. We don't have to worry about money. That's how things get done.

The corporations do it differently. They pay very good wages. Then if their top people don't produce, they have carcasses all over the place. If they don't produce in a month, they say, "Look Brother, you're not cutting it. We're paying you a lot of money because we want results." The other way is not to pay anything. If you try to be in between, you're not going to get anything done. I'm convinced that's how these things work. In unions and in churches and in groups that are made up principally of people, you don't fire people for nonperformance like they do in the big corporations. However, we know you have guys who are not that effective—guys who won't do the work. They don't get fired. If you get a job in the church or in the unions you're in for life, brother, whether you can cut it or not. Very, very seldom does someone get fired. That's true even in our union. When a strike is called, everybody comes in to work. Then after a while we begin to see that some guys aren't cutting it. We actually haven't hurt the growers that much by taking them out on strike. And we have a very difficult time trying to get them to understand if they're going to organize workers they've got to work.

Money is not going to organize the disadvantaged, the powerless, or the poor. We need other weapons. That's why the War on Poverty is such a miserable failure. You put out a big pot of money, and all you do is fight over it. Then you run out of money and you run out of troops. It's just like those revolutions. If you haven't got the money you haven't got the troops.

We didn't worry about money at the beginning. Now we're beginning to feel a little of that coming. And I'm very worried. For instance, we gave a $5.00 weekly allowance and we still do, though it's more than that when you consider rent and food. But now, some don't think $5.00 is enough. They'd like to get $10.00. Maybe they should get $10.00. But there has to be some point where you say, "If you want to make money, go back to the fields." When we started the strike, workers were getting 95 cents an hour. Now people packing grapes during harvest, at piece rate, average $3.00 and $3.50 an hour plus some fringe benefits. Those are very good wages. In lettuce, the piece rate wages went up almost 300 percent in the first contract. So we tell the workers, "If you want to make that kind of money, go back. That's where the money's going to be. Not here."

We'll organize workers in this movement as long as we're willing to sacrifice. The moment we stop sacrificing, we stop organizing. I guarantee that. There are workers in Florida, in Texas, in New York, and in the southern states who are going to be very difficult to organize. But they have to be organized. We have to help our brothers in other countries too. We got a letter from Guatemala a couple of days ago. People there are having a devil of a time organizing because the government is very repressive. Since their struggle is against American companies, they feel we could boycott them here to get them organized there. And I know that's true. But we're not going to do it by paying wages. We can't. When we first started talking about a boycott, everyone told us, "You'll never do it. Boycotts never work." Every single union told Jim Drake, the first organizer of the boycott, "It can't be done. We've tried it and we are a bigger union. And we have a lot of money." We told ourselves that's one more reason why we should try it. So we put a lot of manpower into cities around the country. At one time we had about five hundred full-time people on the boycott not counting a tremendous number of supporters. You know why we were helped? Because they knew our guys weren't getting paid. So they didn't mind doing the same. But you do mind helping if you know that the other guys are getting a big fat salary.

When you sacrifice, you force others to sacrifice. It's an extremely powerful weapon. When somebody stops eating for a week or ten days, people come and want to be part of that experience. Someone goes to jail and people want to help him. You don't buy that with money. That doesn't have any price in terms of dollars.

Those who are willing to sacrifice and be of service have very little difficulty with people. They know what they are all about. People can't help but want to be near them—to help them and work with them. That's what love is all about. It starts with you and radiates out. You can't phony it. It just doesn't go. When you work and sacrifice more than anyone else around you, you put others on the spot and they have to do at least a bit more than they've been doing. And that's what puts it together.

These observations tie in directly with the whole question of organizing. Why do we have leaders? We put some people out in the fields and all of a sudden they hit, they click. Everyone's happy with them, and they begin to move mountains. With other people there are problems and heartaches. They just don't go. When we look and see what's happening, almost invariably the differences are along the lines of willingness to sacrifice and work long hours.

We didn't start out knowing these things. We have discovered them. During those six years of strike and boycott it never seemed like that much of a struggle. We accepted it as a fact. Now that we're over that big hurdle, we look back and say, "My God. People really sacrificed. And the things that I asked them to do! Did I really ask them to do that much?" I asked them to do it to the maximum, and they did it.

Question: What's your dream for the farm worker's union?

Answer: My dream is that farm workers will someday have enough power to take care of themselves, and if they gain that, that they don't become selfish . . . that the movement doesn't go to hell, in other words. And that's difficult. We're already beginning to see a few danger signs.

Only when we have a union that isn't selfish can we help other people. The first step in building a union is to help yourself. You sacrifice for ten years to have a union. You get better wages. So what? It's nice. But the real trick is to have a union, to have that power, and to selflessly help brothers completely unconnected with you. In order to get there, the movement has to be guided by some kind of philosophy. Everything comes back to how you deal with money.

Let me extend my dream. If the workers in California get organized, they can assist the organizing of people in Florida. The people in California and Florida together can assist the organizing of other workers. With a boycott they can help organize farm workers around the world. My God! There just aren't any other unions for farm workers in the rest of the world. One of the greatest miscarriages of justice is that the people who provide food for the world don't have enough food for themselves. It's horrible. I just can't understand it. Take the Philippines for instance. There are no unions there. They import people to work just like we do here. And they move them from island to island, from province to province. In West Germany, they bring in farm workers from Spain and Portugal. In Mexico, they can't get Mexicans to work in the hemp so they import workers from Guatemala and treat them like braceros. They're exploited just as the Mexicans are in this country. The damn exploitation of farm workers is consistent.

Imagine what could happen with one selfless act on our part. We could take on the Philippine sugar industry and knock the hell out of them with a boycott. It could bring a union to Filipino farm workers. Then we'd say to them, "Take care of yourselves first. Organize your union. And when that's done, we want you to help Malaysia or the rest of Asia." Same thing with Latin America. That's the dream. Frankly, we're not going to do that now. We have so many problems ourselves. More people are out to destroy us than ever before. The right wing is spending hundreds of thousands of dollars to get us.

And we have other problems. When we started the movement, no one questioned the $5.00 per week. Now some people who have worked and sacrificed for a long time want a little more security. No one can blame them. But we are still in a giant struggle, and workers in Florida and Texas are still going hungry. How can we be making money! I'm just talking about the staff now. With the workers? That's a tough one! To reverse that trend is going to be very difficult. It's going to take a long time.

We'll have many fights with them, many arguments. We may not be here if we argue too strongly. Look for a minute at how difficult it is: We start telling workers, "Now look. You've got a lot of money. You shouldn't get more money." Then they say, "Why not? The employers are making more profit." And what do we answer? "We're going to get less money so the employers can make more money so we can help our brothers?" It's a *very difficult* question. . . . The workers get strong. I don't know if that's going to change the employers. I don't think so. But it doesn't have to start with the workers. If the staff and the leadership of the union stick to the style of sacrifice and service, then the workers who are in leadership positions may begin to get the idea of self-sacrifice. Then we will really have something. Like everything else it has to begin in your own life and in those people who have given their lives to build the union. But it is hard, and we have a long way to go.

Chávez at the University of Santa Clara, October 26, 1972

A transcript and audio tape of this impromptu speech are in the possession of the editors.

We're pleased to be here this afternoon to spend a few minutes with you, to talk to you about the farm workers, to talk to you about the problems that are everyday occurrences in California. Before I do that, before I came here I met with the Chicano brothers and sisters, and they were airing their complaints to me that they have against the administration, and it reminded me so much of the complaints that farm workers have. And I think that the problem here is pretty much like the problem out in the fields, and it is that the time has come when powerless and small groups of people, minority people, cannot be shunted away, cannot be set aside or pushed aside without explanation. I truly hope that the administration, in fact I pray that the administration, [will] lead the way in the universities so this problem existing in Santa Clara is evident—and it's pretty much a problem in other universities in the state—that the University of Santa Clara lead the way by negotiating with the students. [. . .] Only through talking the problem out can there be an understanding and can a grievance be adjusted. There's got to be a way of adjusting grievances: [. . .] if the University of Santa Clara, the administration, would submit this matter to a third party and let there be discussions and let there be negotiations, let there be a way of resolving the problems.

Now I talked with my brothers and sisters, and they told me that there will be picketing out there, and I told them that if they were picketing this session I would not speak here because I'm not one to cross picket lines. And I was assured by them that they were not picketing against me here or against you, but they were demonstrating that they had grievances. And we acknowledge that grievances do exist and that there has to be a way of adjusting those grievances. It is so much easier in life, so much easier to understand that these days are not days for one to make decisions based on whatever happened to be our desire and our inclination because of power against other people; that those decisions more and more throughout the world are not standing up; that the only thing that stands up eventually and throughout is a decision based on reason and on justice and on a willingness to meet with however lowly the man or the woman may be raising the complaint and the grievances, however lowly they may be to meet with them. After all, they are all of the same human race. I want to assure you that I don't know their complaints in detail. And it would not be in keeping to say that I know all the issues, but I do know that there are grievances and those grievances should be adjusted.

What I am saying is to all of you who do not feel the grievance, to all those of you sitting there who do not understand what the grievance is, take a little time and find out. Find out what the grievance is. Find out why they have a picket sign; what is it [that is] hurting [. . .] them. Otherwise you have created in this university, as they have created in the fields, a group of men and women, the vast majority of people, who don't understand why we grieve and become a problem for everyone concerned.

The employers, the agricultural employers in California, have had the attitude for many years that farm workers really don't have a right to organize, and they've demonstrated this attitude in many ways; but just recently after about five years of struggle in the lettuce—in the grape strike and boycott—and after a successful boycott and after a successful organizing in those areas where workers want to have a union, the employers have come to the conclusion that they can no longer stop the forward thrust of the farm workers' movement by the traditional methods that they have used for many years, and that is one of ridiculing the movement, trying to make the movement illegal, trying to say that the movement is comprised of Communists and trying to ignore us. And so they've gone now to a very potent method, and the method is one of electing legislation against our interest as workers, to stop them or the workers from organizing. They have tried three times in the last three years in the state legislature to get repressive legislation. The state legislators turned them down. So then they went to the petition initiative. They have now gone to a method of getting signatures from registered voters to put the question of agricultural labor relations on the ballot in 1972, in November.

And this is what I want to talk to you about. To the employers who have a difficult time, the growers and their friends have a difficult time justifying what they are saying. First of all, they say that our union does not want to have secret-ballot elections and that if we did the workers wouldn't support us, and that is not true. The employers know that, the growers know that, and we know that. On the other hand, they know that the only thing that will save and preserve agriculture as is today with the employer here and the worker without any power, the only way we will keep agriculture from coming into the twentieth century is by enacting legislation that will do two things: that will take away our right to strike and our right to boycott. And so what Proposition 22 does very effectively if it passes, they are going to take the right to boycott, the right to strike by doing the following: Proposition 22 says that there's great concern among the citizens of the state of California, if this is enacted, [over] the uninterrupted flow of agricultural products from the fields to the market place. And they make a great, a *great* thing about that, and then they go and they say sort of as an after thought, "Incidentally, workers have the right to organize." And then they come back in the next paragraph and throughout the proposition and systematically take away those rights that we have. Now, an employer under 22, a grower if he thinks

Chávez speaking at a rally against Proposition 22 in Fresno, California, in September 1972. *Photo by Glen Pearcy. Courtesy Walter P. Reuther Library, Wayne State University*

there is going to be a strike, if he feels there's a threat of a strike, if he dreams there is going to be a strike, or if he just plain wants to think there is going to be a strike, he can go to the judge and get a sixty-day injunction against strikes at harvest time. And the clincher is why sixty days. Why not eighty days? Why not forty-five days? And the answer is very simple. Sixty days because of 192 crops that are harvested in California, ninety-eight of those crops can be harvested within a period of less than sixty days. And so, effectively, if we cannot strike at harvest time, when can we strike? You haven't seen groups of people striking when they are unemployed have you? A strike is not a bad thing. The labor movement of this country and of the world has been built on strikes.

Then, you go a step further to accomplish the aims that they have and then they . . . Proposition 22 says that boycotts, either primary or secondary boycotts, are illegal and we cannot boycott by trade name, by generic name, or in any other way, including boycotting either in front of a store, or boycotting, say, in the living room. If you out there support the lettuce boycott, you tell your friend in the living room . . . , "Don't eat lettuce." If Proposition 22 comes into effect, you will be breaking the law. And it is punishable by one year in jail and $5,000 fine. I doubt that they will go that far, but this is what the law says. That is what the proposition says. Now in order to be able to go to the public and sell the idea of taking the boycott and the strike away from us, they come back and they say that there should be secret-ballot elections for the purpose of representation elections to determine if the workers want a union, and, if so, what union they want. And it's to this that I want to speak very clearly.

They've got an election procedure that first of all says that in order to have an election 30 percent of the workers have to petition the board that they want representation. And we are not arguing with that. Then the board will order an election provided, however, that if another union was involved and they got 15 percent of the signatures they could also be on the ballot, and we are not against that. But further on in that clause Proposition 22 says that if two unions were to have an election and neither one got a majority, there could be a runoff election. And we'd have to wait twelve months for another election without a runoff election. And that has nothing to do with democracy in that instance. Then to qualify as a voter, a worker must work fourteen days out of the last thirty days in order to vote. But in order to qualify as a farm worker, he must work one hundred days in any one geographic area in the proceeding year. Then elections could not be held, and this is really ridiculous.

Proposition 22 says elections cannot be held at any time when the number of migratory and seasonal workers outnumber the permanent workers. Five percent of the people working in agriculture today are permanent workers, and 95 percent are migratory and seasonal. So what they are saying is that elections can never be held. Let me give you an example. In the Coachella Valley between March 15 and the last day of June, more or less, about 6,500 workers work in grapes. By July 4 less than one hundred people are working there. What Proposition 22 says that when it comes into effect, we could not hope to have an election in the last part of March, April, or May or June because there are too many workers there, and they are not permanent workers, and we would have to have an election in July or August or September when only less than one hundred workers are working, and they would be making the determination for the other 6,500 workers. And that could never stand up. The election procedure eliminates, prohibits employers from recognizing the union if they desire, prohibits a card check election, which is granted by the federal government under the National Labor Relations Act, and disqualifies the strikers from voting. Under the federal law, as you know, if there are one hundred people that are working in our factory and fifty-one people walk out on strike, there is no election. They're automatically certified as a union. Here they will be disqualified as workers because the moment the employer will replace them with strikebreakers, those strikers are disqualified and are no longer considered to be agricultural workers under the act, under Proposition 22, therefore, ineligible to vote.

The people, the growers and the people helping them, had a very great difficult time in qualifying the petition. In order to get people to sign the petition after going out and finding out that many people refused to sign it, they began to misrepresent the petition. They began to do things like when a prospective volunteer that wanted to make a little extra money came to their office, they were told specifically, "Stay away from college campuses; stay away from Chicano groups. It would be better for you to go to the elderly middle class people, preferably women, because they don't ask questions." Then they were also told [that] the legal description of what Proposition 22 was all about has to appear by law on the petition. Blancher & Associates from San Francisco, who got almost $300,000 to qualify the petition, came up with a gimmick. They printed a now famous pink card that was placed right on top of the Attorney General's description of what Proposition 22 was all about so that when the prospective signer came up to the table they were not able to see the actual legal description of what 22 is all about. In place, there was on top of the description a pink card that talked about a better keeper for farm workers, a minimum wage for farm workers, and this petition is going to lower food prices, and this petition is really helping César Chávez and the farm workers. And through that vast misrepresentation, they got people to sign it. We decided in the union not to oppose the signing. We thought that it would be more democratic if people wanted to sign to let them sign and we would fight it out in the general election. But a writer for the *Los Angeles Times* went in and posed as a petition gatherer and leaked out that information. When that happened we began then to become interested. In the last four weeks we've uncovered [that] in every single county when they got petitions—but including more so in Los Angeles County, Orange, San Diego, San Bernadino, Riverside, Kern, Fresno, San Francisco, Santa Clara, Alameda, for in every single county in order to qualify the petition—they did the following: they misrepresented the facts with the pink card. Many people signed not knowing what they were signing. They committed fraud and forgery.

We presented to the Secretary of State, [Jerry] Brown, overwhelming evidence that the petition qualified only because of all the misrepresentations, frauds, and forgeries. Let me give you some examples. There are long lists filed with the different county clerks in these counties where obviously one man wrote all the names, all the addresses, all the dates. There are petitions where they were circulated by kids ten, eleven, and twelve years old. What they did was that the petition circulators went to the kids and they subcontracted in fact—incidentally, that's a term we really hate in agriculture because the labor contractors, they subcontracted—the petition circulation; circulating the petitions, and 30 cents was being paid for each name, so there are cases where men and women would keep 20 cents or 15 cents and give the rest to these kids who were going all around the neighborhoods [to] get signatures, which is totally illegal.

And so Proposition 22 has three hurdles to go through: the Secretary of State is in court, asking the court to take 22 off the ballot; and if it doesn't come off the ballot there is going to be a vote obviously on November the 7th. If it does pass, we are going to go to court ourselves. So we don't think 22 can make . . . might make one or two of those hurdles but not three. But we'd much rather like to see the people turn it down in the election. We'd much rather like to see those who support us go to the polls first and even those who don't support us turn out for the elections. Those who want to support and maintain and preserve the right of initiative in this state, to vote against it, even if you don't agree with the farm workers, so that tomorrow we will be able when we vote for those issues, whatever they may be, be able to know that, in fact, no one was lied to and you are voting on something that was gathered in a legal way. Proposition 22 is not going to end the turmoil in the fields. It can't. The more repression we get, the more solidified we get and the more we fight. It's an obvious fact. Because, you see, the more we get persecuted, the more martyrs there are. And that's the history of mankind. We are going to do it nonviolently—that's our destiny; we're committed to it. We're doing it nonviolently because we know the effects of nonviolence. We are doing it nonviolently because nonviolent action is superior to any type of action and more lasting than you can fight nonviolently morally and legally and you can hope to get wide support from all of the interest groups and from all the people in the country. We are going to do it that way because we are committed to it and because it is effective and because we want with our own actions in a small way to show other people who have grievances like here today, that nonviolent action has with it truth and has with it tremendous power that cannot be generated in any other way. So we thank you for being here. I have a few moments, and if you have questions I would like to answer.

Speech in Coachella, 1973

A transcript of this impromptu speech is in the United Farm Workers Papers, Wayne State University.

Brothers and sisters in the field—for you are our brothers and sisters of the fields, just as your mothers and fathers were the brothers and sisters of our mothers and fathers. We are the people of the fields, the people who have made the trees and the vines the work of our lives. We know together what the truth is and you know, as we know, that there was never anyone to care about us until the Farm Workers Union came. ONLY the Farm Workers Union gave us new hope and new dreams for our families and our children. You know that and we know that and nothing can ever change it. Before the Farm Workers Union we had only each other to care for. It was our common problems and our common suffering that gave birth to this union, our own union, the Farm Workers Union. All around us were those who said that it could never be done. Everywhere people said that the growers were too strong for us, that the police would be against us, that the courts would beat us down, and that sooner or later we would fall back into the poverty and despair of our forefathers. But we fooled them. We fooled them because our common suffering and our love for each other and our families kept us together and kept us sacrificing and fighting for the better tomorrow that all of us dream about as we work among the vines.

Stop and think: What do you dream of as you work day after day in the hot sun? You dream of a nicer home for your wife, a good school for your kids, some dignity and rest for the older ones. Those have always been the dreams of the farm workers, but they never started to come true until we built this union. No one can ever erase from your minds or our minds that there was no one who cared, no one who fought for us, no one who helped hold out to us hope for a brighter tomorrow. It was the Farm Workers Union, YOUR Farm Workers Union which did it. Never until the Union came did our wages move ahead. Think of it: We are the youngest union in America and yet we have DOUBLED our basic wage, and even more!

Never was our health or the health of our families given any consideration until your Farm Workers Union. Remember the days when the vines were our toilets. Remember the indignities that our wives and mothers and daughters experienced. Think back upon it brothers and sisters. It is a brighter day today in the fields and all of us who look deeply into our hearts know that the difference is entirely because of our union—THE FIRST UNION THAT EVER CARED!

But more than that we need to remember that there was something which made that UNION, for unions are not pieces of merchandise to be bought at a corner store. Our union was born out of our common suffering, our common hopes for our children, and our common love for each other.

Brothers and sisters, that love is still strong in our hearts. We think it is still strong in your hearts. We all must know that to let outsiders come in and destroy that love we have for each other is to destroy what we can make tomorrow mean for our children and our loved ones.

We came as far as we are today through sticking together. We will go even further tomorrow if we remember that under everything else our strength is our love and respect for each other.

Speech at Convention of International Union, United Automobile, Aerospace and Agricultural Implement Workers of America, Los Angeles, June 1974

A transcript of this impromptu speech is in the United Farm Workers Papers, Wayne State University.

Thank you very much, Brother McDermott, Brother Woodcock, Brother Mazey and Delegates to this 24th Constitutional Convention:

We want to congratulate all of the officers that were elected here. We want to

tell you that we bring greetings to you from the farm workers who are now struggling in the fields in California and Arizona to *bring back a union,* workers who
are struggling across the United States and Canada on the boycott, from all of
them we bring greetings to you, congratulations on your convention and ask that
all good luck remain with you and your Union for the time to come.

We have been touring the United States lately and we are amazed that there is
still great support for the farm workers' cause.

As we come to the Convention, we remember so many of you have been with us
on the picket lines in California in 1968, 1969, and with us throughout this country with the boycott picket lines.

We want to especially thank the many locals, too numerous to count, of your
great union which have been assisting us in the boycott, the CAP Council, and all
of the men, women, and rank and filers and officers of your great union, for the
tremendous support we have gotten throughout the ten years of rough going for
our union.

I want to tell you that we're asking all of you to boycott grapes, to boycott lettuce and to boycott the yellow wines. There is a little confusion about which lettuce to boycott, and I would like to tell you that we're boycotting the western iceberg head lettuce. It's a very long name for a small lettuce. The western iceberg
head lettuce is the only lettuce that looks like lettuce so there's no confusion; it's
a round head lettuce. If it does not bear the emblem of the Black Thunderbird, the
union label of our union, you should not eat it.

And on grapes the same thing. There is only one grape grower with a contract
in this union, and those grapes are marked with the union label. If you don't see
the union label, don't buy the grapes.

And on the wine, the Gallo wine, you know, that is the biggest wine company
in the world. And they put out at least twenty labels. In some cases, the word
Gallo does not appear on the label.

There are two ways to find out if you're drinking Gallo wine. If you don't see
the name Gallo on the label, you will read on the small print the words "Modesto,
California." And if it says "Modesto, California," that's Gallo wine. And another
way to find out if you're drinking Gallo wine is drink the stuff, and if you get sick,
that's also Gallo wine.

As you may know, among the labels that are made by Gallo is the one called
Ripple, and there's a button out and it's very popular these days. The buttons say
simply, "Nixon Drinks Ripple."[17]

As we travel throughout the country, we're asked constantly whether the farm
workers are going to survive. I want to tell you that the farm workers are well and
alive in California; they're striking and they're doing what they must do as workers to defend their interests.

Today in Monterey, California, the president of the Teamsters Union, Frank

Fitzsimmons, was there today at 11 o'clock to issue a charter to *their* farm workers in California.

We called a special work stoppage today of all the Teamster companies or workers of growers under a Teamster contract, and right this moment 90 percent of those workers that are in the Teamsters Union are not working because they're with us demonstrating against Fitzsimmons.

The farm workers know what it is to have a democratic union. They're not going to settle for anything less than the type of union that they want and the union they feel represents them.

We don't know anything about driving trucks or trucking. We don't know anything about organizing growers, but we know a few things about organizing farm workers.

You see, it is very plain and clear. If the farm workers are given the right to determine by their own free will which union they want, if they could get an election to let everybody know which union they want, we tell you, brothers and sisters, that the farm workers would vote 90 to 95 percent for this union as the farm workers union.

I was in Coachella, a scene of great struggle for our union not long ago, and the picket lines in our union, as you know, are family affairs. The mother comes out and the father and the kids and the grandfather and the first and third and fourth and fifth cousins, they all come to the picket lines to help one another.

I was there not long ago when a group of the kids—ages eight, ten, twelve years old—in the picket line tell a little story that they wanted to tell me and they told me the story.

It's about three men who are traveling out in the countryside in an automobile, and the car breaks down and they realize that they're going to have a difficult time making it back to the city, so they go to the nearest farmhouse and ask the farmer if he could put them up for the night, and the farmer said that he could put them up for the night.

I have to tell you that one was an Indian, a Hindu from India; the other one was a Rabbi, a Jewish Rabbi; and the third one was an unnamed Teamster official. And so after they got to the house and had a good supper, the farmer told them that he had space for two of them in the house and that the third one would have to stay in the barn because he did not have enough space for them in the house. And after they ate, the Hindu said that he would go to the barn because he had never slept in an American barn. He went to the barn and after a while the people turned out the light, and they were ready to go to sleep when there was a knock on the door. And when the door was opened, the Hindu was in the door, and he said that he couldn't sleep in the barn because there was a cow there and because of his religion he couldn't stay there.

The good Rabbi said that he would go to the barn. So the Rabbi went to the barn, and the people closed the door and turned out the lights and were getting ready to go to sleep again when there was another knock on the door.

The door was opened and the Rabbi was at the front door saying that he couldn't stay in the barn because there were pigs in the barn.

And so the Teamster said that he would go to the barn. And so he went to the barn, and the people turned out the light and were just getting ready to go to sleep when there was a commotion at the front door. The people opened up the front door and the cow and the pig were at the front door.

Brothers and sisters, the idea and the struggle to organize workers is not new. Since 1880, there have been writings of strikes in California of workers trying to get a union together for themselves. We have the American Indian. When you read your history books that there was a revolution and that there was an uprising, there was no uprising. The workers were striking to get a union.

Then came the Chinese who were brought here to build a railroad, and when the railroads were ended they went to work in the fields. And they had strange ideas that they wanted to have a union, and the growers then went to Japan and imported thousands of Japanese to come and replace the Chinese. The Japanese came to California and they had worse ideas. Not only did they want a union, but they also wanted to own the land.

And then the Hindus came and the Filipinos and the blacks and the Oakies and the Mexicans, and every single group of workers tried to organize a union and in every single instance they were beaten back.

The socialists, the Communists, the CIO, the AFL, the AFL-CIO, every single attempt to organize workers has been pushed back and destroyed. And then, finally, in 1962, our union made its appearance. And we're the first union in the history of agriculture, and thanks to you and to many people across the country we were able to get contracts and establish a union.

The growers found out soon enough that they, by themselves and the tricks they had, were no longer going to work to destroy the union, and they sought and found different alternatives to destroy our union. And so it's ironic that in this same hall, in December of 1972, Charles Colson—I'm sure you know who he is—Charles Colson was the intermediary to get Frank Fitzsimmons from the Teamsters Union at a National Farm Bureau Convention here in this hall—this is where the plot was hatched so that they could go and take our contracts from us the following spring of 1973.

Brothers and sisters, we know that it's very strange that when those contracts were gotten in 1970 for three years, that in Coachella last year, in April of last year, we had as an example thirty-four contracts in other valleys.

On April 15 at midnight, we had thirty-four contracts. The next morning we had two contracts, and the Teamsters had thirty-two contracts. How could it be when there were no elections held? How could it be when the workers didn't know what had happened? How could it be when we were in negotiations with the growers? How could it be when we had been struggling with those workers for about ten years? We were an incumbent union; we had a contract with the growers. That's the way the contracts were taken away from us.

We don't know about the Teamsters Union in other places in industry. We know about the Teamsters Union and the Teamster workers, the Teamster people who work in agriculture. And we got to conclude from what we have seen that the Teamsters in agriculture is nothing but a company union. It's a tool doing the dirty work of the employers to destroy unions and of workers to think union.

Brothers and sisters, we went back in April of 1973 and told the growers and the Teamsters, when did you have elections? Let's have elections, and let the workers decide. If the workers decide that they don't want anything to do with the Farm Workers Union, we'll pack up and leave. We'll call the strike off and we won't have a boycott and you can have the workers. But if we win the election, we want the Teamsters to leave, and we want the growers to negotiate with our union.

And we were told then that it's too late to have elections. We went back this April, a year later, and we again challenged them for an election and we made a ridiculous proposition to them. We said you won't give us an election; obviously, you're afraid you'll lose. That's why you won't give us an election.

Let me make a ridiculous proposition. We proposed a deal to the growers in Coachella and the Teamsters; we said, "Let the strikebreakers go, and let them decide for everybody which union they want." And they wouldn't take us on.

You know why? Because not even the people working in the fields are against this union. And everybody knows this.

The only way that this conflict can end is either to have elections to let the people decide or to make the strike and the boycott so powerful that the growers will not be able to sell their grapes and their lettuce and their wines until they come to us and they negotiate with us and we get a contract.

We did not only lose contracts; we lost some cherished things that we had fought so long to get: the whole idea of the labor contractor, the hiring boss, the whole idea of the man who had been exploiting workers is the third party, the crew chief—we had got rid of him, and we established hiring halls in his place. We lost that. The workers don't have that now. They're back to their old tricks of letting the labor contractors hire the workers and fire the workers.

We lost the great fight that we had put on for control of pesticides; simple conveniences for workers, like toilets in the fields. You don't find a toilet in those grape fields and lettuce fields today since our union was kicked out. The idea of having ice-cold potable water with individual drinking cups for the individuals is gone. These are the things that went out with those contracts.

But also, we don't mourn. We know that if we have to fight again to establish our union to fight with the workers to have a truly democratic union, a union that belongs to the workers, we will do it again, because if it must be done, we will do it.

We know that the workers are committed to the struggle. We know that they're willing to sacrifice. We know that they have determination. But we also know that this determination comes because of unions like the UAW who are still with us for so many years. You give us the encouragement to continue struggling. We know that come hell or high water, the Farm Workers of America are going to have a free union; they're going to have a democratic union, and they're going to have their own union. They're going to be able to determine like you do and all the workers in America which union they want. That we guarantee you.

Because, brothers and sisters, once the workers have tasted a little freedom, once the workers have seen what the union can do for them, once the workers are able to compare two unions, once the workers have struggled for so many years, then they're able to make this miracle come true. Once the workers know and have felt what it is to be free and know what it is to sit across the table from an employer, once workers know they cannot be fired at the whim of the employer—these things make an impression on the workers. And because of this, workers are willing to sacrifice and fight as long as it takes to bring back that kind of life that they had for three precious years. We have had a whole series of obstacles.

There are two Californias; there is rural California and there is also urban California. And in rural California . . . I want to let you know that the judges in those places, with few exceptions, are owned by the growers.

We have some of the most ridiculous injunctions against us. We're now striking in ten different places in California. Not only in grapes and lettuce; there are some strawberry strikes, cantaloupe strikes in every single place. We have the same injunctions because, you won't believe this, a group of district attorneys from various counties got together and got a grant from the federal government to get together and standardize an injunction. And now they have a standard injunction. Every time we have a strike, they just throw it in the hopper, and they come up with a restraining order against us which means that in places where we have two, three, four hundred people striking we are reduced to five or six people in the picket lines. That means that we can't use the bullhorn. That means that we get tremendous harassment; that means that like last year we had almost five thousand people arrested for breaking the injunction, which means that they're free then to go to Mexico and import numbers of illegals to come and break the strike, which means that there are now people in California who make a business—it's a flourishing business—to run this private police force and this private patrol. A flourishing business to be in is the business of a professional strikebreaker or strikebreaker recruiter. These are the new industries in California because of our struggle. And because of that, the boycott must continue; the boycott must go on to be able to overcome, because we cannot do the organizing in the traditional way that you do it.

Until we get 100 percent of the workers on strike, it really doesn't mean anything, because two days later they will replace all those with people from Mexico. That is what we are up against.

Brothers and sisters, we know that right now in California there are at least sixty to seventy thousand illegals from Mexico breaking strikes and working elsewhere. And we make a petition to all of you; we make a petition that every Congressman and every U.S. Senator must know what is going on so they can register the proper complaint with the Attorney General of the United States to get him to start enforcing the laws in regard to the wide-open door policy, the invitation to the illegals, to come and break our strikes.

If we were able to remove the illegals from California, at least from the strike fields, we would win the strike overnight. This is another reason why we must continue the struggle of the boycott to be able to win.

The strike last year was a terrible bloody strike, costly. We had almost five thousand people jailed; over two hundred people were beaten up and were sent to the hospital. We had forty-four people shot and wounded, twelve people seriously, and two people were killed.

All on our side.

The gimmick of the county sheriff bringing helicopters in our picket lines and dispersing pickets, calling our picket lines illegal assemblies and either beating us or taking us to jail or forcing us to give up the picketing, blocking the county roads at midnight so we wouldn't go to picket at five o'clock in the morning—all these outrageous acts against the union, and even with all of that we continued to struggle, continued to fight and continued to have hope that we're going to win.

We want to tell you that your help from your union is substantial and we appreciate it.

Brother [Leonard] Woodcock and Brother [Emil] Mazey and the rest of the officers, and all of you: We have been receiving from your union since last April $10,000 a week, and without that money we'd be dead today. And we stand here today to tell you that we appreciate that. We want you to know that.

We want you to know that as the union won at Farah, we'll win; as you've beaten the General Motors people, we'll beat the growers in California. But let me tell you that although you don't think you'll be paid back, we want to make a commitment. We're going to pay you back in the following way.

We're going to have our own union. And after we build our union, we're going to be with you side by side, struggling to help other workers build other unions.

We know that we have a commitment to help people as we've been helped. We'll never lose that. And that's the promise we make you right here today.

What we wouldn't do and give to have a union like the UAW. We had a founding convention last year; we built a constitution, and I will tell you that we borrowed a lot from your constitution. What we wouldn't do to have a union like the UAW. The workers out in the fields know about the union; they know about the labor movement. They know about unions today, and they didn't know ten years ago.

They're not afraid; they want a union.

And these workers will struggle as long as it takes; they'll do whatever has to be done, legally and morally and nonviolently; they'll stay with it until we win. That we know.

Not only in California but in Arizona and throughout the United States, farm workers are now in their own revolution. In the fields of California and Arizona and other states it's like the 1930s for this Union. The workers in Florida, the black workers, the Chicano workers in California, the Filipino workers in California, the white workers in Arizona want a union. And there's no power in this earth . . . once the workers get the spirit and the idea and the great desire.

It's like a great thirst, and that thirst is not going to be abated; that thirst is not going to go away until the workers have a union that they can work with and they can work under and they can support, and it's their union.

And brothers and sisters, it doesn't matter what it takes. How long it takes, what we have to give up in terms of sacrifices—we'll stay with it. We'll stay with it because we know that if we give up the fight today, the Farm Workers may be organized, but they're going to be organized in a very different union that's not going to represent them. There are just too many forces against the workers having a free union under the other unions. There's no way that it will work.

So we want to close by telling you that there's a great irony here. You know men, women, and children who sacrifice and struggle and work too hard. So many things are asked of them: to travel the length and the width of this country; they're asked to move from place to place; they're asked to travel one thousand miles, two thousand miles without job security, to go to the other side of the country, in the hope of finding a job—and if they do find a job, they're going to be paid a pittance for it; to go on hoping that they'll find a home—most likely they wind up under a tree or under a bridge on a river bank; to go with no money, save enough for the gas to get there, risking all of the things that come from being poor and not having the security of a job and of a union. And they're asked that year in and year out, and they do it. They do it because—you see, brothers and sisters—they're laborers, the crucifying labor of the short handle hoe being bent in two. Stoop labor. Ten hours, twelve hours. They do that and they do it willingly. And you know what they do because of that great sacrifice. They are involved in the planting and the cultivation and the harvesting of the greatest abundance of food known in this society. They bring in so much food to feed you and me and the whole country and enough food to export to other places. The ironic thing and the tragic thing is that after they make this tremendous contribution, they don't have any money or any food left for themselves. And that's ridiculous. Here they produce a tremendous amount of food and there is no food left for themselves and for the children.

We're not going to stop struggling until the day comes when they can at least participate in the fruits of their labors, have enough money and enough food to eat for themselves and their families.

We want to thank you very, very much, and we ask God's blessings upon your union.

Good afternoon.

■■■■■■

CHAPTER 3

Ongoing Challenges, Heady Triumphs, Discouraging Defeats, 1976–83

In the last half of the 1970s Chávez turned increasingly toward politics to achieve his goals. With substantial credibility in California and indeed in many parts of the nation, he was a potent force who could rightly call Governor Jerry Brown a friend and who enjoyed growing national influence from his educational speaking tours. And statewide politics had produced progress for his crop pickers. The California legislature had passed and Governor Brown had signed ALRA, the Agricultural Labor Relations Act, and the governor had appointed a pro-UFW board to oversee its operation. When the UFW defeated the Teamsters in many of the early elections under the ALRB, the UFW's future at last seemed assured.[1]

In what was now a familiar pattern, the UFW had little time to enjoy its successes. Opponents of the ALRB unleashed a textbook example of the use of power to undercut labor laws and to bust unions, engaging in a variety of activities, both legal and illegal, such as burglarizing union offices, placing spies in the UFW, and initiating lawsuits and legislative action to weaken ALRA, specifically by denying funds necessary for the ALRB to function. In response, Chávez and UFW supporters placed Proposition 14 on the ballot in 1976. It proposed that the ALRB be adequately funded and that union organizers be allowed access to workers on farms in attempts to recruit them. The growers and their legislative supporters marshaled massive resources and defeated the proposition.[2]

Notwithstanding the defeat, the UFW's overall progress was impressive. The Teamsters again agreed not to organize agricultural workers, and by 1978 the UFW had over one hundred thousand members. In this moment of peak UFW strength Chávez called an end to the general boycotts against grape and lettuce growers and promised that in the future only selected brands would be boycotted. His increased skill with boycotts was part of his growing reliance on sophisticated methods. Newly hired public relations experts helped him refine his message for the public, and newly purchased computerized mailing equipment could send out a million appeals a week.

At the very time the UFW was overcoming external challenges, it faced growing internal problems. Growers complained that the union lacked the professional staff needed to implement the terms of contracts; the union's staff changed so often that few were able to master their jobs; and there were too few accountants, experts in management, lawyers, personnel officers, and other officials needed to consolidate UFW gains and to run its operations effectively. Some UFW members began to question Chávez's leadership openly, criticizing him for centralizing power in himself and mistreating staff members. Between 1978 and 1981 many prominent leaders left in disagreements with Chávez, among them Gil Padilla, one of the union's founders; Jerry Cohen, the chief legal counsel; Jessica Govea, director of the union's health service board; Marshall Ganz, the union's chief organizer; and Eliseo Medina, a former member of the union's executive board. Much of the union's energy was spent in internal battles rather than in winning union elections and negotiating contracts.

In 1979, in the midst of the internal dissension, the UFW mounted a massive lettuce strike. It was the strike Chávez had always dreamed of. He confided to a group of strikers: "I feel the way I have never felt before. . . . We have thirty years of struggle behind us, but I am spirited and encouraged. I feel I can fight for another hundred years."[3] The strike was eventually successful, though not before violence returned to the fields and UFW member Rufino Contreras was murdered.

Although UFW membership continued strong and conditions in the fields seemed to be improving, the fortunes of both farm workers and Chávez reversed quickly. By the 1980s, as Chávez's opponents gained key political victories in California and the nation, the UFW was winning fewer elections and losing thousands of members. In 1982 pro-grower George Deukmejian replaced Jerry Brown as governor and appointed a union foe, David Sterling, to head the ALRB. The board immediately adopted an antiunion stance. Though the UFW still had enough contracts to stay alive, it had lost much of its power. In a broader context the protest and idealism that characterized the 1960s and early 1970s had given way to the conservatism and materialism that characterized the Reagan years as president.

During this period as throughout his career, Chávez's primary rhetorical means remained the spoken word. His nomination speech for presidential candidate Jerry Brown in 1976 was particularly telling. He does not focus on Brown or the Democratic Party, referring to Brown by name only once and omitting discussion of Brown's positions on issues. Instead, Chávez focused on "social justice and human rights."[4] Given a national forum and an influential audience of policy makers, Chávez remained true to his life's cause by offering reasons and evidence he believed would instruct the public and thereby lead to improvements in the lives of the poor.

In a letter to the *Los Angeles Times* in 1978 he focused on the events surrounding his arrest for violating a ban on picketing near Yuma, Arizona. He found it ironic that in Yuma, his birthplace, he would be arrested by police who had grown up in the same part of Arizona where he had been born. By his own account he was treated well in jail, and in the courtroom the county attorney made it clear that he did not want to prosecute him and thereby make him a martyr. The authorities, unsure how to treat a jailed leader who was a heroic saint to many, released him and handed down a six-month suspended contempt sentence.

That same year an article by Chávez appeared in a special issue of *Maryknoll* magazine devoted to "The Legacy of Martin Luther King, Jr." In the article he explained his ideas on nonviolence, linking them to the nonviolent beliefs of Dr. King and Gandhi, relating nonviolence to the UFW's efforts at improving the lives of farm workers. Notice in this essay, as in all of Chávez's written works, how his rhetorical profile retains its essential qualities.

In February 1979 Chávez addressed the Texas Organizing Convocation in Pharr, Texas. He resumed his role of teacher, here particularly as teacher of union organizers. The first part of the speech is a restatement of his eulogy for Rufino Contreras. (Chapter 5 includes that speech and a discussion of its context and content.) He then covers the struggles of farm workers, the stages through which the union evolved from its beginning until 1979, the improvements in working conditions it had won, its opponents' hostile actions, the sacrifices workers endured, and its organization and goals.

Speaking before a very different audience, a gathering of members of the United Church of Christ, he maintained his role of educator. His rhetorical means were entirely appropriate for instruction as part of a divinely guided plan for progress—in this case to an audience that likely shared his spiritual starting point. He relied on clearly organized and worded arguments and evidence, a blueprint for the future that if followed would ensure success. He began by thanking the members of the audience for their support in the past, then talked about the current status of the union including the current internal problems and claimed that the internal problems had been solved, partially through a reorganization of the union's structure. He took great care to clarify the union's goals.

In 1982 he spoke to a graduating class in negotiations in La Paz about the need for trained organizers in the union. He believed that people should be trained, given responsible positions, and then allowed to complete those tasks effectively. Some of the rhetorical devices of his remarks—particularly his use of anaphora, the stylistic device of beginning consecutive sentences or fragments with the same words, and of antithesis—parallel the style in John F. Kennedy's inaugural address. Chávez's speech writer, Marc Grossman, often used famous speeches like Kennedy's Inaugural as models for Chávez's speeches.

The texts in this section further illustrate how Chávez evolved as a leader and as a rhetor. He began the period with a strong belief in the power of political action as a vehicle in improving the lives of farm workers. At its end, he had markedly less confidence in political solutions and had returned to the union's most traditional tactics and arguments. His strong faith in public address, however, remained unshaken. His fundamental rhetorical means and ends held steady as he added polish to his style and adapted and created arguments and appeals to fit new exigencies and audiences.

Nomination Address for Governor Jerry Brown, Democratic National Convention, July 14, 1976

This speech was delivered from notes. The original notes are in the Jacques Levy Papers in the Beinecke Rare Book and Manuscript Library, Yale University, New Haven Connecticut.

Buenos Noches. A todos mis hermanos de la habla Español.

Brothers and Sisters:

We bring greetings from California, greetings from the men, women, and children who toil the fields to bring our daily food to our tables.

There's a great task to be done in this nation. First, we have to set a goal. We have to give people a sense of purpose.

There's a great deal to do. We need to construct instead of destroy. We need to inspire hope in the people for the future.

Right now we have millions of people unable to find work. That inability to find work destroys the spirit. We have men, women, and youth who are skilled, who have energy and ideals, looking for work, and all they get are hand-outs.

Hand-outs! Imagine how stifling that can be to the spirit.

Or they get make-work, busy-work. This is just as bad. It makes people feel of no purpose. It makes people feel useless.

Others suggest that only technology can solve our problems. But too often technology means drudgery. It means turning human beings into robots. Imagine how many people in America today find no purpose in their daily work. Imagine how crippling that can be.

Human beings are unique because they are creative. When we stifle that creativity, we destroy the individual's spirit. We need to give workers a voice. Let them be creative at their place of work. Not only will that enrich their lives, but it will benefit us all.

We need work that improves the quality of life, for this type of work is the cornerstone of human dignity. And because people are important, working for people—even sacrificing a little bit for them—brings much meaning to one's life.

There is so much meaningful work to be done! And so many people unemployed!

Think of the thousands of people who are bedridden with sores on their backs because there's no one to turn them.

Think of the older people who are abandoned, who need a cup of water, who need a warm meal, but have no one to give them help.

Think about the countless children who have to be cared for, who can be trained, educated, and given a purpose and love.

What about housing, what about rebuilding our cities, what about mass transit?! And what could be more meaningful than providing decent health care for everyone in America?

What could have more purpose than working to end the use of narcotics? What could be more joyful than working to restore and preserve the sacredness of land, water, and air? For patriotism is not protecting the land of our fathers, but preserving the land for our children.

But we know that only when we feel that that street is our street, when we feel that that river is our river, and we know that this land is our land, only then will we take care of them, and only then will we be able to deal with those problems.

People are the best answer to solving their own problems. Until our government hears the voices of those with problems, all the people, we will never be able to solve those problems and more and more people will be turned off.

César Chávez Goes Home
Los Angeles Times, June 25, 1978

This letter was reprinted in *American Dissent from Thomas Jefferson to César Chávez: The Rhetoric of Reform and Revolution,* edited by Thomas E. Hachey and Ralph E. Weber (Huntington, N.Y.: Robert E. Krieger Publishing Company, 1981), 162–65.

"Congress shall make no law . . . abridging the freedom . . . or of the right of the people peaceable to assemble. . . ."

My thoughts kept returning to those lines in the First Amendment as my wife Helen and I stood with about 40 workers beneath the United Farm Workers' black-eagled banners beside a melon field near Yuma, Arizona. History provided the backdrop, ongoing injustice wrote the script.

We were there—the date was Tuesday, June 13—because Yuma field workers had asked for UFW help in mounting a strike for better wages, hours and working conditions. Many of the workers with us were striking for the sixth time in eight seasons. Each time their efforts had been broken by court injunction. But just standing, we were challenging the latest court order—it had been issued by Superior Judge Bill Helm on June 7—that banned all picketing.

By this time we had a federal court decision behind us. Just last April, a three-judge federal panel in Phoenix declared the 1972 Arizona Farm Labor Law unconstitutional "in its entirety" and enjoined the state from enforcing it. The Arizona statute had denied voting rights to most migrant farmworkers, banned their right to strike and boycott and outlawed negotiations on issues crucial to the workers.

Our union attorneys told us that the judge's order was the most restrictive anti-picketing ruling issued by any American court in generations. It banned all picketing by all persons on all parts of the growers' properties. The growers had obtained the order at a hearing where they alleged picket-line violence and claimed workers were satisfied with their lot and did not want to unionize.

The scenario was a familiar one. Every year we faced the same scene in Arizona: All we could do was sit dejected as growers hid behind court injunctions. For nearly a decade rural judges and growers in Arizona have used legal maneuvering to outlaw farmworker organizing.

Because the harvest period is the best time to organize, jurists issue illegal injunctions, knowing they will be overturned by higher courts. But in the meantime, growers gain time. It usually takes months before anti-strike orders are reversed. Meanwhile, workers, deprived of their rights, harvest the crops, then move on to their next job and the strike is lost. Each time a strike is broken by courts' and growers' strategy, the workers' hopes to organize are destroyed.

So when I received a call for help from the Arizona workers, we started the car trip to Yuma from our headquarters in Keene. On the way, I thought of the paradox between that state and California. Since 1975, farm workers in California have had the right to choose a union in state-supervised elections. But just across the line in Arizona, farm workers are denied even the most basic rights afforded other segments of American labor.

As we traveled that Monday evening through the California desert, we wondered what lay in store for us in Yuma. We have found in California and elsewhere that if unconstitutional injunctions are left unchallenged, they provide growers with terrible precedent.

Still, my thoughts turned to jail; the idea of losing one's freedom is a sobering thought. In this case it was a particularly poignant idea, for Yuma is my birth-place.

If you look at a map, Yuma is at the center of a triangle formed by the juncture of California, Arizona and the state of Sonora, Mexico, all separated by the Colorado River. When I was born there in 1927—on land my grandfather home-steaded before the turn of the century—agriculture around Yuma was distinguished by small family farming. Times were not easy, but my early memories are of a rich and full life—until the Depression hit. Then we lost our land and were forced into the California migrant stream.

Today, agriculture near Yuma is mostly run by large-scale agribusiness. The men, women and children who work the land are brought chiefly from San Luis Rio Colorado, across the international border in Sonora, where they live in misery and poverty.

About 40 workers joined us to picket at the G&S Produce Co. fields in violation of the judge's order. Before long a half dozen Yuma County sheriff's deputies faced us across U.S. Highway 95 under the hot desert sun. A deputy formally read Judge Helm's injunction and said we would be arrested if we refused to move.

Behind us in the fields three harvesting crews—mostly women and children—braved the heat and the dust, repeatedly stooping to cut cantaloupes, then placing them in heavy sacks strapped around their shoulders.

The workers picketing with us left the area at my request; Helen and I remained and were arrested.

One of the arresting officers who rode with us to the jailhouse hailed from the north Gila Valley, my birthplace. We reminisced about people and places I left behind many years ago. As we drove, I thought about how strange it was to come home this way.

Soon brought before Judge Helm, we asked to present constitutional challenges to the injunction. We also declined release on our own recognizance or upon payment of bail because, as a matter of conscience, we felt that to accept release would legitimize an illegal order. As we told Judge Helm, the only way we would leave jail would be if he vacated his injunction. He refused.

Judge Helm had ruled the picketing unlawful because employees were asked to walk off their jobs. But that has always been the objective of a strike and even Arizona laws recognize that as lawful conduct.

The judge held that picketing violated Arizona's right-to-work law and its anti-secondary boycott statute, but neither applied to the Yuma organizing.

Finally, we were told that picketing was illegal because employers were losing money. But a strike's purpose is to generate economic pressure on employers and the courts have held this is not unlawful.

Judge Helm's order flies in the face of 30 years of legal precedent. And the

U.S. Constitution has never sanctioned such a total ban on freedom of speech. We knew that such an injunction had to be challenged even though it meant we would be jailed.

This struggle transcends the organizing effort and even the union. Judge Helm threatens more than our rights and the rights of union members. At issue is the ability of all Americans to engage in First Amendment activities without fear of criminal prosecution.

In our 16 years of organizing the UFW, we had been imprisoned several times. It has never been a pleasant experience and it was not pleasant in Yuma, although the jail personnel were professional and treated us well.

But the courteous treatment in jail belied the resentment astir outside in the local grower community. By Wednesday, June 14, some threats had been received in the jail and the sheriff's officers were concerned as we prepared for another hearing before Judge Helm.

Judge Helm denied our motion to quash or modify his injunction after listening to 20 minutes of oral argument. "The growers showed their employees are satisfied with their working conditions," he said. "The picketing was for the purpose of intimidating field workers. . . . What can the UFW offer these workers that the growers haven't given them?" But not a single worker testified to being satisfied with wages or conditions.

Then the judge said, "Picketing now would raise the fear of intimidation even if picketing were legal." Like a former Kern County sheriff who told a U.S. Senate subcommittee he had arrested striking farmworkers because they "might" break the law, Judge Helm suspended the First Amendment because there "might" be intimidation.

Then, at the urging of the county attorney, we were ordered released from jail over our protests and instructed to return for trial Friday. "If (César Chávez) wants to be a martyr," the county attorney argued, "let him do it in someone else's jail." It was almost a comic scene: The prosecuting attorney arguing for our release; our attorney arguing to keep us in.

When we stepped from the jail we were greeted by 600 cheering farmworkers waving the familiar UFW banners.

Later, as we prepared to return to California, a farmworker told us of an experience he had that morning with an Anglo woman employed at the courthouse:

"Is Chávez still in jail trying to get sympathy?" she asked.

"Ma'am, he's in jail because he won't obey an unconstitutional injunction," the worker answered.

"He should go back to Russia. We have to protect our farmers," she said.

"The Constitution protects farmworkers too."

The worker, of course, is right—unless he is speaking of that part of the

United States bounded by the four walls of Judge Helm's court. On Friday, the judge ignored the mandate of the First Amendment and the ruling of the federal court and handed Helen and me six month suspended contempt sentences.

Our convictions will be appealed.

Martin Luther King, Jr.: He Showed Us the Way, April 1978

This essay appeared in *Maryknoll,* April 1978, 52–55.

In honoring Martin Luther King, Jr.'s memory we also acknowledge nonviolence as a truly powerful weapon to achieve equality and liberation—in fact, the only weapon that Christians who struggle for social change can claim as their own.

Dr. King's entire life was an example of power that nonviolence brings to bear in the real world. It is an example that inspired much of the philosophy and strategy of the farm workers' movement. This observance of Dr. King's death gives us the best possible opportunity to recall the principles with which our struggle has grown and matured.

Our conviction is that human life is a very special possession given by God to man and that no one has the right to take it for any reason or for any cause, however just it may be.

We are also convinced that nonviolence is more powerful than violence. Nonviolence supports you if you have a just and moral cause. Nonviolence provides the opportunity to stay on the offensive, and that is of crucial importance to win any contest.

If we resort to violence then one of two things will happen: either the violence will be escalated and there will be many injuries and perhaps deaths on both sides, or there will be total demoralization of the workers.

Nonviolence has exactly the opposite effect. If, for every violent act committed against us, we respond with nonviolence, we attract people's support. We can gather the support of millions who have a conscience and would rather see a nonviolent resolution to problems. We are convinced that when people are faced with a direct appeal from the poor struggling nonviolently against great odds, they will react positively. The American people and people everywhere still yearn for justice. It is to that yearning that we appeal.

But if we are committed to nonviolence only as a strategy or tactic, then if it fails our only alternative is to turn to violence. So we must balance the strategy with a clear understanding of what we are doing. However important the struggle is and however much misery, poverty and exploitation exist, we know that it cannot be more important than one human life. We work on the theory that men and women who are truly concerned about people are nonviolent by nature.

These people become violent when the deep concern they have for people is frustrated and when they are faced with seemingly insurmountable odds.

We advocate militant nonviolence as our means of achieving justice for our people, but we are not blind to the feelings of frustration, impatience and anger which seethe inside every farm worker. The burdens of generations of poverty and powerlessness lie heavy in the fields of America. If we fail, there are those who will see violence as the shortcut to change.

It is precisely to overcome these frustrations that we have involved masses of people in their own struggle throughout the movement. Freedom is best experienced through participation and self-determination, and free men and women instinctively prefer democratic change to any other means. Thus, demonstrations and marches, strikes and boycotts are not only weapons against the growers, but our way of avoiding the senseless violence that brings no honor to any class or community. The boycott, as Gandhi taught, is the most nearly perfect instrument of nonviolent change, allowing masses of people to participate actively in a cause.

When victory comes through violence, it is a victory with strings attached. If we beat the growers at the expense of violence, victory would come at the expense of injury and perhaps death. Such a thing would have a tremendous impact on us. We would lose regard for human beings. Then the struggle would become a mechanical thing. When you lose your sense of life and justice, you lose your strength.

The greater the oppression, the more leverage nonviolence holds. Violence does not work in the long run and if it is temporarily successful, it replaces one violent form of power with another just as violent. People suffer from violence. Examine history. Who gets killed in the case of violent revolution? The poor, the workers. The people of the land are the ones who give their bodies and don't really gain that much for it. We believe it is too big a price to pay for not getting anything. Those who espouse violence exploit people. To call men to arms with many promises, to ask them to give up their lives for a cause and then not produce for them afterwards, is the most vicious type of oppression.

We know that most likely we are not going to do anything else the rest of our lives except build our union. For us there is nowhere else to go. Although we would like to see victory come soon, we are willing to wait. In this sense time is our ally. We learned many years ago that the rich may have money, but the poor have time.

It has been our experience that few men or women ever have the opportunity to know the true satisfaction that comes with giving one's life totally in the nonviolent struggle for justice. Martin Luther King, Jr., was one of these unique servants and from him we learned many of the lessons that have guided us. For these lessons and for his sacrifice for the poor and oppressed, Dr. King's memory will be cherished in the hearts of the farm workers forever.

Summary of the President's Address to the Texas Organizing Convocation, Pharr, Texas, February 25, 1979

A copy of the outline of this speech is in the United Farm Workers Papers, Wayne State University.

THE WORTH OF A FARM WORKER

As we open this organizing convocation in Texas this morning, our thoughts return to February 10, 1979, a day of infamy for all farm workers. On this day greed and injustice struck down our brother, Rufino Contreras, in a struck lettuce field in California's Imperial Valley.

We wonder what is the worth of a man? What is the worth of a farm worker. Rufino, his father, and brother together gave their company twenty years of their labor. They were faithful workers who helped build up the wealth of their boss, helped build up the wealth of his ranch.

What was their reward for their service and their sacrifice? When they petitioned for a more just share of what they themselves produced, when they spoke out against the injustice they endured, the company answered them with bullets; the company sent hired guns to quiet Rufino Contreras.

Capital and labor together produce the fruit of the land. But what really counts is labor! The human beings who torture their bodies, sacrifice their youth, and numb their spirits to produce this great agricultural wealth, a wealth so vast that it feeds all of America and much of the world. And yet the men, women, and children who are the flesh and blood of this production often do not have enough to feed themselves.

But we are convinced that true wealth is not measured in money or status or power. It is measured in the legacy that we leave behind for those we love and those we inspire.

In that sense, Rufino Contreras is not dead. Wherever farm workers organize, stand up for their rights, and strike for justice, Rufino is with them.

Rufino lives among us. It is those who have killed him and those who have conspired to kill him that have died, because the love, the compassion, the light in their hearts have been stilled.

Rufino still lives because those who mourn him have rededicated ourselves to the ideals for which he gave his life; Rufino Contreras lives insofar as we continue to build a union that will, someday, bring justice to all farm workers.

It is our mission to finish the work Rufino Contreras has begun among us, knowing that true justice for ourselves and our opponents is only possible before God, who is the final judge.

THE IMPERIAL VALLEY STRIKE

What are the Imperial Valley farm workers fighting for? To begin to bring their wages and benefits into the twentieth century with the same relative kinds of economic standards that workers in other industries who do similar work earn.

The economic situation of our membership is years behind other workers. While other workers had unions generations ago, and those workers made economic progress through their unions, the farm workers remained stagnant. Consequently, the farm workers have a great deal of catching up to do.

For example, since 1970 farm worker wages in the California-Arizona vegetable industry have gone up from $2 per hour to $3.70 per hour in the contracts which have expired, an 85 percent increase. But consumer prices went up 71 percent in the same period, and the farm workers are earning only 13 cents more per hour in real wages, adjusted for inflation, than they earned eight or nine years ago.

In 1970, lettuce workers earned 40 cents per box piece rate. Today, under the old contracts which have expired, they continue to earn 57 cents per box. But in real earnings they are making 6.4 cents *less* per box today than they earned eight or nine years ago.

It took the farm workers in the vegetable industry ten years to build their union to the point where we are at today. The issue in these negotiations is to put that union that has been built to work.

FOUR PHASES OF THE WORK

Our farm workers' struggle can be divided into four distinct phases:

First, when we begin the work, we suffer ridicule from our own friends, family, and neighbors—even from many of the workers themselves. After so many years many believe it just can't be done. The workers are afraid. They laugh when we say we seek to build a true farm workers' union.

During the second phase, once we have started organizing a little, we are ridiculed by friends and foe alike.

As we do more work and the organizing begins to take form, the ridicule from our opponents turns to worry and we encounter stern opposition. It is at this stage that the workers' blood, sweat, and tears are shed.

Finally, during the fourth stage, victory is achieved and there is acceptance of the union by the employers.

The farm workers in California have reached the third phase; they are no longer afraid of the growers, which is perhaps the greatest single achievement the union has made. The Texas farm workers are still struggling through the first phase.

The major provisions of UFW contracts free farm workers from the exploitation and discrimination that impoverishes so many of our people in this rich country:

Hiring Halls mean an end to the infamous farm-labor contractor system, which directly exploits and oppresses farm workers. It frees workers from shape-ups, bribes, and favoritism. It means when workers are dispatched by the hiring hall, they are guaranteed jobs.

Seniority means real job security for farm workers. It means fairness and equity during layoffs and rehiring. It means a reduced need for farm workers to migrate. It means promotions based on seniority and not friendships, nepotism, and bribery.

Grievance and Arbitration guarantees farm workers a process through which they can obtain justice if they are unfairly fired, disciplined, or mistreated by the employer. It means workers are no longer at the mercy of the grower.

Health & Safety means the grower recognizes the need to protect the lives of the workers from pesticides and dangerous working conditions.

Rest Periods mean the workers cannot be forced to work long hours without breaks from the monotony and harshness of the work.

Robert F. Kennedy Medical Plan means farm workers and their families will have access to quality medical care through their own medical program designed to meet their special needs.

The Juan de la Cruz Pension Fund means that, for the first time, farm workers will have some security in their later years.

The Nagi Daifallah Vacation Plan means workers who could never qualify for traditional vacation plans will earn some vacation benefits.

Paid Holidays mean that farm workers can join workers in other industries who celebrate important national and religious holidays without losing badly needed family income.

Union Label means that growers will place the union's Black Eagle symbol on all products shipped by the company to show the world that they were produced by farm workers: union labor.

Decent Wages mean that farm workers will no longer have to subsidize one of America's wealthiest industries with their depressed wages. This is what we have won in California. And this is what we want in Texas!

OUR MARTYRS

But we should never forget that these gains have come at a high price. The farm workers have paid a terrible cost in blood, sweat, and tears for the progress they have achieved.

Rufino Contreras was the fourth person to die in a UFW strike. In 1972 Nan Freeman, an eighteen-year-old supporter of the union, was crushed to death on a UFW picket line in Florida. In 1973, two union members—Juan de la Cruz and Nagi Daifallah—were brutally murdered during massive grape strikes. Hundreds of other farm workers were injured; thousands were arrested because they stood up for the union.

The farm workers faced the growers' hired goons, private security guards, biased police, and company unions. They faced shotguns, rifles, pistols, clubs, dogs, mace, and tear gas. But through all this, they built a union, a union that has spread throughout California and taken root in Arizona, Florida, Washington State, and Texas.

The union has survived all the combined opposition of agribusiness, the Teamsters Union, and the Nixon Administration. It has gone on to win the great majority of the five hundred union elections held under California's landmark Agricultural Labor Relations Act. It has signed over two hundred contracts with agricultural employers.

BEYOND WAGES AND WORKING CONDITIONS

But we have tried to look beyond wages and working conditions, as important as they are. We must build a true brotherhood among all our people. Our goal is to build an organization that truly cares about its people, an organization that is concerned with the families of its members, an organization that will take care of its members during the years when they cannot work, an organization that deals not only with wages, hours, and conditions but also with families, retirees, and all the pressing social problems that menace workers in our society, an organization whose members know that there are literally thousands of farm workers throughout the nation who are still not under its protection, an organization whose membership will not rest until all farm workers in the nation are brought under its banner.

TWO KINDS OF CONTRACTS

That is why our union negotiates two kinds of contracts for its members. We negotiate a collective bargaining agreement with the growers to meet our members' economic needs. We negotiate a social contract with our government to meet the other human and social needs of our people.

Our legislative program must progress hand in hand with our organizing program. Farmworkers in Texas need workmen's compensation. They need disability insurance. They need unemployment compensation. They need pesticide protection. They need abolition of the infamous short-handled hoe. They need anti-strikebreaker legislation. They need to be free from any renewed Bracero Program.

AN ORGANIZATION OF OUR OWN

But what farm workers need more than anything else is a union of our own.

Since this union was founded, it has been the dream of the leadership to build an organization led by farm workers, paid for by farm workers, and dedicated to fulfilling the needs and aspirations of farm workers. We are convinced that the vanguard of this movement must be the workers themselves; we must completely turn over the task of running the union to them.

Planning and training will be critical ingredients in this process. Every organizing committee and every organizing-committee member must be equipped with the necessary training to effectively operate the union at his or her level.

The union will be strong and united because its members and worker leadership is strong and united. We must infuse the workers with excitement, hope, mission, and promise and define exactly the goals, objectives, programs, policies, and procedures that will enable them to eventually assume the burdens of leadership and administration.

RECOGNITION FOR SACRIFICE

It has been written that those who refuse to remember the past are destined to relive it. Those of us who meet today in Texas must remember the farm workers who have sacrificed and suffered to bring the union to where it is today. All of us have been truly encouraged and inspired and are indebted to the band of farm workers who from the very beginning of the movement have been "al pie del canon"—men and women who have given their all to the cause during organizing campaigns, strikes, demonstrations, sit-ins, marches, and boycotts.

It is right and proper that these workers be recognized.

ORGANIZING STRUCTURE

When the union was formed in California, the farm workers there created the same types of organizing committees which you will formally recognize today. When the farm workers won recognition from their employers, these organizing committees became negotiating committees. And when contracts were successfully negotiated, the negotiating committees became ranch committees.

Ranch committees, in our union, perform the functions of the traditional union local. They are composed of workers elected by their fellow workers to administer the union at their respective companies. The ranch committee is at the core of a ranch community, all the union members at a company who compose the basic fabric of the union.

Organizing committees are unchartered subordinate bodies of the union created by the National Executive Board. The board may create an organizing committee in any area, in any state, where there are workers within the union's jurisdiction and not covered by a union contract. It is the president's duty to appoint directors of the organizing committees, define their territorial jurisdiction, and supervise their activities.

The board has formally approved a set of uniform rules and bylaws for organizing committees, pending presentation of the rules and bylaws to the 1979 UFW Fourth Constitutional Convention.

OUR GOALS

Our union, in its Texas organizing efforts, seeks to fulfill the goals the farm workers have set everywhere they organize under the Black Eagle banner. Our objects are:

To unite under the union's banner all workers employed as agricultural laborers, regardless of race, creed, sex, or nationality;

To negotiate, bargain collectively, contract, or otherwise deal with the employers of farm workers concerning wages, hours, working conditions, grievances, labor disputes, and all other related matters;

To protect the moral and legal right of farm workers to exert economic pressure on recalcitrant employers, including the unrestricted right to strike, boycott, and engage in other nonviolent activities;

To work and cooperate with other unions for the mutual benefit of the respective memberships and the building of solidarity among the entire labor movement;

To promote a better understanding by government and the public of the purposes and objects of this union and the labor movement as a whole;

To engage in legislative activity to promote, protect, and advance the physical, economic, and social welfare of the workers;

To promote registration, voting, political education, and other citizenship activities;

To take all such other action which will conserve and promote the welfare and interests of this union and its members;

To promote the full and equal participation by women in all affairs, activities, and leadership positions of the union.

We face an immensely powerful industry largely committed to opposing our movement. Our tasks are plain: to carry on the struggle to build one national union that will bring farm workers the blessings of union democracy and collective bargaining, one union to liberate farm workers from the pain and suffering that enslaves so many of our people in this land of wealth and promise, one union that will form a powerful force for dignity and justice for all people in America and around the world.

One brotherhood, one people, one union.

Viva la Causa!

OUR CHALLENGE

The lessons of the past are clear; the challenge before us is great. Farm workers have made many gains. But so many more workers, in Texas and elsewhere, cry out for the union, and our opponents in agribusiness and their allies are rich and powerful and determined to stop workers from building a union of their own.

Notes for Speech to the United Church Board for Homeland Ministries, United Church of Christ, October 24, 1981

A transcript of these speech notes is in the United Farm Workers Papers, Wayne State University.

1. INTRODUCTION

Thank you for inviting me to be with you.

I am glad to have this opportunity.

More than any other denomination you have led the churches in being with us and staying with us year after year.

Naturally, the Migrant Ministry (now the Farm Worker Ministry) was the key . . . . They devoted almost all their time.

Your board through John Moyer has been the main pillar of the Migrant Ministry since John first came to Delano in 1965.

John was President of National Farm Worker Ministry 1975 through 1977. Olgha Sandman was President of the National Farm Worker Ministry 1977–1979.

They still serve on the NFWM Executive Committee and provide strong leadership.

II. HOWARD SPRAGG

Your support has been a different character from that of most churches.

I think a lot of churches adopted us as the liberal cause of the time (many have gone on to the next cause by now).

Your support was deeper—your support was based on a deeper biblical commitment to the poor and to workers who are exploited.

You have viewed our union as a path of progress and hope for poverty-stricken workers.

Your leaders have not been embarrassed by the word "union" but have made collaboration with unions part of your mission strategy.

I know that Howard is responsible for that depth and that strategy. From the first time I met him in 1970 I could tell that he was a lot more realistic about the world we live in and was much more ready to get his hands dirty for the sake of justice.

Howard, I want to thank you personally for the quality of seriousness of your commitment to our struggle

—For coming to visit me in jail in Salinas in 1970

—For taking time to speak to our members at our convention in August 1975

—For the persistent, dependable support you have provided John and Olgha and the Migrant Ministry for these many years.

PLANE TRIP TO COACHELLA IN 1973

A special thanks to all of you for that amazing plane trip to Coachella in 1973 from your General Synod in St. Louis.

Without a doubt, it was the single, most powerful example of the church's solidarity with us

—And it came at a time of overwhelming need

—Teamsters trying to destroy us

—Our people frightened and scattered by brutal Teamster violence.

During the Synod Chris and I were talking almost hourly with John Moyer and Dave Keohler.

But I know that many others were responsible for that dramatic and unusual act of courage.

—Physical courage

—But more important and harder: political and administrative courage

—On behalf of our members, thank you.

IV. THE STATUS OF OUR MOVEMENT

Let me now take a few minutes to bring you up-to-date on our movement.

In some respects we are like a poor, developing nation.

(And I have noticed that missionaries who have served in recently independent, third world countries understand our situation very well.)

Our focus of work has shifted from the highly public struggle to the areas of management and planning and administration.

We are more involved in

—Negotiating contracts and

—Developing the means of serving our members

—Than we are in fighting the growers and expanding into new areas.

But, still, we are engaged in 3 strikes and 2 major boycotts with the possibility of a conflict with Coca Cola in the near future.

—Red Coach Boycott

—Steak Mate strike and boycott of Ralston-Purina

Like a developing country we are besieged with problems and adversaries:

—Internal political struggle (always with us—especially at Convention time)

—Growers are getting more sophisticated in their resistance

—Some Growers simply won't deal with us and are going out of business; others are transferring ownership (of 295 UFW certifications, 92 companies have either changed ownership or gone out of business)

—Others refuse to negotiate and then appeal ALRB bad faith bargaining decisions all the way through the courts—using the intervening time to push union sympathizers out of the company

—In the vegetable industry there is a massive move to cut production in areas covered by a union contract (SunHarvest—of 1,500 workers, 600 laid off)

—The Teamster Pact expires in the Spring of 1982—not too far away (get your plane ready).

Like a developing country we need professionals from the outside like doctors, computer programmers and management experts. And we have to pay for them (with some exceptions like Sr. Florence).

V. THE MANAGEMENT TEAM

Our most serious and important internal struggle is over—at least for now.

I would like to tell you a little about it because it will help you better understand our situation.

We grew up in a union, thanks to the sacrifices of the workers and the genius and courage of a group of heroic lone rangers (Eliseo [Medina], Marshall [Ganz], Jim Drake, Jerry [Cohen], etc.).

But we reached a point in the mid-70s (actually we reached it earlier, but none of us noticed) when the old ways of doing things weren't working and couldn't work.

We needed to move from independent heroics to a team management system.

For the past four years I have been stubbornly pushing for management systems in our union for the team management at the top.

Change is hard and the fight within our Board was long and bitter.

It was finally resolved at the end of last year.

We have divided the Union's work into 9 areas of responsibility: Regions I, II, III; Out of State; Political; Boycott; Property Management; Staff Operations I, II.

One person is responsible for managing each area. Everyone meets at La Paz, our headquarters. We meet as a team every week for 2 days to share information and make administrative policy. In between meetings Chris [Hartmire] keeps the communication flowing.

We developed some commonsense rules for the survival of the team:

—Will make all decisions in his/her area
—No member will make decisions outside his/her area

—We don't need to like each other

—The top management team is not a committee, it is a team— no President, or boss—but a coach

—Requires systematic and intensive communication

—It is not team management if someone else can do it.

The team is working and will work if we don't get lazy or don't get distracted.

It is a great relief to me.

And for the first time we have a Union leader assigned to "other states" (I used to deal with it with time left over).

—Conventions in Texas

—Conventions scheduled in Florida and Arizona for 1982

—Tomorrow we will be in Onarga, Illinois with Olgah opening a UFW center there.

Our dreams are still alive but they have been tempered by the tough battles of these past 20 years.

I always knew that building one national union for farm workers was a lifetime work—in our nation, in this period of history it may be the work of more than one lifetime.

VI. CAN WE WORK TOGETHER IN THE FUTURE?

There is one other thing I would like to talk to you about.

Many have looked on us as a social movement for all times and all people.

We have been idealized—and frankly we have cooperated with that in order to win boycotts and survive as a union.

But the truth is that we are just plain people trying to build a *Labor Union*.

Our people come from many races but they are all workers, they are all employed by growers.

They pay dues and they are very human in their wants and desires.

We are pushing the responsibility for the work on the union onto them—but they would like us to do it for them.

As leaders we are deeply committed to nonviolence and to helping other struggling groups but only a core group of our members have internalized these convictions.

Still, we are building a strong organization with a real membership and significant financial resources.

We don't intend to lose track of our ideals and for years to come we will be organizing poor people who are mostly black and brown.

My question is this: Given these realities, how will we maintain our solid working relationship with the churches.

We *are* a union and we won't apologize for it.

The demands on us are primarily internal, with our members—and we have precious little time to spend cultivating external relationships.

We know that our commitments and goals spring from the same source, from our faith in God and our choice to follow His Son.

But a large number of your members are suspicious of *all* unions (especially when they are more than weak and struggling).

And some of your leaders have begun to think of us in negative terms

   —Just another union (whatever that means)
   —Just after more money for their members
   —Just after more dues and more power.

In short they have begun to look down their noses at us.

We are certainly not perfect and we have many problems of our own making.

But I suspect—I don't know for sure—I suspect that you also are not perfect and that your churches have problems that God did not intend.

Given these realities: How do we maintain our working relationship?

It seems like a simple question but it may be more important than it looks.

In some nations, like El Salvador—these everyday working relationships developed only at the extremity—when violence seemed like the only way left to bring about change.

We don't know for sure where our nation is headed but I think we had better raise the banner of nonviolence very high and I think we had better do it together and soon.

It will not be easy. From our side we will have to stretch ourselves and give of our time and energy. We will have to keep coming at you for help and solidarity.

But, at least, *our* members are open to this relationship and we *do* need your support for our strength and our growth (the boycott being the most obvious example).

You have a more difficult challenge:

   —You don't need us in an obvious way
   —You don't need us for your institutional survival
   —And it might be easier with your members if you let this particular relationship slide.

I promise that we will do our share—to the best of our ability.

I ask you to do yours.

Together, there is an immense amount of work we can do for justice and peace.

Notes for Speech to Graduating Negotiations Class, 1982

A transcript of this speech is in the United Farm Workers Papers, Wayne State University.

Throughout the long history of the world true progress [has] only [been] made when leaders [have been] willing to take risks, to depart from past practices, to chart a new course.

Not an easy task. There are many who fear change. They take security from stability, no matter how false it may be. They cringe from the challenge of a new vision, a new dream. Dag Hammarshkjold once wrote: "Never look down to test the ground before taking your next step; only he who keeps his eye fixed on the far horizon will find his right road. Never measure the height of a mountain until you have reached the top. Then you will see how low it was."

The school was born out of a conscious decision by the national executive board to depart from past practices and chart a new course.

[The] School [was] born out of the leadership's commitment to realizing the principle that our purpose is to enable common people to do uncommon things.

In order to progress we have to rid ourselves of past decisions that have ceased to be productive. Yesterday's actions and decisions, no matter how wise they may have been, inevitably become today's problems.

We must commit today's resources to the future. This means we can no longer spend time and energy and ingenuity patching up the mistakes of yesterday. We must discard those functions that cease to promise results.

It is not difficult to get rid of total failures. They liquidate themselves. Yesterday's successes, however, always linger on long beyond their productive life. We must seek out those sacred tasks of the past that drain resources and scarce time and prune them ruthlessly so we can focus on the future. We must never forget that our most valued resource is our human strength; the only effective way to guarantee progress is to assign important tasks to people who have the ability and training to perform, and develop and train others who will carry the work of the union on through succeeding generations. Gone are the days of the loner who did his work and achieved his objectives at the expense of everyone else's work and objectives. Today the union works and grows as a team, with everyone fulfilling his or her part of a larger plan that involves us all.

We gather today not to recognize the accomplishments of individuals—although we celebrate your growth as men and women in the struggle—but to celebrate the progress and advancement your training will mean to the entire movement and to farm workers everywhere.

In a real sense today's ceremony symbolizes the passing of the torch to a new generation born in the movement, hardened by the struggle, disciplined through many difficult and demanding battles, and firmly committed to the principles of sacrifice and servanthood that has built our union and kept the movement strong and vibrant.

Justice, not charity.

Dignity, not mercy.

Servanthood, not service.

▬

CHAPTER 4

The Difficult Last Decade: 1984–93

During the last decade of his life Chávez faced difficulties that rivaled any in his long career. The country's political mood continued conservative. President Reagan and his administration openly worked to reduce the power of labor unions; Reagan was succeeded by George Bush, whom Chávez believed to be no friend of labor; and in California, Governor George Deukmejian remained a strong foe of unions. Lawmakers everywhere seemed to follow the lead of the conservative executive branches of government. For example, the 1986 Immigration Reform and Control Act allowed a virtually inexhaustible supply of cheap labor to enter the country. Heartened by the more favorable political climate, growers became more aggressive in challenging the union and added their considerable weight to the forces that by 1984 had neutralized the Agricultural Labor Relations Board (ALRB).[1]

The weakness of the ALRB and the dwindling strength of the UFW reinforced Chávez's commitment to the battle-tested method of the boycott. On June 12, 1984, he announced a new boycott on grapes, understanding the risks. Over the years the UFW had called more than fifty boycotts, leaving the interested public confused about which if any products were being targeted at any given time. Often, even the union's strongest supporters did not know whether a boycott was in effect or what was being boycotted.

To educate the public, the UFW launched a massive campaign using "computer-generated mailings, slick advertising, and media packets."[2] Chávez described the effort:

We will use modern techniques of direct mailings, media advertising, and other means of once again bringing together liberals, church groups, workers and others to support us until the full meaning of the California labor law is restored and provides protections workers must have.[3]

Although Chávez was willing to intensify a multimedia approach to reach a broader audience more quickly, he would maintain his standard rhetorical profile, as the speeches and essays in this chapter make clear.

The veteran labor leader focused his campaign on the problems caused by pesticide residues on fruits. According to Matt Meier and Feliciano Ribera, the boycott sought to protest "excessive and negligent use of dangerous pesticides by growers and to call attention to the emasculation of California's Agricultural Labor Relations Act" (ALRA).[4] Although the UFW had long fought to regulate the use of pesticides, Chávez believed that in the 1980s the message would gain persuasiveness by resonating with middle-class audiences' concerns for the environment. Adding a visual dimension to its appeal, the union produced "The Wrath of Grapes," a video that graphically showed the birth defects and high rates of cancers caused by pesticide poisoning.

In 1987 and 1988 Chávez traveled to the Midwest and East, speaking on pesticides and the boycott. He informed audiences why he singled out grapes: "There are more reported pesticide poisonings with grapes than any other type of produce."[5] To emphasize his point, he identified "cancer clusters" in farming communities like McFarland, California, where rates of cancer six times higher than normal were found.[6] To identify further with victims of pesticides, and to dramatize the boycott, he began a fast on July 16, 1988, that lasted thirty-six days and drew nation-wide media attention. (See chapter 5 for a discussion of the fast.)

Chávez continued to depend on the boycott into the 1990s, assuring audiences that it could triumph by depending on an alliance among "Latinos, blacks, and other minorities, plus allies in labor and the Church." Relying on his conviction that he was carrying out the will of an all-powerful God, he remained certain that he would not fail in his righteous cause. The public had learned to boycott in the 1960s and 1970s, he reasoned, and the habit would continue into the 1990s. Although the boycott did bring some successes, it did not lessen overall sales of grapes nor rebuild the union.

During these unsettling years Chávez was jolted by the deaths of perhaps his two most significant supporters. In December of 1991 his mother died at the age of ninety-nine. The following September Fred Ross also died. Both deaths strongly affected Chávez. In chapter 5 we offer further discussion of these events and the eulogies Chávez delivered.

In the last few years of his life Chávez encountered increased opposition from what had always been friendly quarters. He provoked criticism, from within and outside the union, for centralizing power in the UFW and for placing his family members in major positions; his appointments of volunteer workers rather than professional people into important positions

Chávez speaking to striking farmer workers circa 1988. *Courtesy Walter P. Reuther Library, Wayne State University*

caused many of the union's "most loyal and efficient staff members" to re-
sign;[7] and his long-standing core of supporters, like liberal journalists, became increasingly critical. Because of the criticism, Chávez increasingly
withdrew into an ever smaller, tight group of loyalists.[8]

Chávez's enemies also stepped up their challenges to him. Antiunion
forces launched a barrage of lawsuits, winning a major case in 1991.
Chávez was forced to return to university campuses and other friendly
venues for money to help the union defend itself.[9] In April of 1993 he traveled to San Luis, Arizona, near his birthplace, to testify in the union's appeal of a $5.4 million award that had been won by Bruce Church, Inc. He
had started another fast to gain moral strength and find additional support.
On the night that his closest coworkers had persuaded the weakened
leader to break his fast, April 23, 1993, César Chávez died in his sleep.[10]
He was sixty-five years old.

As would not surprise those who have read the previous pages, Chávez
relied on his public discourse in his last decade—and he remained confident that his righteous, well-reasoned, and clearly presented case would
lead to UFW victories by raising needed money, promoting the boycott,
convincing the public, and organizing farm workers. In September of
1984, at the Seventh Convention of the UFW in Bakersfield, he delivered a
carefully crafted and laboriously revised address that focused on Proposition 39, the "Deukmejian Reapportionment Initiative" to reapportion the
state in a manner that would reduce the strength of Hispanics, other minorities, and liberals. He collaborated with speech writer Marc Grossman
in editing this speech, and he wrote many comments in the margins of
drafts of his text.

Chávez began by reviewing the anti-UFW actions meant to destroy the
union and to subjugate poor people while increasing the wealth and power
of the rich. He pointed specifically to how the state government under
Deukmejian's leadership had weakened the Agricultural Labor Relations
Act to the point where it no longer protected workers. Proposition 39 illustrated one means Deukmejian and his supporters employed to curtail
the power of Hispanics and other minorities. But that tactic would fail,
Chávez argued, because Hispanics were gaining the numbers, wealth, and
power to dominate California politics one day and to defeat the reactionary forces led by Deukmejian and his ilk.

On November 9, 1984, at the Commonwealth Club of San Francisco,
Chávez delivered one of his most significant and painstakingly constructed
addresses.[11] It was the first speech, other than ones at union conventions,
in which Chávez almost exclusively read from a manuscript. He worked
as hard on the speech as on any in his career, laboring with Grossman

through several drafts. Many of the ideas and much of the language had appeared in earlier speeches.[12] Especially striking is his increased use of anaphora, a stylistic device that repeats sets of words in consecutive sentences or clauses to heighten the impact of ideas. Such added stylistic polish characterized many of Chávez's later speeches.

In his introduction Chávez lamented a needless bus accident in 1973 that killed thirty-two workers. After using that tragedy as a symbol for the treatment of farm workers in the past, he vividly described their present horrific conditions. Personalizing his ideas, he referred to his own desperate life as a migrant worker and related how he created a union to change conditions for farm workers. Examples of Hispanics whose lives improved because of the union reified his image of the UFW; examples of Deukmejian and his supporters attacking the ALRA and the union justified the UFW's boycott and its sophisticated public relations techniques. His cause would inevitably triumph, he characteristically promised, because of the boycott and the increased strength of Hispanics in California. Note, however, that the inevitable victory in this instance rested on Chávez's deep worldview rather than on particular circumstances. In the past Chávez had always found localized evidence of victory, notwithstanding circumstances that might discourage, depress, and even defeat another leader of farm workers.

In November of 1985 Chávez returned to many of the same themes in a speech before the L.A. County Chicano Employees Association. He started by reviewing the early successes of the union, mentioning that the union had forced the growers to back ALRA. He identified the means through which Deukmejian and his supporters had weakened the law, the consequences of the weakening, the violence against workers, and in particularly great detail the effects on workers and others of the spraying of pesticides in California. He concluded by reassuring listeners of the power of the boycott and the inevitability of his cause's victory.

In 1986 and 1987 Chávez traveled the country giving a speech called the "Wrath of Grapes Boycott." In it he described the strengths, value, and effects of the boycott, how the UFW successfully employed that power to gain contracts and pass ALRA, and what UFW enemies did to blunt the law. Dangerous pesticides served as a frightening example of the outcome of the lack of enforcement of the law. In his usual fact-filled and concrete manner, he named and discussed the pesticides causing the problems and gave examples of the damage that pesticides had inflicted on workers and their children. He implored listeners to join the boycott so that endangered farm workers could be rescued.

Chávez traveled to Arizona in 1987 to stand with the Pecan workers in their battle against growers. In English and Spanish he expressed his solidarity with workers, singling out growers like Richard Walden of the Santa Cruz Valley Pecan Company who attempted to destroy unions. The Reagan administration created an anti-worker climate, he argued, that served as an invitation to growers like Walden, who brought in consultants to break strikes. A boycott of pecans could help defeat growers who followed Walden's example.

In March of 1989 Chávez spoke at Pacific Lutheran University in Tacoma, Washington,[13] one of the first public appearances following his thirty-six-day fast the previous year. The text was printed in the *Sacramento Bee* on April 16, 1989.[14] It lays out a meticulously composed attack on the use of pesticides, beginning with the story of Johnnie Rodríguez, the son of farm workers, who died from cancer at the age of five. Rodríguez was one of thirteen children in McFarland, California, who had been diagnosed with cancer, a rate four hundred times higher than normal. Chávez documented the savage conditions, resulting from actions by growers and their political supporters, in which workers lived, and he provided other examples of farm workers injured and killed by pesticides, illuminating their poisonous effects. He concluded with the reasons for his fast and directed the audience to boycott grapes as a means of stopping the indiscriminate spraying of pesticides.

Showing his adaptability to issues and audiences, Chávez spoke in Sacramento in 1991 at a rally against budget cuts for schools and other vital state services. He was joined by Rev. Jesse Jackson, and Speaker Willie Brown of the California Assembly. Note how Chávez tied the need for public schools to the means of improving the lives of all minorities. He illustrated how budgets were being cut from schools and the money spent more and more for prisons. That money was cut, he charged, because most students represented ethnic minorities; thus, minorities themselves must take the lead in reversing the reductions.

The last speech included in this section was delivered before the Building Industry Association of Northern California at a meeting in San Jose. Chávez opened by reminiscing about his roots in San Jose and in Sal Si Puedes and about his early career as a community organizer for the Community Services Organization (CSO), noting the changes the CSO had brought. But as one would expect, he centered on the need for change in the present—for farm workers still lived under miserable conditions in camps or slept in the open or were homeless. He had formed the UFW to overcome such mistreatment of workers, he reminded listeners, and the UFW boycotted produce to improve conditions for farm workers. Adapting to his audience and occasion, he turned to a program that the union had started to develop: low-cost housing for farm workers. He highlighted as examples the UFW's housing and apartment projects near Fresno and the workers who had benefited from the union's housing; and he listed the union's proposed housing projects for the future. Home builders were implored to help the union achieve its goals.

As you read Chávez's last speeches, note that he retained the rhetorical profile he had established three decades earlier. Though issues, audiences, and circumstances all shifted, his substantive themes, arguments, and explanations—together with the rhetorical means seen in his first and second personae, language, delivery, organization, and use of evidence—remained remarkably stable. If UFW rhetors personified a clear and reasonable case for their righteous cause, Chávez believed, no alteration in audiences or issues could prevent victory.

Address to the UFW's 7th Constitutional Convention, September 1984

A transcript of this speech is in the United Farm Workers Papers, Wayne State University.

There is a shadow falling over the land, brothers and sisters, and the dark forces of reaction threaten us now as never before.

The enemies of the poor and the working classes hold power in the White House and the governor's office.

Our enemies seek to impose a new Bracero program on the farm workers of America; they seek to return to the days before there was a farm workers union, when our people were treated as if they were agricultural implements instead of human beings.

Our enemies seek to hand over millions of dollars in government money to segregated private colleges that close their doors to blacks and other people of color.

Our enemies have given the wealthiest people the biggest tax cuts in American history at the same time they have increased taxes for the poor and working people. They have created a whole new class of millionaires while forcing millions of ordinary people into poverty.

President Reagan is a man with a very special sense of religion. Reagan sees a proper role for government and a proper role for God. It's very simple: Reagan's government helps the rich, and God helps the rest of us.

Chávez speaking at a United Farm Workers meeting circa 1990. *Courtesy Walter P. Reuther Library, Wayne State University*

Our enemies want all of us to carry identification cards issued by the government which only we will be forced to produce to get a job, to apply for unemployment insurance, to keep from being deported by the border patrol.

Our enemies have created the P.I.K. give-away program to give away millions of dollars in cash money to the richest corporate growers in America for not growing crops, while unemployment benefits for farm workers are cut and while food and medical care for the poor are reduced.

Our enemies are refusing to enforce the nation's fair housing laws, which protect black and brown people from discrimination.

Our enemies are refusing to enforce the laws that protect working people on the job from unsafe conditions which cause injuries and take lives.

Our enemies are responsible for the brutal murder of thousands of dark-skinned, Spanish-speaking farm workers through their military support of blood-thirsty dictators in Central America. The men, women, and children who have been slaughtered committed the same crimes we have committed: they wanted a better life for themselves and their families, a life free from hunger and poverty and exploitation.

The same dark forces of reaction which dominate the government in Washington also dominate the government in Sacramento. Governor Deukmejian is a lackey of Ronald Reagan. They collect their money from the same reactionary interests; their decisions are made by the same slick public relations men. They attack working people, minority people, and poor people with the same fervor.

Farm workers are not the only people who have suffered under Deukmejian. But Deukmejian has taken a terrible toll in human suffering among the farm workers of this state.

The law that guarantees our right to organize helped farm workers make progress in overcoming injustice.

At companies where farm workers are protected by union contracts we made progress

—Against child labor
—Against miserable wages and working conditions
—Against sexual harassment of women workers
—Against favoritism and discrimination in hiring and employment
—Against dangerous pesticides which poison our people.

Where we have organized, these injustices soon pass into history.

But under Deukmejian, the law that guarantees our right to organize no longer protects farm workers. It doesn't work anymore! Instead of prosecuting growers who break the law, Deukmejian's men give them aid and comfort. Instead of enforcing the law as it was written against those who break it, Deukmejian invites growers who ignore their farm workers' rights by seeking relief from the governor's appointees.

What does all this mean for you and for other farm workers?

It means that the right to vote in free elections is a sham!

It means that the right to talk freely about the union among your fellow workers on the job is a cruel hoax.

It means the right to be free from threats and intimidation by growers is an empty promise.

It means the right to sit down and negotiate with your employer as equals across the bargaining table—and not as peons in the fields—is a fraud.

It means that 6,300 farm workers who are owed $72 million in back pay because their employers broke the law are still waiting for their checks.

It means that 36,000 farm workers who voted to be represented by the UFW in free elections are still waiting for contracts because their employers won't bargain in good faith.

Are these make-believe threats? Are these exaggerations?

Ask your friends and coworkers who are waiting for the money they are owed from the growers.

Ask your friends and coworkers who are waiting for the growers to bargain in good faith and sign contracts.

Ask your friends and coworkers who've been fired from their jobs because they spoke out for the union.

Ask your friends and coworkers who've been threatened with physical violence because they support the UFW.

Ask the family of René López, the young farm worker from Fresno who was shot to death last year because he supported the union, because he spoke out against injustice, because he exercised his rights under the law.

Farm workers are not the only people who have suffered under Deukmejian. And they are not the only people who are under attack by the dark forces of reaction. Millions of dollars have been spent to place propositions on the November election ballot for the people of California to vote on. The dark forces of reaction have placed Proposition 41 on the ballot. It will reduce the welfare benefits poor people in California receive by 40 percent.

The Republicans want to give poor people—women and children living in poverty—a 40 percent cut in their support money as a Christmas present this December.

There is another proposition on the ballot this November, Proposition 39, the Deukmejian Reapportionment Initiative.

Proposition 39 would redraw the boundary lines for legislative and congressional districts. The existing reapportionment law that sets the current boundary lines was passed by the Democrats in the legislature. It represents a great victory in the long struggle for more political power by Hispanics and other minority people. Deukmejian wants to redraw the boundary lines because he wants to get rid of the friends we have in the Legislature and in Congress—friends who vote to defend the interests of farm workers and other working people. Deukmejian wants to redraw the lines so Mexican people will be split apart into many small communities: so our political strength will not be felt, so we will be forced to vote only for reactionary politicians who back Deukmejian.

The same Deukmejian who is working to deny a better life to farm workers is also working to deny all Hispanics in California the right to full participation in the political process. Deukmejian and the corporate growers who are paying for Proposition 39 want to redraw the lines to send more of our enemies to Sacramento. The Western Growers Association has already given $50,000 to the Deukmejian Reapportionment Initiative. And growers continue to support Proposition 39 with their money and influence.

But brothers and sisters, the dark forces of reaction also want to pass Proposition 39 because they are afraid of us! Deukmejian and the growers have looked into the future and the future is ours!

History and inevitability are on our side. The farm workers and their children—and the Hispanics and their children—are the future in this state. And corporate growers are the past. The monumental growth of Hispanic influence in California means increased population, increased social and economic power, and increased political influence.

Those politicians who ally themselves with corporate growers are in for a big surprise. They want to make their careers in politics; they want to hold power twenty and thirty years from now. But twenty and thirty years from now—in Modesto, in Salinas, in Fresno, in Bakersfield, in the Imperial Valley, and in many of the great cities of California—those communities will be dominated by farm workers and not by growers, by the children and grandchildren of farm workers, and by the children and grandchildren of growers.

Look at the values we cherish! Look at the things they hold dear! We came from big families; they keep down the size of their families. We take pride in our children. They take pride in the money they make. The growers have money and everything it buys. We have people and numbers. We'll see who triumphs in the end. The day will come when we're the majority when our children are the lawyers and the doctors and the politicians—when we hold political power in this state.

These trends are part of the forces of history that cannot be stopped. No governor and no organization of rich growers can resist them for very long. They are inevitable. Once change begins, it cannot be stopped:

You cannot uneducate the person who has learned to read.

You cannot humiliate the person who feels pride.

You cannot oppress the people who are not afraid anymore.

Our people are on the move. Our day is coming. It may not come this year. It may not come during this decade. But it will come, someday!

And when that day comes, we shall see the fulfillment of that passage from the book of Matthew in the New Testament that "the last shall be first and the first shall be last."

Our duty is clear. We must stand up and defend our rights as free men and women. We must defeat Proposition 39! We must unite with our Hispanic brothers and sisters who don't work in the fields by joining together in this noble crusade.

For twenty-one months we have taken all the abuse and injustice Governor Deukmejian can dish out. He has attacked us where it hurts the most:

He has deprived us of our rights under the law.

He has taken away the ability of many of us to provide for our families.

He has tried to deny us the dignity that can only be ours in a union that we build and control.

Now it is our turn to fight back; it's our turn to strike a blow for all Hispanics in California by defeating Proposition 39.

Proposition 39 was placed on the ballot to destroy the majority coalition of progressive legislators under the leadership of Assembly Speaker Willie Brown and Senate President Pro Tem David Roberti. That majority coalition has pre-served farm workers' rights by protecting the Agricultural Labor Relations Act from destruction by the growers. That majority coalition has stood up for the rights of all working people and for the rights of the poor, the sick, the elderly, and the disadvantaged.

Please join with me now in welcoming to this convention the Speaker of the California State Assembly, Willie Brown, and a delegation representing the Democratic members of the California State Assembly.

Address to the Commonwealth Club of San Francisco, November 9, 1984

A transcript and audio tape of this speech are in the United Farm Workers Papers, Wayne State University.

Twenty-one years ago last September, on a lonely, stretch of railroad track paralleling U.S. Highway 101 near Salinas, thirty-two Bracero farm workers lost their lives in a tragic accident.

The Braceros had been imported from Mexico to work on California farms. They died when their bus, which was converted from a flatbed truck, drove in front of a freight train. Conversion of the bus had not been approved by any government agency. The driver had "tunnel" vision. Most of the bodies lay unidentified for days. *No one, including the grower who employed the workers even knew their names.*

Today, thousands of farm workers live under savage conditions: beneath trees and amid garbage and human excrement, near tomato fields in San Diego County, tomato fields which use the most modern farm technology. Vicious rats gnaw on them as they sleep. They walk miles to buy food at inflated prices, and they carry in water from irrigation pumps.

Child labor is still common in many farm areas. As much as 30 percent of Northern California's garlic harvesters are under-aged children. Kids as young as six years old have voted in state-conducted union elections since they qualified as workers. Some eight hundred thousand under-aged children work with their families harvesting crops across America.

Babies born to migrant workers suffer 25 percent higher infant mortality than the rest of the population.

Malnutrition among migrant worker children is 10 times higher than the national rate.

Farm workers' average life expectancy is still forty-nine years—compared to seventy-three years for the average American.

All my life, I have been driven by one dream, one goal, one vision: To overthrow a farm labor system in this nation which treats farm workers as if they were not important human beings. Farm workers are not agricultural implements; they are not beasts of burden to be used and discarded. That dream was born in my youth. It was nurtured in my early days of organizing. It has flourished. It has been attacked.

I'm not very different from anyone else who has ever tried to accomplish something with his life. My motivation comes from my personal life, from watching what my mother and father went through when I was growing up, from what we experienced as migrant farm workers in California.

That dream, that vision grew from my own experience with racism, with hope, with the desire to be treated fairly and to see my people treated as human beings and not as chattel. It grew from anger and rage—emotions I felt forty years ago when people of my color were denied the right to see a movie or eat at a restaurant in many parts of California. It grew from the frustration and humiliation I felt as a boy who couldn't understand how the growers could abuse and exploit farm workers when there were so many of us and so few of them.

Later, in the '50s, I experienced a different kind of exploitation. In San Jose, in Los Angeles and in other urban communities, we, the Mexican American people, were dominated by a majority that was Anglo. I began to realize what other minority people had discovered: that the only answer, the only hope was in organizing.

More of us had to become citizens. We had to register to vote. And people like me had to develop the skills it would take to organize, to educate, to help empower the Chicano people.

I spent many years—before we founded the union—learning how to work with people.

We experienced some successes in voter registration in politics in battling racial discrimination—successes in an era when Black Americans were just beginning to assert their civil rights and when political awareness among Hispanics was almost nonexistent. But deep in my heart, I knew I could never be happy unless I tried organizing the farm workers. I didn't know if I would succeed. But I had to try.

All Hispanics—urban and rural, young and old—are connected to the farm workers' experience. We had all lived through the fields, or our parents had. We shared that common humiliation. How could we progress as a people, even if we lived in the cities, while the farm workers—men and women of our color—were condemned to a life without pride? How could we progress as a people while the farm workers—who symbolized our history in this land—were denied self-respect? How could our people believe that their children could become lawyers and doctors and judges and business people while this shame, this injustice was permitted to continue?

Those who attack our union often say, "It's not really a union. It's something else—a social movement, a civil rights movement. It's something dangerous."

They're half right.

The United Farm Workers is first and foremost a union. A union like any other. A union that either produces for its members on the bread and butter issues or doesn't survive.

But the UFW has always been something more than a union, although it's never been dangerous if you believe in the Bill of Rights. The UFW was the beginning! We attacked that historical source of shame and infamy that our people in this country lived with. We attacked that injustice, not by complaining, not by seeking hand-outs, not by becoming soldiers in the War on Poverty.

We organized!

Farm workers acknowledged we had allowed ourselves to become victims in a democratic society—a society where majority rule and collective bargaining are supposed to be more than academic theories or political rhetoric. And by addressing this historical problem, we created confidence and in an entire people's ability to create the future.

The UFW's survival—its existence—was not in doubt in my mind when the time began to come—after the union became visible—when Chicanos started entering college in greater numbers, when Hispanics began running for public office in greater numbers, when our people started asserting their rights on a broad range of issues and in many communities across the country.

The union's survival—its very existence—sent out a signal to all Hispanics:

That we were fighting for our dignity,

That we were challenging and overcoming injustice,

That we were empowering the least educated among us, the poorest among us.

The message was clear: If it could happen in the fields, it could happen anywhere—in the cities, in the courts, in the city councils, in the state legislatures.

I didn't really appreciate it at the time, but the coming of our union signaled the start of great changes among Hispanics that are only now beginning to be seen.

I've traveled to every part of this nation. I have met and spoken with thousands of Hispanics from every walk of life from every social and economic class.

One thing I hear most often from Hispanics, regardless of age or position—and from many non-Hispanics as well—is that the farm workers gave them hope that they could succeed and the inspiration to work for change.

From time to time you will hear our opponents declare that the union is weak, that the union has no support, that the union has not grown fast enough. Our obituary has been written many times. How ironic it is that the same forces which argue so passionately that the union is not influential are the same forces that continue to fight us so hard.

The union's power in agriculture has nothing to do with the number of farm workers under union contract.

It has nothing to do with the farm workers' ability to contribute to Democratic politicians.

It doesn't even have much to do with our ability to conduct successful boycotts.

The very fact of our existence forces an entire industry—unionized and non-unionized—to spend millions of dollars year after year on improved wages, on improved working conditions, on benefits for workers. If we're so weak and unsuccessful, why do the growers continue to fight us with such passion? Because so long as we continue to exist, farm workers will benefit from our existence even if they don't work under union contract.

It doesn't really matter whether we have a hundred thousand members or five hundred thousand members. In truth, hundreds of thousands of farm workers in California—and in other states—are better off today because of our work. And Hispanics across California and the nation, who don't work in agriculture, are better off today because of what the farm workers taught people—about organization, about pride and strength, about seizing control over their own lives.

Tens of thousands of the children and grandchildren of farm workers—and the children and grandchildren of poor Hispanics—are moving out of the fields and out of the barrios and into the professions and into business and into politics. And that movement cannot be reversed!

Our union will forever exist as an empowering force among Chicanos in the Southwest. And that means our power and our influence will grow and not diminish.

Two major trends give us hope and encouragement:

First, our union has returned to a tried and tested weapon in the farm workers' nonviolent arsenal—the boycott! After the Agricultural Labor Relations Act became law in California in 1975, we dismantled our boycott to work with the law.

During the early and mid-'70s, millions of Americans supported our boycotts. After 1975, we redirected our efforts from the boycott to organizing and winning elections under the law. The law helped farm workers make progress in overcoming poverty and injustice.

At companies where farm workers are protected by union contracts, we have made progress in overcoming child labor, in overcoming miserable wages and working conditions, in overcoming sexual harassment of women workers, in overcoming dangerous pesticides which poison our people and poison the food we all eat. Where we have organized, these injustices soon pass into history.

But under Republican Governor George Deukmejian, the law that guarantees our right to organize no longer protects farm workers—it doesn't work anymore!

In 1982 corporate growers gave Deukmejian one million dollars to run for governor of California. Since he took office, Deukmejian has paid back his debt to the growers with the blood and sweat of California farm workers. Instead of enforcing the law as it was written against those who break it, Deukmejian invites growers who break the law to seek relief from the governor's appointees.

What does all this mean for farm workers?

It means that the right to vote in free elections is a sham!

It means that the right to talk freely about the union among your fellow workers on the job is a cruel hoax!

It means the right to be free from threats and intimidation by growers is an empty promise!

It means the right to sit down and negotiate with your employer as equals across the bargaining table—and not as peons in the field—is a fraud!

It means that thousands of farm workers—who are owed millions of dollars in back pay because their employers broke the law—are still waiting for their checks.

It means that 36,000 farm workers—who voted to be represented by the United Farm Workers in free elections—are still waiting for contracts from growers who refuse to bargain in good faith.

It means that, for farm workers, child labor will continue.

It means that infant mortality will continue.

It means malnutrition among our children will continue.

It means the short life expectancy and the inhuman living and working conditions will continue.

Are these make-believe threats? Are they exaggerations?

Ask the farm workers who are still waiting for growers to bargain in good faith and sign contracts!

Ask the farm workers who've been fired from their jobs because they spoke out for the union!

Ask the farm workers who've been threatened with physical violence because they support the UFW!

Ask the family of René Lopez, the young farm worker from Fresno who was shot to death last year because he supported the union.

These tragic events forced farm workers to declare a new international boycott of California table grapes.

That's why we are asking Americans once again to join the farm workers by boycotting California grapes.

The Louis Harris poll revealed that 17 million American adults boycotted grapes. We are convinced that those people and that good will have not disappeared.

That segment of the population which makes our boycotts work are the Hispanics, the Blacks, the other minorities and our allies in labor and the church. But it is also an entire generation of young Americans who matured politically and socially in the 1960s and '70s—millions of people for whom boycotting grapes and other products became a socially accepted pattern of behavior. If you were young, Anglo, and on or near campus during the late '60s and early '70s, chances are you supported farm workers.

Fifteen years later the men and women of that generation are alive and well. They are in their mid-thirties and forties. They are pursuing professional careers. Their disposable income is relatively high. But they are still inclined to respond to an appeal from farm workers. The union's mission still has meaning for them.

Only we must translate the importance of a union for farm workers into the language of the 1980s. Instead of talking about the right to organize, we must talk about protection against sexual harassment in the fields. We must speak about the right to quality food—and food that is safe to eat.

I can tell you that the new language is working; the 17 million are still there. They are responding—not to picket lines and leafletting alone, but to the high-tech boycott of today, a boycott that uses computers and direct mail and advertising techniques which have revolutionized business and politics in recent years. We have achieved more success with the boycott in the first eleven months of 1984 than we achieved in the fourteen years since 1970.

The other trend that gives us hope is the monumental growth of Hispanic influence in this country—and what that means in increased population, increased social and economic clout, and increased political influence.

South of the Sacramento River in California, Hispanics now make up more than 25 percent of the population.

That figure will top 30 percent by the year 2000.

There are 1.1 million Spanish-surnamed registered voters in California; 85 percent are Democrats; only 13 percent are Republicans.

In 1975, there were two hundred Hispanic elected officials at all levels of government. In 1984, there are over four hundred elected judges, city council members, mayors and legislators. In light of these trends it is absurd to believe or suggest that we are going to go back in time as a union or as a people!

The growers often try to blame the union for their problems, to lay their sins off on us, sins for which they only have themselves to blame. The growers only have themselves to blame as they begin to reap the harvest from decades of environmental damage they have brought upon the land—

The pesticides, the herbicides, the soil fumigants, the fertilizers, the salt deposits from thoughtless irrigation,

The ravages from years of unrestrained poisoning of our soil and water.

Thousands of acres of land in California have already been irrevocably damaged by this wanton abuse of nature.

Thousands more will be lost unless growers understand that dumping more poisons on the soil won't solve their problems—on the short term or the long term. Health authorities in many San Joaquin Valley towns already warn young children and pregnant women not to drink the water because of nitrates from fertilizers which have contaminated the groundwater.

The growers only have themselves to blame for an increasing demand by consumers for higher quality food—food that isn't tainted by toxins, food that doesn't result from plant mutations or chemicals which produce red, luscious-looking tomatoes that taste like alfalfa.

The growers are making the same mistake American automakers made in the '60s and '70s when they refused to produce small, economical cars and opened the door to increased foreign competition.

Growers only have themselves to blame for increasing attacks on their publicly financed handouts and government welfare: water subsidies, mechanization research, huge subsidies for not growing crops. These special privileges came into being before the Supreme Court's one-person, one-vote decision at a time when rural lawmakers dominated the legislature and the Congress.

Soon, those handouts could be in jeopardy—as government searches for more revenue and as urban taxpayers take a closer look at farm programs and whom they benefit. The growers only have themselves to blame for the humiliation they have brought upon succeeding waves of immigrant groups which have sweated and sacrificed for a hundred years to make this industry rich. For generations, they have subjugated entire races of dark-skinned farm workers. These are the sins of the growers—not the farm workers:

We didn't poison the land.

We didn't open the door to imported produce.

We didn't covet billions of dollars in government handouts.

We didn't abuse and exploit the people who work the land.

Today, the growers are like a punch-drunk old boxer who doesn't know he's past his prime. The times are changing. The political and social environment has changed. The chickens are coming home to roost and the time to account for past sins is approaching.

I am told, these days, why farm workers should be discouraged and pessimistic: The Republicans control the governor's office and the White House. They say there is a conservative trend in the nation.

Yet we are filled with hope and encouragement. We have looked into the future and the future is ours!

History and inevitability are on our side. The farm workers and their children—and the Hispanics and their children—are the future in California. And corporate growers are the past!

Those politicians who ally themselves with the corporate growers and against the farm workers and the Hispanics are in for a big surprise.

They want to make their careers in politics. They want to hold power twenty and thirty years from now.

But twenty and thirty years from now—in Modesto, in Salinas, in Fresno, in Bakersfield, in the Imperial Valley, and in many of the great cities of California—those communities will be dominated by farm workers and not by growers, by the children and grandchildren of farm workers and not by the children and grandchildren of growers.

These trends are part of the forces of history which cannot be stopped! No person and no organization can resist them for very long. They are inevitable! Once social change begins, it cannot be reversed.

You cannot uneducate the person who has learned to read. You cannot humiliate the person who feels pride. You cannot oppress the people who are not afraid anymore.

Our opponents must understand that it's not just a union we have built. Unions, like other institutions, can come and go. But we're more than an institution! For nearly twenty years our union has been on the cutting edge of a people's cause. And you cannot do away with an entire people. You cannot stamp out a people's cause.

Regardless of what the future holds for the union—regardless of what the future holds for farm workers—our accomplishments cannot be undone! "La Causa"—our cause—doesn't have to be experienced twice. The consciousness and pride that were raised by our union are alive and thriving inside millions of young Hispanics who will never work on a farm!

Like the other immigrant groups, the day will come when we win the economic and political rewards which are in keeping with our numbers in society. The day will come when the politicians do the right thing by our people out of political necessity and not out of charity or idealism.

That day may not come this year.

That day may not come during this decade.

But it will come, someday!

And when that day comes, we shall see the fulfillment of that passage from the Book of Matthew in the New Testament, "The last shall be first and the first shall be last." And on that day, our nation shall fulfill its creed and that fulfillment shall enrich us all.

Thank you very much.

Speech to the Los Angeles County Chicano Employee Association
October 25, 1985

A transcript of this speech is in the United Farm Workers Papers, Wayne State University.

Twenty years ago last month long-suffering men and women in the vineyards surrounding Delano—120 miles north of here—struck out against one hundred years of humiliation and oppression. Our strike was not brutally crushed—as were dozens of other organizing efforts—because of the grape workers' secret weapon: the boycott!

We dramatically transformed the simple act of refusing to buy grapes into a powerful statement against poverty and injustice.

The first grape boycott touched the hearts and consciences of millions of Americans who never worked on a farm. Ten years later it forced growers to accept a law in California which was supposed to guarantee farm workers the same rights as workers in other industries.

But twenty years after the first grape struggle—and ten years after the law was passed—greed and injustice have taken over the governor's office in Sacramento. This good law has stopped working because Republican Governor George Deukmejian won't enforce it.

Deukmejian was elected with $1 million in campaign gifts from corporate growers. Since he took office there's been a massive cut in funding for enforcement of the law; State civil servants who try to enforce the law are punished and purged for being disloyal to Deukmejian; Deukmejian won't allow farm workers to collect tens of millions of dollars in back pay they are owed from growers convicted of violating the law; the governor's political appointees settle cases where *the courts* have ordered growers to pay back workers for as little as 10 cents on the dollar.

Farm workers who cooperated secretly with prosecutors by informing on growers who broke the law discovered that Deukmejian's men turned their names over to the company—a company already convicted of retaliating against its workers.

I do not need to recount for you what happens to workers when the labor laws that were created to protect their rights are not enforced. The experiences of our brother and sister trade unionists under the National Labor Relations Board— particularly since Ronald Reagan took office—are well known to us.

Like Ronald Reagan, George Deukmejian also left a legacy of nonenforcement. Deukmejian's legacy of nonenforcement can be seen every day:

Farm workers face coercion and violence for exercising protected rights.

It can be seen in the thousands of California farm workers whose hopes for a better life were shattered when Deukmejian sold out his oath of office to corporate agribusiness.

It can be seen in the family of René Lopez, the twenty-one-year-old farm worker shot to death in 1983, shortly after he voted in a state-supervised election. That brutal murder by two grower goons hired to harass farm workers occurred *after* Deukmejian's men failed to take action against armed guards who were threatening workers with guns.

But Deukmejian's legacy of non-enforcement can also be seen in the death last August 5 of Juan Chavoya, thirty-two and the father of four young children, who died in a San Diego County field sprayed only an hour before with a highly toxic insecticide in violation of state law.

Deukmejian's legacy of nonenforcement can also be seen in the thousands of California farm workers who are poisoned each year by toxic pesticides because enforcement of pesticide protection laws in this state is a joke! The underreporting of pesticide poisoning of farm workers is so pervasive that only about 1 percent of the actual number of cases in agriculture is recorded by the state.

But it's not just farm workers who're threatened by agricultural poisons. Hispanic kids in McFarland, near Delano, are contracting cancer at alarming rates. The water is contaminated in dozens of *other* San Joaquin Valley cities and towns.

We won the first grape boycott by letting consumers know about the indignities endured by California farm workers and their families. Twelve percent of the public, according to one nationwide poll, made that boycott a success in the 1970s.

The message of the *new* grape boycott is that consumers can protect farm workers—and themselves—by boycotting nonunion fresh grapes. And a California poll released last month showed 42 percent of the public *will* boycott grapes. That boycott will force growers to bargain in good faith for contracts which will protect farm workers *and* consumers from the *fearful perils of pesticides*.

There is nothing more important that we as farm workers share in common with the consumers of America than the safety of the nation's food supply which we both depend upon.

With this boycott weapon in our nonviolent arsenal—and with the unselfish support our union cause continues to enjoy from the House of Labor—we shall win in the end.

You can count on it!

Wrath of Grapes Boycott Speech, 1986

A transcript of this speech is in the United Farm Workers Papers, Wayne University.

I am speaking to you about our Wrath of Grapes Boycott because I believe our greatest court, the court of last resort, is the American people. And I believe that once you have taken a few moments to hear this message you will concur in this verdict along with a million other North Americans who are already committed to the largest grape boycott in history. The worth of humans is involved here.

I see us as one family. We cannot turn our backs on each other and our future. We farm workers are closest to food production. We were the first to recognize the serious health hazards of agriculture pesticides to both consumers and ourselves.

Twenty years ago over 17 million Americans united in a grape boycott campaign that transformed the simple act of refusing to buy grapes into a powerful and effective force against poverty and injustice. Through the combined strengths of a national boycott, California farm workers won many of the same rights as other workers—the right to organize and negotiate with growers.

But we also won a critical battle for all Americans. Our first contracts banned the use of DDT, DDE, Dieldrin on crops, years before the federal government acted.

Twenty years later our contracts still seek to limit the spread of poison in our food and fields, but we need your help once again if we are to succeed.

A powerful self-serving alliance between the California governor and the $4 billion agricultural industry has resulted in a systematic and reckless poisoning of not only California farm workers but of grape consumers throughout our nation and Canada.

The hard won law enacted in 1975 has been trampled beneath the feet of self-interest. Blatant violations of California labor laws are constantly ignored. And worst of all, the indiscriminate and even illegal use of dangerous pesticides has radically increased in the last decade causing illness, permanent disability, and even death.

We must not allow the governor of California and the selfish interests of California grape growers to threaten lives throughout North America.

We have known for many years that pesticides used in agriculture pollute the air, earth, and water, contaminate animals and humans, and are found in the tissue of newborn infants and mothers' milk. This March, the *New York Times* reported that the Environmental Protection Agency finally considers pesticide pollution its most urgent problem, noting virtually everyone is exposed to pesticides.

The Environmental Protection Agency experts have warned that

#1—Pesticide residue is being found in a growing number of food products.

#2—Some poisons registered for use in the last thirty years cause cancer, mutations, and birth defects.

#3—Most chemicals on the market have insufficient and sometimes fraudulent test results.

#4—Underground water supplies of twenty-three states are already tainted, and farm workers suffer some pesticide-induced illness in alarming numbers.

Consumers must be alerted now that no one can actually define or measure so called safe exposure to residual poison that accumulates in the human body, as environments differ and each person's tolerance is unique. What might be safe statistically for the average healthy forty year old male might irreparably harm an elderly consumer, a child, or the baby of a pregnant mother.

What we do know absolutely is that human lives are worth more than grapes and that innocent looking grapes on the table may disguise poisonous residues hidden deep inside where washing cannot reach.

Let me share the frightening facts with you. Last July the *New York Times* and national television reported that nearly one thousand California, Pacific Northwest, Alaskan, and Canadian consumers became ill as the result of eating watermelons tainted with the powerful insecticide Aldicarb, labeled the most acutely toxic pesticide registered in the United States. Yet Aldicarb cannot be legally used on watermelons.

In June local agriculture officials quarantined fields in Delano, California, grape ranches because residues of the pesticide Orthene were found in the vineyards; yet Orthene cannot be legally used on table grapes.

And a new study shows pesticides used in growing may be responsible for the illness of over three hundred thousand of the nation's 4 million farm workers.

But of the twenty-seven legally restricted toxic poisons currently used on grapes, at least five are potentially as dangerous or more hazardous to consumers and grape workers than deadly Aldicarb and Orthene.

Here are five major threats to your health that cling to California table grapes:

—Parathion and Phosdrin—are highly poisonous insecticides, similar to nerve gas, and are responsible for the majority of deaths and serious poisoning of farm workers. They cause birth defects and are carcinogens.

—Captan—a proven cancer-causing and birth-defect producing agent (fungicide).

—Dinoseb—a highly toxic herbicide that has caused worker deaths.

—methyl bromide—a more potent mutagen (an agent affecting genetic material) than mustard gas and is a highly poisonous and proven carcinogen.

Statistics and news articles do not relate the real cost, the human anguish that originates from poisons on our food. They do not tell the tragedies I personally learn of daily.

How can I explain these chemicals to three-year-old Amalia Larios, who will never walk, born with a spinal defect due to pesticide exposure of her mother.

What statistics are important to Adrian Espinoza, seven years old and dying of cancer with eight other children, whose only source of water was polluted with pesticides.

What headlines can justify the loss of irrigator Manuel Anaya's right hand, amputated due to recurrent infection from powerful herbicides added to the water he worked with in the fields.

How do we comfort the mother of maimed and stillborn infants, the parents who watch their teenage children sicken or die.

What report can be cited at the hospital beds I visit, at growing numbers of wakes I attend.

What court will hear the case of thirty-two-year-old Juan Chaboya, murdered by deadly chemicals in the freshly sprayed fields outside San Diego, his dead body dumped by the growers forty-five miles away at a Tijuana clinic. What excuse for justice will we offer his four children and his widow if we do nothing.

Now is the time for all of us to stand as a family and demand a response in the name of decency. Too much is at stake. This is a battle that none of us can afford to lose because it is a fight for the future of America. It is a fight we can win, and it is a fight that everyone can join.

Add your voice to our demands of decency as we call for

#1—A ban on the five most dangerous pesticides used in grape production—Parathion, Phosdrin, Dinoseb, methyl bromide, and Captan.

#2—A joint UFW/grower testing program for poisonous residues on grapes sold in stores with the results made public.

#3—Free and fair elections for farm workers to decide whether to organize and negotiate contracts limiting the use of dangerous poisons in the fields.

#4—Good faith bargaining.

Until these demands of decency are met, we will carry the message of the Wrath of Grapes Boycott from state to state. Ten years ago, 12 percent of the country boycotted grapes and the growers were forced to accountability. California Governor Deukmejian and agribusiness cannot withstand the judgment of outraged consumers who refused to purchase their tainted products. Every month over 1 million grape consumers like yourselves receive our message across North America. State and federal law makers, mayors and city councils, religious and labor leaders, students and senior citizens, mothers and fathers, rich and poor, concerned individuals in every walk of life have endorsed the Wrath of Grapes Boycott. With their commitment and their donations, they in turn have reached out to their friends and relatives to help bind the foundation of a growing coalition of decency.

Now I am reaching out to you for help because consumers and farm workers must stand together as one family if we are to be heard. I am not asking you to give up wine or raisins. I am asking you to give us your commitment and valuable support.

I am asking you to join us now and be counted to join the growing family of individuals who will boycott grapes until the demands of decency have been met.

And hard as it is for me to ask for money, I am asking you to contribute to the cause—$100, $50, $15, whatever you can afford, whatever you would have spent on grapes this year. Insure that every week 1 million more consumers will know the truth.

You have my personal pledge that every cent of your contributions will be spent on the Wrath of Grapes Campaign bringing this message into every home in America because this message is the source of our combined strength.

My friends, the wrath of grapes is a plague born of selfish men that is indiscriminately and undeniably poisoning us all. Our only protection is to boycott the grapes, and our only weapon is the truth. If we unite we can only triumph for ourselves, for our children, and for their children. We look forward to hearing from you soon.

United Farm Workers of America: Pecan Workers Speech, Arizona, 1987

This speech was given to the workers at the Santa Cruz Valley Pecan Company in Arizona. A transcript of the speech is in the United Farm Workers Papers, Wayne State University.

I bring you greetings from the Farmworkers.

I bring you our love, concern, and solidarity.

I bring you our support.

We are proud to stand with you on this picket line.

We are proud to join you in your fight which is also our fight because your fight is also the fight of every working person in our land.

Still we are prouder of your spirit, determination and unity.

We are confident of your victory. We know your commitment and strength will bring you through.

We shall overcome.

Together we will send Richard Walden a message.

A strong message.

A message to stop trying to bust the union.

A message to sit down and bargain in good faith until a contract is reached.

A message that we won't stand for his cheap wages, harassment, unsafe jobs, and unhealthy conditions.

A message that we will not continue making him rich with our sweat.

And a message that the farm workers will support the boycott and that he won't be able to sell his damn pecans.

We come together in solidarity to tell the Richard Waldens and other bosses in America that working people—that the American people want

Dignity and respect

[To] be secure in our jobs

Be secure in our unions

[For you] to accept the corporate responsibilities

To bargain with their workers

To stop pushing us workers around

And

[We want] to tell management that their corporations can't and won't survive without the good will of the American public

Tell them that we stand for equal and human rights

Peace in Nicaragua—world and here

Justice and Freedom right here in Arizona.

I see us as one family—a family of workers who depend on our work to provide the basic necessities for ourselves and our loved ones.

We cannot turn our backs on each other, because we all share in the same future.

Together we will win this critical battle.

Together we shall stand till victory.

A powerful self-serving alliance between President Reagan and the billionaires of this land has resulted in systematic and sometimes reckless attempts to break unions, like Richard Walden is doing.

The National Labor Relations Act has been trampled beneath the feet of self-interest—blatant violations of the NLRB are constantly ignored. And worst of all, indiscriminate and even illegal tactics are often used against workers' organizations.

Today employers like Walden violate the law with impunity, and enforcement of its provisions to protect workers is almost nonexistent. Intimidation and firing are in store for workers who show an interest in voting for a union. Bad faith bargaining by employers is prevalent all over this land.

And employers like Richard Walden, rather than provide just wages and decent benefits to workers, try to create the impression that the unions don't represent their workers, and when workers persist and insist on being represented the employers like Richard Walden will resort to the infamous industrial-relations consultant that brings workers nothing but agony and abuse.

Worse yet, the atmosphere under this administration is so antiunion that employers like Richard Walden show no qualms of conscience about the use of the strikebreaking scum of the earth—consultants, the purveyors of industrial conflict, the heartless self-serving like Robert Deeny and Juan Garza, one of the most vicious systems ever conceived by the human mind, a system in which employers like Richard Walden wash their hands of the dirty work. They hire consultants like Robert Deeny and Juan Garza to do for them—industrial soldiers of fortune, a system in which these puppets of employers hire and fire at will, cheat workers out of a fair wage, force workers to strike, taunt workers, and in general reduce workers to mere industrial tools instead of human beings.

We must not allow the Ronald Reagans, Richard Waldens, Robert Deenys, and Juan Garzas to threaten workers and break their unions.

What we know absolutely is that workers are worth more than those damn pecans and that we won't eat pecans until we are treated fairly with justice and dignity.

We say to you that now is the time for all to stand together as a family and demand a response in the name of decency from Richard Walden. Too much is at stake. This is a battle that none of us can afford to lose because it is a fight for the future of America. It is a fight that we can win, and it is a fight that everyone can join.

Until these demands of decency are met, we will carry your message to boycott Green Valley Pecans—pecan candies and pecan pies—to every farm worker and friends everywhere.

Our unity, our solidarity, and our faith in justice shall prevail until the day comes when Richard Walden will negotiate a just contract and we can return to our job with dignity—secure in our job and in our union, the United Farm Workers of America.

Thank you.

Unión de Campesinos de America: Discurso a los Trabajadores de la Nuez

Les traigo saludos de los campesinos les traigo amor, sentimiento, y solidaridad Traigo apoyo para ustedes.

Estamos orgullosos de estar con ustedes en este pickedte [picket line].

Estamos orgullosos, de unernos a su lucha, que también es nuestra lucha, porque su lucha también es la lucha de cada trabajador o trabajadora en nuestro país.

Y estamos aun mas orgullosos de su espíritu de determinación y unidad.

Confiamos en que lograrán la Victoria. Porque sabemos que su confianza y fuerza los verán hasta en fin.

Nosotros Venceremos (& we shall overcome).

Un mensaje fuerte:

Un mensaje para parar tratando de quebrar el gremio.

Un mensaje de sentar y negociar en la buena fe hasta un contrato está agarrado.

Un mensaje que no paramos por sus sueldos baratos, hostigados, trabajos inseguros de y condiciones malsanas.

Un mensaje que nosotros no continuaremos a ponerlo rico con nuestro sudor.

Y un mensaje que los campesinos apoyarán el boicot y que el no puede vender sus malditos pecans.

Nosotros juntamos en la solidaridad para contar el Richard Waldens y otros jefes en América

Que trabajadores—que la gente Americana quiere

Dignidad y respeto

Seremos seguro en nuestros trabajos

Seramos seguro en nuestros gremios

A aceptar las responsabilidades corporacionales

Para negociar con sus trabajadores

A parar de empujar nosotros trabajadores alrededor

y

A decir la dirección que su corporación no puede y no va a sobrevivir sin la voluntad buena del publico Americano

Dígales que permanecemos para derechos iguales y humanos

La paz en Nicaragua—El mundo y aquí

Justicia y libertad

Aquí mismo en _____, AZ.

Yo nos veo como una familia—una familia de trabajadores quienes depende de nuestro trabajo para proveer las necesidades básicas para nosotros y nuestras amadoras.

No podemos volver nuestras espaldas sobre nosotros porque nos partimos en el mismo futuro.

Juntos nos ganaremos esta batalla crítica.

Juntos nos permaneceremos hasta la victoria.

Una personalidad poderosa—sirviendo alianza entre el presidente Reagan y los billonarios de esta tierra ha resultado en un tratado sistemático y a veces imprudentes de romper.

Los gremios como le está haciendo Richard Walden el acto del National Labor Relations Board se ha pisoteado abajo los pies del interés propio—las violaciones evidentes del NLRB se ignoran constantemente. Y peor de todo tácticas indistintas y también son usados frecuentemente contra organizaciones de trabajadores.

Hoy empleadores como Walden infringen la ley con la impunidad, y la aplicación de sus provisiones para proteger trabajadores es casi totalmente sin existir. La intimidación y la descarga están en el futuro para trabajadores quienes muestran un interés en votar para un gremio—negociando en mala fe que es frecuente por todo esta tierra.

Y empleadores como Richard Walden mas bien que proveer sueldo justos y beneficios decentes a los trabajadores tratan de crear la impresion que los gremios no representan sus trabajadores y cuando trabajadores persisten y insisten que sean representados los empleadores como Richard Walden recurren' al asesor infame de relación industrial que trae trabajadores nada pero agonía y abuso.

Peor aún, la atmosfera debajo esta administración es tan contra el gremio que empleadores como Richard Walden muestran ningunos ecrúpulos de conciencia del uso de los quebradores de huelgas.

Que son la nata de los asesores de tierra los proveedores del conflicto industrial los egoístas hombres sin corazón como Robert Deeny y Juan Garza uno de los sistemas mas viciosos siempre concebido por la mente humana . . . una sistema en que empleadores como Richard Walden lavan sus manos del trabajo sucio ellos contratan asesores como Robert Deeny y Juan Garza para hacer por ellos soldados de la fortuna industrial.

Un sistema en que estos títeres de los empleadores contratan y disparan cuando quieren estafar trabajadores de un sueldo justo, forzar los trabajadores de ir en huelga, se mofan los trabajadores y en general reducen trabajadores a herramientas industriales meras en vez de seres humanos.

Nosotros no debemos permitir los Ronald Reagans, Richard Waldens, Robert Deenys, y Juan Garzas amenazar trabajadores y quebrar sus gremios.

Que sabemos absolutamente es que trabajadores valen mas que esos malditos pecans y que no comeremos pecans hasta se tratan nosotros bastante con la justicia y la dignidad.

Nosotros decimos a ud.

Que ahora es el tiempo para todos nosotros paramos juntos como una familia y demandar una respuesta en el nombre de la decencia.

De Richard Walden tanto es un juego esta es una batalla que ningunos de nosotros podemos afrontar de perder. Porque es una pelea para el futuro de América. Es una pelea que nosotros podemos ganar y es una pelea con que todos pueden reunir.

Hasta estas demandas de decencia se encuentran nosotros llevaremos ud. Mensaje para boicotear los Pecans de Green Valley—dulces de pecan y pasteles de pecan a cada campesino y a cada amigo en todos lados.

Nuestra unidad, nuestra solidaridad, y nuestra fe en la justicia predominará.

Hasta el dia viene cuando Richard Walden negociará un contrato justo y podemos regresar a nuestro trabajo con dignidad, seguros en nuestro trabajo y en nuestro gremio los Farm Workers of America.

Adradezco a udes.

Speech at Pacific Lutheran University, March 1989

The text of this speech is in the United Farm Workers Papers, Wayne State Univesity. The speech was reprinted in the *Sacramento Bee*, April 16, 1989, 1, 6.

What is the worth of a man or a woman? What is the worth of a farm worker? How do you measure the value of a life?

Ask the parents of Johnnie Rodríguez.

Johnnie Rodríguez was not even a man; Johnnie was a five-year-old boy when he died after a painful two-year battle against cancer.

His parents, Juan and Elia, are farm workers. Like all grape workers, they are exposed to pesticides and other agricultural chemicals.

Elia worked in the table grapes around Delano, California until she was eight months pregnant with Johnnie.

Juan and Elia cannot say for certain if pesticides caused their son's cancer. But neuroblastoma is one of the cancers found in McFarland, a small farm town only a few miles from Delano, where the Rodríguezes live.

"Pesticides are always in the fields and around the towns," Johnnie's father told us. "The children get them when they play, outside, drink the water or hug you after you come home from working in fields that are sprayed."

"Once your son has cancer you hope it's a mistake, you pray," Juan says. "He was a real nice boy. He took it strong and lived as long as he could."

I keep a picture of Johnnie Rodríguez. He is sitting on his bed, hugging his teddy bears. His sad eyes and cherubic face stare out at you. The photo was taken four days before he died.

Johnnie Rodríguez was one of 13 McFarland children diagnosed with cancer in recent years; and one of six who have died from the disease. With only 6,000 residents, the rate of cancer in McFarland is 400 percent above normal.

In McFarland and in Fowler childhood cancer cases are being reported in excess of expected rates. In Delano and other farming towns, questions are also being raised.

The chief source of carcinogens in these communities are pesticides from vineyards and fields that encircle them. Health experts think the high rate of cancer in McFarland is from pesticides and nitrate-containing fertilizers leaching into the water system from surrounding fields.

Last year California's Republican Governor, George Deukmejian, killed a modest study to find out why so many children are dying of cancer in McFarland. "Fiscal integrity" was the reason he gave for his veto of the $125,000 program which could have helped 84 other rural communities with drinking water problems.

Last year, as support for our cause grew, Governor Deukmejian used a statewide radio broadcast to attack the grape boycott.

There is no evidence to prove that pesticides on grapes and other produce endanger farm workers or consumers, Deukmejian claimed.

Ask the family of Felipe Franco.

Felipe is a bright seven year old.

Like other children, Felipe will some day need to be independent. But Felipe is not like other children: he was born without arms and legs.

Felipe's mother, Ramona, worked in the grapes near Delano until she was in her eighth month of pregnancy. She was exposed to Captan, known to cause birth defects and one of the pesticides our grape boycott seeks to ban.

"Every morning when I began working I could smell and see pesticides on the grape leaves," Ramona said.

Like many farm workers, she was assured by growers and their foremen how the pesticides that surrounded her were safe, that they were harmless "medicine" for the plants.

Only after Ramona took her son to specialists in Los Angeles was she told that the pesticides she was exposed to in the vineyards caused Felipe's deformity. The deep sadness she feels has subsided, but not the anger.

Felipe feels neither anger nor sadness. He dreams of what only a child can hope for: Felipe wants to grow arms and legs. "He believes he will have his limbs someday," his mother says. "His great dream is to be able to move around, to walk, to take care of himself."

Our critics sometimes ask, "Why should the United Farm Workers worry about pesticides when farm workers have so many other more obvious problems?"

The wealth and plenty of California agribusiness are built atop the suffering of generations of California farm workers. Farm labor history across America is one shameful tale after another of hardship and exploitation.

Malnutrition among migrant children. Tuberculosis, pneumonia and respirator infections. Short life expectancy.

Savage living conditions. Miserable wages and working conditions. Sexual harassment of women workers. Widespread child labor. Inferior schools or no school at all.

When farm workers organize against these injustices they are met with brutality and coercion—and death.

Under Governor Deukmejian, California's pioneering law guaranteeing farm workers the right to organize and vote in secret ballot union elections is now just one more tool growers use to oppress our people.

Thousands who thought the law protected them were threatened and fired and beaten by the growers; two were shot to death by gunmen their employers had hired.

For 100 years succeeding waves of immigrants have sweated and sacrificed to make this industry rich. And for their sweat and for their sacrifice, farm workers have been repaid with humiliation and contempt.

With all these problems, why, then, do we dwell so on the perils of pesticides?

Because there is something even more important to farm workers than the benefits unionization brings.

There is something more important to the farm workers' union than winning better wages and working conditions.

That is protecting farm workers—and consumers—from systematic poisoning through the reckless use of agricultural toxics.

There is nothing we care more about than the lives and safety of our families. There is nothing we share more deeply in common with the consumers of North America than the safety of the food all of us reply upon.

What good does it do to achieve the blessings of collective bargaining and make economic progress for people when their health is destroyed in the process?

If we ignored pesticide poisoning then all the other injustices our people face would be compounded by an even more deadly tyranny. But ignore that final injustice is what our opponents would have us do.

"Don't worry," the growers say.

"The U.F.W. misleads the public about the dangers of pesticides," the Table Grape Commission says. "Governor Deukmejian's pesticide safety system protects workers," the Farm Bureau proclaims.

Ask the family of Juan Chabolla. Juan Chabolla collapsed after working in a field sprayed only an hour before with Monitor, a deadly pesticide.

But instead of rushing Juan to a nearby hospital, the grower drove him 45 miles across the U.S.-Mexico border and left him in a Tijuana clinic. He was dead on arrival.

Juan, 32, left his wife and four young children in their impoverished clapboard shack in Maneadero, Mexico.

Just after Juan died, Governor Deukmejian vetoed a modest bill, strongly opposed by agribusiness, that would have required growers to post warning signs in fields where dangerous pesticides are applied.

Two hundred and fifty million [. . .] pounds of pesticides are applied each year to crops in California; in 1986, 10 million pounds went on grapes.

Grapes is the largest fruit crop in California. It receives more restricted use of pesticides than any fresh food crop.

About one-third of grape pesticides are known carcinogens—like the chemicals that may have afflicted Johnnie Rodríguez; others are teratogens—birth-defect-producing pesticides—that doctors think deformed Felipe Franco.

Pesticides cause acute poisoning—of the kind that killed Juan Chabolla—and chronic, long-term effects such as we're seeing in communities like McFarland.

More than half of all acute pesticide-related illnesses reported in California involve grape production.

In 1987 and '88, entire crews of grape workers—hundreds of people—were poisoned after entering vineyards containing toxic residues.

In all those episodes, the grapes had been sprayed weeks before. All the *legal* requirements were followed.

But farm workers were still poisoned.

Illegal use of pesticides is also commonplace.

Grape growers have been illegally using Fixx, a growth enhancer, for 20 years. Another illegal pesticide, Acephate, which causes tumors, has also been used on grapes.

Over 2,000 consumers were poisoned in 1984 after eating watermelons illegally sprayed with Aldicarb.

And these are only cases where growers were caught applying illegal chemicals.

Farm workers and their families are exposed to pesticides from the crops they work. The soil the crops are grown in. Drift from sprays applied to adjoining fields-and often to the very field where they are working.

The fields that surround their homes are heavily and repeatedly sprayed. Pesticides pollute irrigation water and groundwater.

Children are still a big part of the labor force. Or they are taken to the fields by their parents because there is no childcare.

Pregnant women labor in the fields to help support their families. Toxic exposure begins at a very young age—often in the womb.

What does acute pesticide poisoning produce?

Eye and respiratory irritations. Skin rashes. Systemic poisoning.

Death.

What are the chronic effects of pesticide poisoning on people, according to scientific studies? Birth defects. Sterility. Still births. Miscarriages. Neurological and neuropsychological effects. Effects on child growth and development. Cancer.

Use of pesticides are governed by strict laws, agribusiness says. Growers argue reported poisonings involved only one (1) percent of California farm workers in 1986.

But experts estimate that only one (1) percent of California pesticide illness or injury is reported. The underreporting of pesticide poisoning is flagrant and it is epidemic.

A World Resources Institute study says 300,000 farm workers are poisoned each year by pesticides in the United States.

Even the state Department of Food and Agriculture reported total pesticide poisoning of farm workers rose by 41 percent in 1987.

Yet the Farm Workers aren't sincere when we raise the pesticide issue, grape growers complain.

They won't admit that the first ban on DDT, Aldrin and Dieldrin in the United States was not by the Environmental Protection Agency in 1972, but in a United Farm Workers contract with a *grape grower* in 1967.

Who will protect farm workers from poisoning if it isn't the farm workers' union?

The Environmental Protection Agency won't do it.

They're in bed with the same agricultural and chemical interests they are supposed to regulate.

It was an accident of history that E.P.A. got stuck with regulating pesticides. It happened after the federal Occupational Safety and Health Administration—which is supposed to safeguard all American working people—refused to protect farm workers.

The law won't do it.

Agribusinesses lobbied mightily to exclude farm workers from federal job safety and health laws. And they won.

You think the National Rifle Association wields a powerful lobby? They're pussy cats compared to organizations that lobby for agribusiness.

Too many people still think of small family farmers—an image corporate agribusiness likes to promote. The American Medical Association tries to do the same thing, except most people don't believe doctors still make house calls. But we all know what farming is today in states like California: a $14 billion a year industry dominated by huge corporations—the state's richest industry.

There has never been a law at the state or national levels that has ever been enforced for farm workers and against growers: child labor, minimum wage and hour, occupational health and safety, agricultural labor relations.

Now will agribusiness protect farm workers from pesticides?

The agrichemical industry won't do it.

It's out to maximize profits. Using smaller amounts of safer chemicals more wisely is not in the interest of chemical companies and agribusiness groups like the Farm Bureau that have heavy financial stakes in maintaining pesticide use.

There is nothing wrong with pesticides, they claim; the blame rests with abuse and misuse of pesticides.

It's like the N.R.A. saying, "Guns don't kill people, people kill people."

Universities won't do it.

America's colleges and universities are the best research facilities in the world. But farm workers are of the wrong color; they don't speak the right language; and they're poor.

The University of California and other land grant colleges spend millions of dollars developing agricultural mechanization and farm chemicals. Although we're all affected in the end, researchers won't deal with the inherent toxicity or chronic effects of their creations.

Protecting farm workers and consumers is not their concern.

Doctors won't do it.

Most physicians farm workers see won't even admit their patients' problems are caused by pesticides. They usually blame symptoms on skin rashes and heat stroke.

Doctors don't know much about pesticides; the signs and symptoms of acute pesticide poisoning are similar to other illnesses.

Doctors who work for growers and most rural physicians won't take a stand.

Two years ago in Tulare County 120 orange grove workers at LaBue Ranch suffered the largest skin poisoning ever reported. The grower altered a pesticide, Omite CR, to make it stick to the leaves better. It did.

It also stuck better to the workers. Later they discovered the delay before reentering the field had to be extended from seven to 42 days.

After the poisoning, the company doctor said workers should just change clothes and return to work. When we demanded the workers be removed from exposure, the doctor replied, "Do you know how much that would cost?"

Workers endure skin irritations and rashes that none of us would tolerate. They continue to work because they desperately need the money. They don't complain out of fear of losing their jobs.

Farm workers aren't told when pesticides are used. They have no health insurance. They are cheated out of workers compensation benefits by disappearing labor contractors or foremen who intimidate people into not filing claims.

In the old days, miners would carry birds with them to warn against poison gas. Hopefully, the birds would die before the miners.

Farm workers are society's canaries.

Farm workers—and their children—demonstrate the effects of pesticide poisoning before anyone else.

But the unrestrained use of agricultural chemicals is like playing Russian Roulette with the health of both farm workers and consumers.

So much of so many pesticides are used and so little is known about them.

Hundreds of farm pesticides leave residues on food; most can't be detected by commonly used tests—many can't be detected by any test at all.

Forty-four (44) percent of the pesticides applied on grapes that can't be detected by tests used to check for toxic residues pose potential health hazards for humans.

Many pesticides used on food—that have government tolerance levels—can cause cancer in human beings.

Almost all of those tolerance levels were set by the federal government without adequate testing for potential harmful health effects on consumers.

Some safety studies on these pesticides were conducted by an Illinois lab that was closed after it was found to be reporting fraudulent data to the E.P.A. Two toxicologists were jailed.

The U.S. General Accounting Office estimates that it will take E.P.A. until well into the 21st century to ensure all pesticides now on the market meet current health and safety standards.

Most pesticides were approved by the U.S. Department of Agriculture in the 1940s and '50s. Little or no testing for chronic health effects was required.

Not long ago the Delaney Amendment, passed by Congress, banned any food additive known to cause cancer in animals or humans. That ban applies to everything—except farm pesticides.

The agrichemical industry convinced Congress that pesticides which cause cancer are not really food additives since they are added to food before it is harvested.

In 1978, E.P.A. allowed new chemicals to be registered conditionally without complete testing for chronic health effects. Testing on half of all new pesticides registered between 1978 and 1984 did not meet current health and safety testing standards.

All this means that we do not know if pesticide residues on the food you buy in supermarkets cause cancer, birth defects, and other tragedies.

And E.P.A. has made no effort to encourage the use of safer alternatives to toxic pesticides.

The chemical companies have convinced the growers—and they want you to believe—that if it wasn't for them, the whole world would succumb to malaria and starvation.

But, brothers and sisters, pesticides haven't worked.

Crop loss to pests is as great or greater than it was 40 years ago. The pesticides haven't changed anything.

Because Darwinian evolution has favored pests of all kinds with this enormous ability, to resist and survive.

It's why antibiotics stop working after awhile. If you don't kill everything, the organisms that survive are tougher and more resistant; and they're the ones that breed.

There are mosquitoes that can survive any combination of pesticides delivered in any dose. There is a startling resurgence of malaria around the world. And it's much worse now because 40 years ago we relied entirely on a chemical solution.

So we ignored alternatives: draining ponds, dredging ditches, observing sound crop practices, encouraging use of natural predators.

In the long run, more lives will be lost because for 30 years we also stopped developing malaria vaccines.

You can't fool Mother Nature. In time, insects can outfox anything we throw at them.

People thought pesticides were the cure-all—the key to an abundance of food. They thought pesticides were the solution; but they were the problem.

The problem is this mammoth agribusiness system. The problem is the huge farms. The problem is the pressure on the land from developers. The problem is not allowing the land to lay fallow and rest. The problem is the abandonment of cultural practices that have stood the test of centuries: crop rotation, diversification of crops.

The problem is monoculture—growing acres and acres of the same crop; disrupting the natural order of things; letting insects feast on acres and acres of a harem of delight . . . and using pesticides that kill off their natural predators.

Meantime, these greedy chemical companies, multi-national corporations, try to sanctify their poisons. They would have us believe they are the health givers—that because of them people are not dying of malaria and starvation.

When all the time, they just want to defend their investments. They just want to protect their profits. They don't want anything to change.

The chemical companies believe in the Domino Theory: all chemicals are threatened if any chemical is questioned. No matter how dangerous it may be.

It's a lot like that saying from the Vietnam War: we had to destroy the village in order to save it.

They have to poison us in order to save us.

But at what cost?

The lives of farm workers and their children who are suffering? The lives of consumers who could reap the harvest of pesticides ten, twenty years from now? The contamination of our ground water? The loss of our reverence for the soil. The raping of the land?

We see these insane practices reflected in the buy-outs and takeovers on Wall Street. It's the same thing: exchanging long term security for short-term gain.

You sacrifice a company for the immediate rewards. But you destroy what produces jobs and livelihoods and economic health.

If you eat the seed corn, you won't have a crop to plant.

Oscar Wilde once said, "A cynic is someone who knows the price of everything and the value of nothing."

We look at the price, but we don't look at the value. Economics and profit drive everything.

People forget that the soil is our sustenance. It is a sacred trust. It is what has worked for us for centuries.

It is what we pass on to future generations.

If we continue in this thoughtless submission to pesticides—if we ruin the top soil—then there will not be an abundance of food to bequeath [to] our children.

Farm workers and consumers cannot get pesticide regulation because those who make the rules are captives of these bankrupt 40- and 50-year old policies that have been shown not to work.

So they don't ban the worst of these poisons because some farm worker might give birth to a deformed child.

So they don't imperil millions of dollars in profits today because, some day, some consumers *might* get cancer.

So they allow all of us, who place our faith in the safety of the food supply, to consume grapes and other produce which contain residues from pesticides that cause cancer and birth defects.

So we accept decades of environmental damage these poisons have brought upon the land.

The growers, the chemical companies and the bureaucrats say, "These are acceptable levels of exposure."

Acceptable to whom?

Acceptable to Johnnie Rodríguez's parents?

Acceptable to Felipe Franco?

Acceptable to the widow of Juan Chabolla and her children?

Acceptable to all farm workers who have known tragedy from pesticides?

There is no acceptable level of exposure to any chemical that causes cancer. There can be no toleration of any toxic that causes miscarriages, still births, and deformed babies.

Risk is associated with any level of exposure. And any level of exposure is too much.

Isn't that the standard of protection you would ask for your family and your children? Isn't that the standard of protection you would demand for yourself?

Then why do we allow farm workers to carry the burden of pesticides on their shoulders?

Do we carry in our hearts the sufferings of farm workers and their children?

Do we feel deeply enough the pain of those who must work in the fields every day with these poisons? Or the anguish of the families that have lost loved ones to cancer? Or the heartache of the parents who fear for the lives of their children? Who are raising children with deformities? Who agonize the outcome of their pregnancies?

Who ask in fear, "Where will this deadly plague strike next?"

Do we feel their pain deeply enough?

I didn't. And I was ashamed.

I studied this wanton abuse of nature. I read the literature, heard from the experts about what pesticides do.

I talked with farm workers, listened to their families, and shared their anguish and their fears. I spoke out against the cycle of death.

But sometimes words come too cheaply. And their meaning is lost in the clutter that so often fills our lives.

That is why, in July and August of last year, I embarked on a 36-day unconditional, water-only fast.

The fast was first and foremost directed at myself—to purify my own body, mind and soul.

The fast was an act of penance for our own members who, out of ignorance or need, cooperate with those who grow and sell food treated with toxics.

The fast was also for those who know what is right and just. It pains me that we continue to shop without protest at stores that offer grapes; that we eat in restaurants that display them; that we are too patient and understanding with those who serve them to us.

The fast, then, was for those who know that they could or should do more—for those who, by not acting, become bystanders in the poisoning of our food and the people who produce it.

The fast was, finally, a declaration of noncooperation with supermarkets that promote, sell, and profit from California table grapes. They are as culpable as those who manufacture the poisons and those who use them.

It is my hope that our friends everywhere will resist in many nonviolent ways the presence of grapes in the stores where they shop.

So I ask of you, take the pledge: boycott grapes. Join the many hundreds who have taken up where my fast ended—by sharing the suffering of the farm workers—by going without food for a day or two days or three.

The misery that pesticides bring farm workers—and the dangers they pose to all consumers—will not be ended with more hearings or studies. The solution is not to be had from those in power because it is they who have allowed this deadly crisis to grow.

The times we face truly call for all of us to do more to stop this evil in our midst.

The answer lies with you and me. It is with all men and women who share the suffering and yearn with us for a better world.

Our cause goes on in hundreds of distant places. It multiplies among thousands and then millions of caring people who heed through a multitude of simple deeds the commandment set out in the book of the Prophet Micah, in the Old Testament: "What does the Lord require of you, but to do justice, to love kindness, and to walk humbly with your God."

Thank you. And boycott grapes.

Statement from César Chávez, Sacramento, April 3, 1991

A transcript of this speech is in the United Farm Workers Papers, Wayne State University.

Some people may ask, "Why should the farm workers be concerned about the condition of public schools in California?"

Let me answer them: Who do you think are in the public schools today in California?

Public schools serve more farm workers than any other publicly financed social institution in society.

Public schools provide the greatest opportunity for upward mobility to Hispanics and to all ethnic minorities in this state.

Yet today, it is a Republican governor and his allies in the legislature who are less concerned than we are about preserving public schools. That is ironic because it was not always the case.

In the 1960s and early '70s, another Republican governor—Ronald Reagan— was leading the fight for more support of public education. But there was a big difference. Back then, the majority of public school children were white, and they were from middle- or upper middle-income families.

Today, the majority of children in our public schools are minority—African American, Hispanic, Asian—and they are from poor and working-class families.

Back then, under Ronald Reagan, Californians spent 5 cents out of every dollar of personal income on public schools. Today, under Pete Wilson, Californians spend a little over 3 cents out of every dollar on education. And if he has his way, it will go down even more.

There is another institution in society that is funded by the state and that is dominated by minorities: the state prisons—and they have fared very well.

Over the last nine years—under Governor Deukmejian and now Governor Wilson—California has carried out a policy of dramatically expanding state prisons while it starves public schools.

What message do those priorities send? Does this mean that the only way our sons and daughters can get recognition from the state of California is by using drugs and committing crimes?

We have looked into the future and the future is ours! Asians and Hispanics and African Americans are the future in California. That trend cannot be stopped. It is inevitable.

Then why do they want to cut funds for schools and other vital services—now? Why do Governor Wilson and his allies seek to reduce the commitment to public education—now? If the majority of children in school were white and if they lived in affluent suburban communities, we wouldn't even be debating how much money to spend on public education.

But it is *our* children—the children of farm workers and Hispanics and other minorities—who are seeking a better life. It is for them, for their future—and for the future of California—that we must say "no" to suspending Proposition 98.

We must say "no" to cutting essential services for the needy instead of tax loopholes for the wealthy.

We must say "no" to making *our* children and *their* teachers scapegoats for the budget crisis.

Address before the Building Industry Association of Northern California, San Jose, November 21, 1991

A transcript of this speech is in the United Farm Workers Papers, Wayne State University.

I always feel like I'm coming home when I visit San Jose. My family often called this place home when we became migrants after the bank foreclosed on my father's small Arizona farm during the late 1930s.

After World War II we returned to San Jose, to a little house on Sharf Avenue in the tough eastside barrio they nicknamed Sal Si Puedes—which for those of you who are culturally deprived translates "get out if you can."

The nickname came about because it seemed as though the only way young men left Sal Si Puedes was to go off to jail, the military, or the cemetery. A lot of people who lived in Sal Si Puedes were farm workers who scratched out a living in the orchards and vineyards that used to flourish on the outskirts of town.

I was one of them—working in the apricots in 1952, when I began my organizing career by starting up the first local chapter of the Community Service Organization (CSO), a civil rights-civic action group among the Hispanics that grew into the most militant and effective organization of its kind in the country.

Throughout California we registered people to vote and turned them out at the polls. We fought segregation. We battled police brutality—the roughing up of young guys and the breaking and entering without warrants. We opposed the forced removal of Hispanics to make way for urban renewal projects. We fought to improve the poor conditions that were so common in Sal Si Puedes and in other minority neighborhoods, the mean streets and walkways, the lack of street lights and traffic signals, the polluted creeks and horse pastures where kids played, the poor drainage, the overflowing cesspools, the amoebic dysentery.

Some things change and some things never do.

I understand San Jose recently named its first Hispanic Chief of Police—Louis Cobarrúviaz, a twenty-six-year veteran of the force. And Hispanics have been elected to the City Council and the Board of Supervisors.

My mother still lives on Sharf Avenue. But most of Sal Si Puedes is gone; it was taken years ago when they put in the freeway.

That neighborhood and many of those conditions may no longer exist in San Jose. But as we meet here this evening—only a short drive from this place—farm workers are living in caves and crude shacks, under trees and bridges, and in wretched farm labor camps.

In the Almaden Valley, right here in Santa Clara County, massive sanitation and safety violations were documented at two labor camps—including raw sewage on the ground.

Some workers in labor camps, who can't find space in crowded barracks, sleep out in the open—while farm labor contractors deduct money from their paychecks for *utility* expenses.

Many are without plumbing or electricity. They bathe in irrigation water that is laden with pesticides.

Entire migrant families are homeless—people living out of their cars near fields and vineyards or under stands of trees.

In Santa Clara and Monterey and San Benito counties—in the Central Valley and throughout California—these savage conditions are often the rule and not the exception.

Farm labor in this state and nation is one shameful tale after another of hardship and exploitation. The wealth and plenty of California agribusiness has been built atop the suffering of these men, women, and children. It was true when my family and I were migrants in the '30s and '40s. It is true even more so today.

We created the United Farm Workers to battle these injustices; it's what we've done with our lives for the last twenty-nine years. It's why we have conducted strikes and marches and fasts and demonstrations. It's why we are once again asking the public to boycott California table grapes.

But we also recognize that many of the social problems plaguing farm workers stem from the denial of housing that is decent and affordable.

The fastest-growing population in California are the Hispanics.

The neediest segment of the Hispanic population are the farm workers.

What better place to go if you really want to build affordable, entry-level housing for the people who need it the most?

We have. And let me tell you—it *can* be done. Those who work to develop housing for migrant farm workers often meet stiff resistance from local established residents. Some people believe their property values will be affected if farm workers move in nearby.

Through a nonprofit, tax-exempt organization—the National Farm Workers Service Center—we've begun an aggressive program to build single-family and rental housing in rural California for low-income farm workers, Hispanics, other minorities, and Anglo families.

Just because it's housing for farm workers and other low-income rural residents doesn't mean it has to be shabby or second-rate. All projects developed by the Service Center come with amenities not generally found in farm-worker housing: wall-to-wall carpeting, central heat and air, two-car garages, large lots, tile roofs, bay windows, garbage disposals, and dishwashers.

We insist on those amenities for the same reason you and other home builders do: so the houses we build will appreciate at the same rate as other houses in the community.

Sometimes we've been frustrated by federal restrictions that place limits on these amenities. We're not interested in building projects that become instant ghettos. We don't accept federal bureaucrats who want to tell us that our houses have to be inferior to the houses offered to more affluent home buyers—just because our homes are for farm workers and other low-income families.

Almost all of our projects seek out available state or local financial assistance. Our staff work with local redevelopment agencies to obtain help for land acquisition and infrastructure. We help families qualify for modest grants that they often need to get into a home.

Sale prices at our seventy-one-lot subdivision in Parlier, near Fresno, start at $49,500—for four models of three- and four-bedroom homes. At this project, for the first time, low-income families could personalize their homes—for example, by deciding on colors for carpets and paint.

We helped low-income home buyers in Parlier obtain below-market interest rates to lower monthly mortgage payments. In addition, we helped these families qualify for government grants to write down the costs of loans.

Under the state's Farm Worker Grant Program, low-income people who work in agriculture and need money for down payments can qualify for up to $15,000 in grants. With a $15,000 grant, a family that purchased a Service Center home for

$49,500 would only need to qualify for a $34,000 mortgage. This state grant program was discontinued, although there is talk about reinstating it for next year.

We built the first single-family subdivision in twenty years in the West Fresno County town of Firebaugh—a 104-lot single family subdivision—with four floor plans and home buyer financial assistance. Most home buyers were local residents. But we also sold to some families from as far away as Oakland and Richmond that were willing to make the daily commute to their jobs.

Our forty-five-lot subdivision for low-income buyers in Avenal even includes front-yard landscaping.

Our 81-unit apartment complex in Parlier, our 106-unit complex in Fresno, and our 56-unit complex in Tehachapi all serve very low- to low-income families, many of them farm workers. In Fresno 90 percent of our tenants earn far below the median income. Rents are also considerably below average. Yet the amenities, especially in Fresno, are on a par with higher-rent apartments. There are no vacancies.

The Padilla family is a typical example of what the Service Center has been able to achieve. Steve Padilla works in the area's grape and citrus fields. He, his wife, and three children used to live in a small, rat- and cockroach-infested two-bedroom apartment. It had no carpeting or central heat and air.

His new residence is an apartment at the Service Center's La Paz Villa Apartments in Parlier. The Padillas live in a three-bedroom apartment with wall-to-wall carpeting, central heat and air, dishwasher and garbage disposal. The rent they pay at La Paz Villa is 30 percent less than what they paid for their previous apartment.

Many of the tenants in our apartment projects used to live in garages, labor camps and other substandard housing. A lot of them were affected by last December's freeze. Lack of jobs and a steady income are constant problems.

The Service Center works with its tenants, helping them stay in their housing—even when that means making arrangements for late rent payments.

The labor movement is working to create some innovative programs to help working people own their own homes. Under a first-of-its-kind contract negotiated by the Boston Hotel and Restaurant Employees Union, employers are paying 5 cents an hour into a joint trust fund. The fund will help hotel workers with new home purchases. Money from the fund will go to help make down payments, cover closing expenses or bank costs, or secure more favorable interest rates.

Before the housing trust fund could be set up, Congress had to amend the Taft-Hartley Act of 1947 so that employers could write off their contributions to the fund as tax deductions.

The national AFL-CIO created the Union Member Mortgage program, which just began operating earlier this year. During the program's first six months, more than twelve hundred union members have obtained over $100 million in home mortgage financing commitments. More than seventy thousand union members have phoned Union Member Mortgage's toll free numbers for more information.

The program is funding refinancing of high-interest mortgages on present homes, purchases of new homes by union members who are "buying up," and new home purchases by first-time home buyers. It offers down payments as low as 5 percent, competitive interest rates and financing through a wholly union-owned bank in New York. It helps first-time buyers by reducing the up-front cash needed to purchase a home.

Housing is not the National Farm Workers Service Center's sole activity. The Service Center has sponsored economic development programs to help rural agricultural-based farm worker communities diversify and expand their tax bases. That, in turn, produces improvements in basic municipal services—such as fire and police protection—as well as new employment opportunities for local residents.

The first and most challenging economic development project was a ten-thousand square-foot commercial center in Parlier.

Most of the existing retail in Parlier used to consist of bars and pool halls. There was no place to buy clothes, no neighborhood family oriented shopping center in town. The commercial project developed by the Service Center features a number of small retailers, including a meat market, clothing store, and sit-down restaurant.

The Service Center is developing another, slightly larger commercial center. It is bringing in a flower shop, pizza parlor, auto parts store, and sit-down cafe.

Parlier is finally being promoted as a place where families can live and prosper. These economic development projects are changing the reputation of the town; other developers are bringing their own projects on line—they're coming to see Parlier as a place where they can build and be successful.

New housing and commercial projects are planned for farm worker areas in other parts of the state.

We're now working in Hollister with city officials and a nonprofit group representing more than five hundred low-income families to develop a ten-lot single-family housing project in that San Benito County community.

A major obstacle to developing affordable housing in the Hollister area is the high cost of land. Land costs in the San Joaquin Valley are around $25,000 per acre. In Hollister, the average cost of land reaches $1—, 000 an acre.

One of the reasons land costs are being driven up is the high demand for housing created by out-of-town families—especially from Santa Clara and Monterey counties—that are seeking more affordable housing.

Added to the high cost of land are city and school fees, which exceed $14,000 for a twelve-hundred square-foot house.

These predevelopment costs make the construction of affordable housing for low-income families unprofitable for traditional home builders and very difficult even for the nonprofit National Farm Workers Service Center.

Still, we're trying hard to come up with an innovative plan that will produce a 105-unit subdivision for farm workers and other low-income people in Hollister.

The BIA has often made the point—quite correctly—that owning your own home is a dream that is being denied to more and more people in California. Across the country, 64 percent of Americans are homeowners. If things continue as they are, the percentage of homeowners in the Bay Area may soon fall below 50 percent.

In today's housing market, only about 10 percent of Bay Area residents can afford the median price of a home—tagged at $268,000. That means households earning more than $70,000 a year can't afford to buy homes.

Those statistics also mean that low- and moderate-income working-class people in urban communities were long ago frozen out of the home market. Most farm workers and other low-income residents in rural areas don't even have a chance to attain home ownership.

Home ownership has been the path to security and prosperity for tens of millions of people in this country. It is the way working men and women have built up wealth for themselves and their children. It is often what people have to show for years of sweat and sacrifice.

Should owning a home of your own be the dream all Americans can work toward—*except* farm workers and Hispanics and other working families, rural or urban?

Should home ownership be *everyone's* right—except farm workers and Hispanics and other working families?

Should *all* people be able to work for the day when they can purchase a home—unless their skin is brown or black, or they work on a farm or in a factory?

When I got out of the Navy at the end of World War II, home builders were universally respected because of the opportunities they helped bring to a whole generation of Americans. My family, and many others, never achieved home ownership because we were farm workers.

I want future generations of farm workers—the people of the land—to have what too many of us were denied: the right to own a decent home, a home of our own. We're working toward that goal. I ask you to join us in that effort. Thank you.

■■■■■

CHAPTER 5

Chávez's Ceremonial Speaking

The first four chapters of this book cover Chávez's speaking and writing during his ongoing campaign to create, build, and maintain the United Farm Workers (UFW). Those chapters are organized chronologically to demonstrate the ways Chávez's rhetoric evolved or remained consistent over a thirty-year period. This chapter considers his use of one specific type of speech, the ceremonial address. Chávez delivered many ceremonial addresses during his years as president of the union: we include here nine of those speeches, three that ended fasts and six eulogies.

Ceremonial speeches have historically been defined as speeches of praise or blame for people, objects, deeds, or ideals. In the classical period of Greece, ceremonial—or as they were then called, epideictic—speeches flourished. They typically "displayed the ideals of the community and invited audiences to acknowledge and reaffirm the greatness of these ideals."[1] In a contemporary definition, Celeste Condit proposed that such a speech would "define the community and the situation it faces, [where] the speaker displays leadership and is judged by the humane vision" in his/her speaking.[2] Today's ceremonial addresses may include eulogies and funeral orations, Fourth of July orations, welcomes and farewells, dedication speeches, commencement addresses, introductions, inaugurals, and other similar speeches.

THE THREE FASTS

The UFW's first major strike began in 1965 and lasted for five years, a period when Chávez often had to remind his followers to incorporate the lessons he had taught them into their everyday lives. In some cases he had to instruct them through his deeds as well as through his words. In 1968 the contest between the UFW and the growers had grown particularly tense, leading to frustrations and threats of violence on both sides. Many of Chávez's followers, including strikers and young Chicanos, were losing faith in nonviolence as a union tactic and were ready to use violence in their cause. Ever committed to nonviolence, Chávez decided to fast until union members renewed their commitment. Although he "had practiced fasting before and found it extremely painful," he chose to "make individual *sacrificio* [sacrifice] the centerpiece of a political statement, one aimed squarely at his own people."[3] Thus, as with virtually all of his acts, he placed foremost emphasis on his action's communicative or rhetorical function. As you will read later in this section, many labor leaders, political figures, and even some of his closest supporters did not understand or accept Chávez's rhetorical view of the world and consequently did not agree with Chávez on the value of his fasts.

Chávez began his fast for nonviolence on February 15, 1968. On the fourth day, at a meeting of union members to announce his intentions, he spoke angrily about people not working hard enough at nonviolence, pointedly criticizing "how they dared to condemn the war in Vietnam while advocating violence in the fields." He not only criticized those who practiced violence, for such actions would achieve nothing, but announced he preferred to show his toughness through a fast rather than through violent deeds.[4] At the conclusion of the meeting he walked to the union's headquarters at Forty Acres in Delano, where he remained throughout the fast.

Many UFW members and volunteers saw his fast as a waste of his and their precious time, believing that he would do more good by actively leading the union. A group charging that Chávez had a messiah complex quit the union in frustration. The UFW's general membership, however, responded favorably. Thousands of workers came to Forty Acres to offer support; some built shrines outside the headquarters, and priests said masses. People slept in tents and in the evenings "had festive prayer rallies with singing and hot chocolate."[5] One of Chávez's aides, Leroy Chatfield, claimed that the fast allowed Chávez to multiply his audiences and reach his broader goals:

> The irony of the fast was that it turned out to be the greatest organizing tool in the history of the labor movement. . . . Workers came from every sector of California and Arizona to meet with César, to talk to him about the problems in their areas. . . . César had more organizing going on while he was immobilized at the Forty Acres fasting than had ever happened before in the union.[6]

When Chávez broke the fast on March 11, so many people joined him that the ceremony was moved from the union's headquarters to a park in

Delano. Among the more than six thousand at the final rally was presidential candidate Senator Robert Kennedy. Chávez was too weak to deliver his speech ending his fast, so migrant minister James Drake read his text in English and Spanish.

Chávez's initial major fast would be remembered "as a defining moment for the union, one that renewed its sense of hope and unity and restored the power of nonviolence."[7] It not only brought national attention; it bequeathed to the sometimes saintly leader an immense moral credibility throughout the country. As Doug Adair stated, before the fast Chávez "was our leader, but he was our brother. . . . But after the fast he had a role to play on the national stage."[8] No doubt partly because of the success of the first fast, Chávez returned to the tactic on several memorable occasions throughout his career.

In Phoenix during May and June of 1972, Chávez undertook his second major fast, this time to protest an Arizona law that outlawed secondary boycotts and to support efforts to recall Governor Jack Williams, an outspoken opponent of unions. Although labor leaders and politicians in Arizona perceived the fast as futile, Chávez was undeterred. Through its three and one half weeks he had noteworthy visitors like Coretta Scott King, the widow of Dr. Martin Luther King, Jr. The physically drained leader's vigil ended with a rally attended by about a thousand farm workers and a group of other supporters who included members of Robert Kennedy's family. The fast failed to remove Williams and end the unfair labor law, but it succeeded in registering hundreds of thousands of new voters who helped elect Latino and Native Americans to the state legislature and Raul Castro as the first Mexican American governor of Arizona.[9]

On July 16, 1988, Chávez began another lengthy fast, this time to protest the use of pesticides on table grapes and to publicize the union's boycott of those grapes. The fast again made national news and featured nightly masses with thousands of worshipers.[10] Chávez's weakening physical condition caused anguish and concern; after twenty-one days, doctors reported that he was "suffering from bouts of nausea, dehydration, dizziness, and malnutrition," warning that "elevated levels of uric acid could cause his kidneys to fail."[11] He proclaimed an end to his fast after thirty-six days. His physician, Dr. Fidel Huerta, stated: "César's condition has deteriorated. . . . He's increasingly experiencing nausea, vomiting and cramping." The frail Chávez had lost twenty-seven pounds, having consumed all of his body fat and begun to burn muscle tissue. Huerta announced that all of Chávez's systems were being affected by the fast,[12] further worrying the labor chief's family, friends, and supporters.

A crowd of eight thousand gathered for a mass at Forty Acres to celebrate the fast's completion. Ethel Kennedy, the wife of Robert Kennedy, and several of her children attended. Other celebrities included well-known politicians like the Reverend Jesse Jackson and California assemblyman Tom Hayden and popular actors such as Martin Sheen and Edward James Olmos. Chávez's son Fernando read his father's statement, which included a plea for others to share in the suffering by undertaking their own three-day fasts. Jackson was the first public figure to undergo such a fast. Others including actors Martin Sheen and Robert Blake also fasted to keep alive a "chain of suffering" that would last for several months.[13]

SPEECHES ENDING THE FASTS

Ceremonial speeches have often been labeled speeches of display, where the speaker attempts to call attention to his or her abilities as a speaker. Condit argues that these speeches require a special kind of eloquence that is "the combination of truth, beauty and power in human speech." The most creative ceremonial speaker may help audiences "stretch their daily experiences into meanings more grand, sweet, noble, or delightful."[14] As we have stated on numerous occasions in our writings on Chávez, he ordinarily placed emphasis on his substantive message rather then on himself. He believed it was his task to present his message continuously and widely; if his good reasons and concrete facts were communicated clearly and convincingly, then people would respond and his righteous cause would triumph. The following three speeches show Chávez directing less attention to himself as a person than to his ideas and reasons.

As you read the speeches ending the fasts you will notice their similarities. In each he explains that because he is too weak to read the text himself someone is reading it for him; thanks the audience for their attendance and for their support during his ordeal; talks about the sense of community created by the UFW, depicting the union as a family that practices nonviolence; explains the purpose of the fast and why he undertook it; contrasts the power of union members to that of their formidable opponents; and implies or promises that the union will win if members return to their nonviolent roots.

The March 10, 1968, speech is a powerful statement of his humane vision of the world, a vision of a union family fighting to overcome its enemies. He concludes with the remarkable lines that capture the essence of his nonviolent beliefs and depict qualities of character needed by his followers:

It is my deepest belief that only by giving our lives do we find life. I am convinced that the truest act of courage, the strongest act of manliness is to sacrifice ourselves for others in a totally non-violent struggle for justice. To me a man is to suffer for others. God help us to be men![15]

The second speech parallels major elements of the 1968 speech but introduces several differences that reflect changes in time and circumstances. Chávez portrays the poverty of the workers and compares their lives to his own. "What is a few days without food," he confides, "in comparison to the daily pain of our brothers and sisters who do backbreaking work in the fields under inhumane conditions and without hope of ever breaking their cycle of poverty and misery." The irony of the situation, he adds, "is that the very people who harvest the food we eat do not have enough food for their own children."

Also new to this speech are his specific references to individuals who died for the union. He presents those martyrs as models—an expanded version of the second persona that concluded his 1968 speech—for UFW supporters to imitate:

Nan Freeman and Sal Santos have given their lives for our movement this past year. They were very young. It hurt us to lose them and it still hurts us. But the greatest tragedy is for a person to live and die without knowing the satisfaction of giving life for others. The greatest tragedy is to be born but not to live for fear of losing a little security or because we are afraid of loving and giving ourselves to other people.

The third speech contains many themes of the first and second but adds content specific to his 1988 campaign on pesticides. Demonstrating that his fasts and the speeches that ended them were never separate from his broader rhetorical campaign, he asked listeners if they felt the plight of workers and their children who daily endured the dangers of pesticide poisoning. Could audiences understand the heartbreak of families who had lost loved ones to cancer, the anguish of workers who were raising children with deformities and feared giving birth to other children with deformities? To his rhetorical question, "Do we feel their pain deeply enough?" he answered: "I know I didn't. And I was ashamed." Whatever the shame Chávez felt, he continued his concrete efforts to end such injustice. He shared his frustration at those who continued to shop in markets that sold grapes grown with pesticides or to eat in restaurants that served them, at those who assisted growers in using pesticides, and at those in power who could end the use of the chemicals.

OCCASIONS FOR CHÁVEZ'S EULOGIES

Some of Chávez's most emotionally moving speeches were eulogies for those closest to him. On December 14, 1991, his mother, Juana Estrada Chávez, died at the age of ninety-nine. His eulogy in Our Lady of Guadalupe Church, not far from his former home in Sal Si Puedes in San Jose, honored the person who had the most profound effect on his life. As Ferriss and Sandoval pointed out, his mother

> had given her son a core set of beliefs—his deep Catholic faith, his commitment to the poor, his pride in Mexican folk culture and its wisdom, and even his fascination with traditional medicine and spirituality. And Juana Chávez, despite her advancing years, had been at César's side at important moments in the UFW's history.[16]

A few months later he faced the wrenching duty of eulogizing Fred Ross, his mentor and friend, who died of cancer at the age of eighty-two. The always overly busy Chávez devoted considerable time and energy to the eulogy, collaborating with Marc Grossman on a speech that went through several drafts. Only a few hours before speaking at the funeral at San Francisco's Delancy Street Foundation, Chávez, "slowed by a severe flu and laryngitis," was still rewriting the speech. He crossed out all references to himself in a text filled with anecdotes fitting to the occasion, making Ross the center of the message.[17]

Chávez also eulogized those who were killed while working for the union. In January of 1972 a young student named Nan Freeman had volunteered to help picket the Talisman Sugar Plant near Belle Glade, Florida. At about 3:00 A.M. the picketers stopped a truck to talk to its driver. As the truck started to move forward it struck Freeman, knocking her unconscious. She died about an hour later. Although she was not a member of the union, Chávez honored her because of her work for the UFW.

In 1973, in the midst of the violent battle over union contracts between the UFW and Teamsters, two workers were killed. In the early morning hours of August 14 a group of workers had attended a party following a union meeting. They were standing outside a bar when a policeman named Gilbert Cooper told them to disperse. When a scuffle broke out, one of the strikers, Nagi Daifulla, began to run. Cooper pursued him, hit him with a flashlight, and then dragged Daifulla across hard pavement. The hospitalized twenty-four-year-old worker later died from head injuries. Chávez called for a three-day fast "to honor the life and sacrifice of Nagi Daifullah," proclaiming: "It must be a time to think about violence and nonviolence. We also want to remember to pray for Deputy Sheriff Cooper during this time."[18]

A few days later, on August 17, sixty-year Juan de la Cruz, another picketer, was shot by someone in a speeding pickup truck. He died three hours later. After the death of de la Cruz, Chávez ended all picketing in the area until "federal law enforcement agencies guaranteed our right to picket and see that our lives are safe and our civil rights are not trampled on."[19] De la Cruz had been a member of the UFW from the beginning, so his death was particularly troubling for Chávez.

The deaths of the workers caused anger and frustration across the UFW. Marshall Ganz, a UFW organizer, believed that the preparation for the funerals prevented more dangerous expressions of bad feelings: "I think that all our activity preparing for the funerals was a Godsend, because I don't know what would have happened if people had been able to stop and think about what had happened. . . . It would have been very difficult to keep people nonviolent."[20] In response to the anger and frustration, Chávez carefully prepared eulogies to champion nonviolence.

We will examine two other eulogies by Chávez. On February 10, 1979, Rufino Contreras and other strikers entered the fields on the Saikhon Ranch in the Imperial Valley to talk to a group of strike-breaking workers. Three company foremen began shooting at the strikers, killing Contreras. After his death, some workers responded with violence—and Chávez again intervened. It was "their respect and love for César" that convinced them to return to nonviolence.[21] On September 21, 1983, twenty-one-year-old René López was killed at the Sikkema Dairy near Fresno. Chosen as a leader by the workers because he was bilingual and had graduated from high school, López had just led a successful campaign for a union election at the dairy.[22] On the day of the election, López was shot in the face by individuals who had been hired by the owner of the dairy to intimidate workers. His funeral was held in Fresno.

EULOGIES

According to communication scholars Kathleen Hall Jamieson and Karlyn Kohrs Campbell, a funeral eulogy traditionally contains several qualities and elements that meet an audience's predictable expectations:

A eulogy responds to those human needs created when a community is sundered by the death of one of its members. In Western culture, at least, a eulogy will acknowledge the death, transform the relationship between the living and the dead from present to past tense, ease the mourners' terror at confronting their own mortality, console them by arguing that the deceased lives on, and reknit the community.[23]

Chávez's eulogies for his mother and for his mentor Fred Ross both met these needs. Note also, however, how Chávez could not, even in eulogizing those closest to him, abandon his career-long themes of providing service to those who suffered injustices and of measuring the value of one's life by one's contributions to those in need. In death as in life, he remained fixed historically on the message that he believed would bring justice— the message he felt chosen to position at the center of his career and life.

In honoring his mother, Chávez explains that the "simple deeds of a lifetime speak far more eloquently than any words of ours about this remarkable woman and the legacy of hope and strength that she leaves behind." The eulogy recounts how his mother fed those even poorer that the Chávezes, ministered to those otherwise in need, tended people in their illnesses, and assisted in the delivery of babies, how hard his mother and father worked to keep the family together, how his mother fought against people who tried to cheat workers, and what lessons in life she pointedly taught her children. The speech is a beautiful description of a remarkable woman whose lessons for life applied well to her son César: "We are here today to say that true wealth is not measured in money or status or power. It is measured in the legacy we leave behind for those we love and those we inspire."

The eulogy for Fred Ross recounts a remarkable life that gave direction for Chávez. He begins by relating how he first met Ross and then followed his model and became an organizer, and how Ross taught him the principles and tactics needed to be effective. In deciding how best to memorialize Ross, Chávez focused on what he felt was Ross's genius at "developing the organizing of people for action into an art form." He quoted at length from Ross's letters in order to allow his mentor to fashion his own eulogy.

In the next four eulogies Chávez sought to transform dead workers into martyrs who would serve the UFW cause. In 1991 he confided, "Although we can't comprehend how they are selected for martyrdom, we do know that Nan, Nagi, Juan, Rufino, and René were and are very special human beings . . . special to their families and friends, but perhaps even more so to the people for whom they laid down their lives." Chávez eulogized all five of the martyrs, and texts of the eulogies are available for all except Daifullah. And the story of each would become part of Chávez's continuing rhetorical campaign by appearing as emotionally moving evidence in his later speeches.[24]

The four eulogies satisfy the needs listed by Jamieson and Campbell, but all have one further quality: they direct members of audiences to honor the deceased by working to build a stronger union. Each address also has unique features, even the eulogy honoring Nan Freeman, which is very brief, probably because Chávez did not know her personally. He refers to Freeman as a "holy person" who gave her life for others, her sacrifice an "immeasurable gift." He requested a period of mourning to honor her.

As a member of the union from "its earliest days," Juan de la Cruz would have known Chávez for many years. In his eulogy Chávez referred to de la Cruz's contributions to the UFW, how he had unselfishly given of himself to make the union stronger. Well-controlled anger creeps into his text: "We live in the midst of people who hate and fear us. They have worked hard to keep us in our place. They will spend millions more to destroy our union. But we do not have to make ourselves small by hating and fearing them in return." The workers should not be fearful, Chávez cautioned in his restatement of a theme repeated uncountable times, because they will win in the end—especially if they sacrifice and work in "the spirit of our brother, Juan de la Cruz."

To honor Rufino Contreras, Chávez opens with a vivid description in his characteristically simple and clear language: "February 10, 1979 was a day of infamy for farm workers. It was a day without joy. The sun didn't shine. The birds didn't sing. The rain didn't fall." To his question, "Why was this such a day of evil?" he responded, "Because on this day greed and injustice struck down our brother Rufino Contreras." Much of the address describes the high quality of Contreras's UFW work and personal life. Chávez concludes with a fitting second persona: "If Rufino were alive today, what would he tell us? He would tell us, 'don't be afraid. Don't be discouraged.' He would tell us, 'don't cry for me, organize!'"

The eulogy for López emphasized his youth and accomplishments, his leadership in fighting for unionism, and the respect he earned from fellow workers in spite of his youth. Although López died young, "he was wise beyond his years. He died in the prime of life, but the number of his years was not the true measure of his life." The speech's conclusion is particularly memorable: "René's father, Francisco, looking down on his fallen son, said these words: 'When he was born, I received him with a kiss, and . . . now I give him back to God with a kiss.'" Chávez finished with stirring words informed by scripture: "'Happy are those who died in the Lord: let them rest from their labor for their good deeds go with them.' Amen."

The ceremonial speeches included in this book present Chávez's humane vision of the world. They give the reader unique insight into Chávez and his ideas, embodying what was crucial to him and to the union, offering an image of Chávez at the most vulnerable times of his life, at times when he was most open to feeling and expressing his emotions. They can be seen as pieces of art that should be read and enjoyed. Yet they also document César Chávez's broader lifelong rhetorical campaign, for in them he maintained his fundamental rhetorical profile and remained fixed on persuading and transforming audiences through what he conceived to be a righteous war of words that defined his own life.

Speech Ending Fast, March 10, 1968

The text of this speech is in the United Farm Workers Papers, Wayne State University. It was reprinted in *Ahora!* 3 (January 8, 1972): 1, and in Winthrop Yinger, *César Chávez: The Rhetoric of Nonviolence* (Hicksville, N.Y.: Exposition, 1975), 46–47.

I have asked the Rev. James Drake to read this statement to you because my heart is so full and my body too weak to be able to say what I feel. My warm thanks to all of you for coming today. Many of you have been here before, during the Fast. Some have sent beautiful cards and telegrams and made offerings at the Mass. All of these expressions of your love have strengthened me and I am grateful.

We should all express our thanks to Senator [Robert] Kennedy for his constant work on behalf of the poor, for his personal encouragement to me, and for taking time to break bread with us today.

I do not want any of you to be deceived about the Fast. The strict Fast of water only which I undertook on February 16 ended after the 21st day because of the advice of our doctor, James McKnight, and other physicians. Since that time I have been taking liquids in order to prevent serious damage to my kidneys.

We are gathered here today not so much to observe the end of the Fast but because we are a family bound together in a common struggle for justice. We are a Union family celebrating our unity and the nonviolent nature of our movement. Perhaps in the future we will come together at other times and places to break bread and to renew our courage and to celebrate important victories.

The Fast has had different meanings for different people. Some of you may still wonder about its meaning and importance. It was not intended as a pressure against any growers. For that reason we have suspended negotiations and arbitration proceedings and relaxed the militant picketing and boycotting of the strike during this period. I undertook the Fast because my heart was filled with grief and pain for the sufferings of farm workers. The Fast was first for me and then for all of us in this Union. It was a Fast for nonviolence and a call to sacrifice.

When we are really honest with ourselves we must admit that our lives are all that really belong to us. So it is how we use our lives that determines what kind of men we are. It is my deepest belief that only by giving our lives do we find life. I am convinced that the truest act of courage, the strongest act of manliness is to sacrifice ourselves for others in a totally nonviolent struggle for justice. To be a man is to suffer for others. God help us to be men!

Statement by César Chávez at the End of His Twenty-Four-Day Fast for Justice, Phoenix, Arizona, June 4, 1972

A transcript of this speech is in the United Farm Workers Papers, Wayne State University.

I want to thank you for coming today. Some of you have been to the Santa Rita Center many times. Some have made beautiful offerings at the Mass. I have received letters and telegrams and lettuce boycott pledges from all over the world. All of these expressions of your love and your support for the farm workers' struggle have strengthened my spirits and I am grateful. I want especially to honor the farm workers who have risked so much to go on strike for their rights. Your sacrifices will not be in vain!

I am weak in my body but I feel very strong in my spirit. I am happy to end the Fast because it is not an easy thing. But it is also not easy for my family and for many of you who have worried and worked and sacrificed. The Fast was meant as a call to sacrifice for justice and a reminder of how much suffering there is among farm workers. In fact, what is a few days without food in comparison to the daily pain of our brothers and sisters who do backbreaking work in the fields under inhumane conditions and without hope of ever breaking their cycle of poverty and misery. What a terrible irony it is that the very people who harvest the food we eat do not have enough food for their own children.

It is possible to become discouraged about the injustice we see everywhere. But God did not promise us that the world would be humane and just. He gives us the gift of life and allows us to choose the way we will use our limited time on this earth. It is an awesome opportunity. We should be thankful for the life we have been given, thankful for the opportunity to do something about the suffering of our fellow man. We *can choose* to use our lives for others to bring about a better and more just world for our children. People who make that choice will know hardship and sacrifice. But if you give yourself totally to the nonviolent struggle for peace and justice, you also find that people will give you their hearts and that you will never go hungry and never be alone. And in giving of yourself you will discover a whole new life full of meaning and love.

Nan Freeman and Sal Santos have given their lives for our movement this past year. They were very young. It hurt us to lose them, and it still hurts us. But the greatest tragedy is not to live and die, as we all must. The greatest tragedy is for a person to live and die without knowing the satisfaction of giving life for others. The greatest tragedy is to be born but not to live for fear of losing a little security or because we are afraid of loving and giving ourselves to other people.

Our opponents in the agricultural industry are very powerful, and farm workers are still weak in money and influence. But we have another kind of power that comes from the justice of our cause. So long as we are willing to sacrifice for that cause, so long as we persist in nonviolence and work to spread the message of our struggle, then millions of people around the world will respond from their hearts, will support our efforts, and in the end we will overcome. It can be done. We know it can be done. God give us the strength and patience to do it without bitterness so that we can win both our friends and opponents to the cause of justice.

Statement Ending Fast, Delano, California, August 21, 1988

Portions of this speech were incorporated into the speech at Pacific Lutheran University, March 1989, included in chapter 4. A transcript of this speech is in the United Farm Workers Papers, Wayne State University.

My heart is too full and my body too weak to read this message for myself. So I have asked that it be shared with you.

I thank God for the support of my family as well as the members and staff of the United Farm Workers. I am grateful to the many thousands of people who came to be with us and for the millions who have kept us in their prayers and have taken up our cause in distant places. They have opened their hearts not just for me, but for the farm workers and the families who suffer from the unrestrained poisons of our soil and water.

Do we really carry in our hearts the plight of the farm workers and their children? Do we feel deeply enough the pain of those who labor every day in the fields with these pesticides? Do we know the heartache of families whose loved ones have been lost to cancer, who fear for the lives of their children, who are raising children with deformities, who agonize over the outcome of their pregnancies, who ask in fear, "Where will the deadly plague strike next?"

Do we feel their pain deeply enough? I know I didn't. And I was ashamed.

In recent years I have studied this wanton abuse of nature. I have read the literature and heard from the experts about what pesticides do to our land and food. I have talked with farm workers, listened to their families, and shared their anguish and their fears. I have spoken out against the cycle of death that threatens our people and our world.

But sometimes words come too cheaply. And their meaning is lost in the clutter that so often fills our lives.

It pains me that some of our members still cooperate with those who grow and sell the poisoned food we all eat. It pains me that we continue to shop without protest at stores that offer grapes, that we eat at restaurants that display them, that we are too patient and understanding with those who serve them to us.

It is true that some farm workers out of fear, ignorance, or economic need, assist the growers in their pesticide madness.

But have we done enough, you and I, to stop this evil in our midst? In the end aren't we judged by our deeds and not by our words.

The fast was first and foremost a personal act. It was something I felt compelled to do—to purify my own body, mind, and soul.

The fast was also an act of penance for those in positions of moral authority and for all men and women who know what is right and just. It if for those who know that they could or should do more. It is for those who, by their failure to act, become bystanders in the poisoning of our food and the people who produce it.

The fast was finally a declaration of non-cooperation with supermarkets that promote, sell, and profit from California table grapes. They are as culpable as those who manufacture the poisons and use them on workers, on our land and our food. It is my hope that our friends everywhere will resist in many nonviolent ways the presence of grapes in the stores where they shop.

The misery that pesticides bring will not be ended by more studies or hearings. The solution is not to be had from those in power because it is they who have allowed this deadly crisis to grow.

The answer lies with you and me. It is for all of us to do more. We will demonstrate by what we do and not by what we say our solidarity with the weak and afflicted.

I pray to God that this fast will encourage a multitude of simple deeds by men and women who feel the suffering and yearn with us for a better world. Together, all things are possible.

Eulogy for Juana Estrada Chávez, San Jose, December 18, 1991

A transcript of this speech is in the United Farm Workers Papers, Wayne State University.

Thanks be to God that our mother's family—those she loved so much—were able to be at her bedside during the final hours. Our mother left us a beautiful heritage of courage and faith, a heritage that, please God, will sustain us come what may, until we meet her again in paradise.

In a passage from the Book of Proverbs, King Solomon offers his description of a good woman:

> Strength and honour are her clothing; and she shall rejoice in time to come.
> She openeth her mouth with wisdom; and in her tongue is the law of kindness.
> She looketh well to the ways of her household, and eateth not the bread of idleness.
> Her children arise up and call her blessed; her husband also, and he praiseth her.
> Favour is deceitful, and beauty is vain; but a woman that feareth the Lord, she shall be praised.
> Give her of the fruit of her hands; and let her own works praise her in the gates.

Juana Estrada Chávez does not need for any of us to speak well of her this day. The simple deeds of a lifetime speak far more eloquently than any words of ours about this remarkable woman and the legacy of hope and strength that she leaves behind.

Rather than bore you by talking about how good she was, let us share some of the events we witnessed and some of the lessons we learned growing up as the children of Juana Chávez.

It was the Depression years of the late 1930s and early '40s. But as poor as we were and with what little we had, mama would send my brother Richard and me out to railroad yards and other places for "hobos" we could invite to our tent to share a meal.

In those days the highways were littered with families whose cars or pickup trucks had broken down—with no place to go and no way to get there. When we were on the road, no matter how badly off we were, our mother would never let us pass a family in trouble.

She brought in a whole assortment of homeless families who didn't have a place to stay. We didn't either. But she'd bring them into our tent and make room for them in what little space we had.

Our mother would tell us, "You always have to help the needy, and God will help you."

Lifelong friendships were born that way. Some of the people she befriended more than fifty years ago are here today.

It was the rainy winter of 1939. We were living in a farm labor camp for cotton pickers outside the small farm town of Mendota in West Fresno County. The camp was unpaved. It was pouring rain. The mud was so bad that cars couldn't get in or out. A young girl was giving birth to her first baby. There was no way to take her to the doctor. So my mother rolled up her sleeves and delivered the baby. And it wasn't the last time it happened.

In those days few people had money for doctors. Many hadn't even set foot in a doctor's office. A lot of the farm workers also didn't speak the language. Many didn't believe in doctors.

Our mother was a folk healer. Besides delivering babies and curing common colds and headaches, she cured children of *sustos empacho mollera pujon y ojo*.

Her favorite herbs were yerba buena, yposote, yerba del pasmo, sauco—and she really believed in manzanilla.

I'd go to her and say, "mama, I have a headache." She'd say, "manzanilla." "Mama, I have a stomachache." "Manzanilla." "Mama, I feel depressed." "Manzanilla." So much so that my nickname came to be . . . Manzi.

It was also that year when Dad was hurt in an auto accident and couldn't work—for a *whole* year.

Our mother and the oldest sister, Rita, supported the family tying carrots in the Imperial Valley. But they didn't know how to do the work. They were farm workers, but they were fresh from a little farm in Arizona and had never done that kind of work before.

So they'd leave home at 3:30 in the morning. And they didn't get back until 7:00 in the evening. They earned $3 a week. But they kept us together until Dad was able to work again.

One January or February we were driving to the Imperial Valley from that labor camp in Mendota when we ran out of money in Los Angeles. Mama quickly sold two beautiful quilts she had crocheted. And we had money to buy gas and continue on our journey.

It was 1941 and there was very little work. We were lucky to find jobs picking cotton in the San Joaquin Valley. When our big, heavy sacks were full, we'd line up and wait to have the sacks weighed by hanging them on a hook at the truck of the labor contractor. You'd get ¾ cents per pound of cotton.

But sometimes the contractor would cheat the workers by putting his knee under the sack so it'd weigh less. Instead of getting credited for a hundred pound sack, the worker would get marked down for only eighty pounds. All this would happen pretty fast, and the victim's view was usually blocked.

Well, Mama was pretty sharp. She saw the contractor cheating a worker who was in line in front of her—and she called him on it. The contractor was furious. The entire Chávez family got fired. It didn't bother her. Our mother used to say there is a difference between being of service and being a servant.

We were living in Delano during the early '40s when I started driving. All of us—especially Rita and I—became a traveling service center. Our mother would have us do all kinds of errands, often driving people to Bakersfield, thirty miles away, to see the doctor or police or district attorney or welfare office.

We drove many a girl having a baby to the General Hospital. One baby was born in the back seat of our car.

After going to work in the fields early in the morning, by 10 A.M. we'd have to change out of our work clothes, jump in the car to Bakersfield, return home, change back into our work clothes and try to get some more work done.

Mama never let us charge a penny for our troubles, not even for gas.

When she wasn't helping people or getting us fired for challenging labor contractors, we were the strikingest family in all of farm labor. Whenever we were working where there was a strike or when the workers got fed up and walked off the job, she'd be the first one to back up our dad's decision to join the strike.

Our mother taught us not to be afraid to fight—to stand up for our rights. But she also taught us not to be violent.

We didn't even know enough at the time to call it nonviolence. But from an early age, through her *dichos* and little lessons, she would always talk to us about not fighting, not responding in kind.

She taught her children to reject that part of a culture which too often tells its young men that you're not a man if you don't fight back.

She would say, "No, it's best to turn the other cheek. God gave you senses like eyes and mind and tongue, and you can get out of anything. It takes two to fight, and one can't do it alone."

This is a day of sadness for Rita and Richard and Eduwiges and Librado and me, for all the grandchildren and great-grandchildren and great-great-grandchildren who are here today. But the services this morning are not an occasion for sadness, much less for despair. Rather, this is a time to celebrate, in the spirit of Christian joy, our mother's life and the goodness and mercy of God. Her ninety-nine years are a story of triumph over cruelty and prejudice and injustice. She was a wise woman who fulfilled God's Commandments by loving and serving her neighbors—even to the point of sacrifice. Our mother's good deeds— good deeds above all of charity and compassion and kindness—are known to many of you.

All who knew our mother as a personal friend or more immediately as a member of the family can vouch for the fact that she had understanding. By this I mean that she had the gift of faith—that gift of knowing what is truly important in life.

We are here today to say that true wealth is not measured in money or status or power. It is measured in the legacy we leave behind for those we love and those we inspire. We are here today because our lives were touched and moved by her spirit of love and service. That spirit is more powerful than any force on earth. It cannot be stopped.

Death comes to us all and we do not get to choose the time or the circumstances of our dying. The hardest thing of all is to die rightly. Juana Chávez died rightly. She served her God and her neighbor.

Now it is for you and me to finish the work Juana Chávez has begun among us in her quiet and simple ways, until we too can say that we have obeyed the commandment set out in the Book of the Prophet Micah in the Old Testament: "What does the Lord require of you, but to do justice, to love kindness, and to walk humbly with your God."

"Happy are those who died in the Lord; Let them rest from their labor for their good deeds go with them."

Amen.

Eulogy for Fred Ross, San Francisco, October 17, 1992

A transcript of this speech is in the United Farm Workers Papers, Wayne State University.

The first time I met Fred Ross, he was about the last person I wanted to see. Fred had come to San Jose in the spring of 1952 to organize a chapter of the Community Service Organization—the CSO. I was working in apricot orchards outside of town and living with Helen and our then four kids in a rough barrio on the eastside of San Jose that they nicknamed Sal Si Puedes (Get Out If You Can).

In those days, it seemed as if the Anglos who came to Sal Si Puedes were college students down from Berkeley or Stanford who were writing their theses on the barrio and asking insulting questions like, "How come Mexican Americans have so many kids?"

I thought Fred was one of them—only I wasn't quite sure because he was this lanky guy who drove a beat-up old car and wore wrinkled clothes.

I finally agreed to have a "housemeeting" so Fred could talk about CSO with a group of friends we invited to our home. But I hatched a plan with some of my young Pachuco[25] buddies to scare him away. At a prearranged signal from me, they'd start insulting him; that way, we thought, Fred would leave and we would get "even."

Fred found a cold reception from the people packed into our living room. Then he started talking—and changed my life.

After a while my Pachuco buddies—waiting for my signal—were getting restless. One of them interrupted Fred. I told him in Calo, Pachuco talk, to shut up or get out; he shut up.

What followed was a frenetic forty days and nights as we registered four thousand new voters—the first such drive in Sal Si Puedes.

Together, Fred and I organized twenty-two CSO chapters across California in the 1950s; he began eight chapters on his own.

CSO turned people who were compliant and submissive into courageous champions of their families and communities. Some five hundred thousand Hispanics were registered to vote; fifty thousand Mexican immigrants obtained citizenship and old-age pensions. We won paved streets and sidewalks, traffic signals, recreational facilities and clinics. CSO curbed police brutality and resisted "urban removal" of Hispanics from redevelopment projects.

Fred used to say that "you can't take shortcuts, because you'll pay for it later." He believed society could be transformed from within by mobilizing individuals and communities. But you have to convert one person at a time, time after time. Progress only comes when people just plow ahead and do it. It takes lots of patience. The concept is so simple that most people miss it.

Fred applied those principles during an organizing career that spanned six decades.

I tagged along to every one of Fred's house meetings during that first campaign in San Jose—sometimes two a night. Studied every word he spoke, every move he made. Questioned him repeatedly, having him explain how in hell the house meetings would turn people out to the general organizing meeting.

The organizing meeting at Mayfair School in East San Jose was a huge success. But there were some folks standing around outside. I told Fred they didn't want to come in. "It's OK," he replied, "Mebos burros mas elotes" [fewer donkeys, more corn]. I went outside anyway to ask them to come inside and happened to overhear some established Chicano leaders finding every excuse why all these people shouldn't be at this meeting—saying things like, "There aren't any leaders in that crowd; they're old people."

At home that night I told Helen how what had happened at the meeting was pure magic—and I was going to learn it. Come what may, I wouldn't stop until I learned how to organize.

For a long time I'd call him Mr. Ross, and he'd say, "Just Fred." It took me a long time to call him Fred. I'd go to work in the fields daydreaming about the house meeting to be held that evening.

I would find any excuse to be with Fred. I even started trying to imitate him. Fred noticed. One day he said, "César, you don't have to parrot me to learn to organize. Just be yourself, follow the procedures and you'll be OK."

The thing I liked most about Fred was there was no bullshit, no pretensions, no ego gimmicks; just plain hard work—at times grinding work.

Fred's accomplishments were even more amazing when you consider that he had a lot to overcome. At times there was much reverse discrimination. Fred was Anglo. He was Protestant. He was middle class.

I watched him at first very closely for the signs of paternalism and superiority. Never, ever did I see any of those signs in Fred. He never looked down on us. But he also never pitied us. He was a tough, unrelenting taskmaster.

One evening after an executive board meeting of the San Jose CSO chapter at Jose and Blanca Alvarado's house, Fred talked to us about old age pensions for noncitizens. He said it would be a great issue, help a lot of old timers who had no money or pensions—and relieve a lot of pressure on their kids. But he warned us that it would be a lot of work setting up the campaign to enact the state old-age pension law. It would take a long time.

We would get impatient. Fred would say, "Calma"—have patience. It'll come. It was eight years before the law was passed, but it was a super victory. And I learned once again about Fred's gift of faith and stick-to-it-ness. Those lessons came in handy years later with the boycott and other union efforts.

Then one day in mid-1952, kind of suddenly, Fred wanted to know if it was OK to ask Saul Alinsky to put me on the payroll. My heart sank to my knees. What followed were many occasions for self-doubt—and a lot of Fred's time spent holding my hand and reassuring me that I could do it.

In Oakland, organizing the first CSO chapter on my own, I'd call Fred every day to make sure I was on track. After the first community-wide organizing meeting was over, I called to give him my report: "Fred, counting all the priests at St. Mary's school, the janitor and myself, we had 327 people."

He said, "I knew it. I knew it. I knew you could do it." I was looking for my pat on the back—and I found it.

After organizing the CSO chapter in Madera in 1954, the whole local leadership was turned against me after a red-baiting campaign from the Immigration authorities, the district attorney, and some immigration coyotes. I was dumbfounded.

Poor Fred had to leave his job and come hold my hand once more. He said, "César, listen, you're stirring a hornet's nest—and some of 'em will come after you. No hay mal que por bien no venga (Literally translated it means there is no bad thing that will not be followed by a good thing—or every negative has its positive).

The company and Teamsters were united against us during our campaign at DiGiorgio Fruit Corporation in 1966. Many of Fred's organizers were volunteers who were also against the Vietnam War. Many trade unionists also helping us were for the war. Fred had to keep peace among them—and fight the war against the Teamsters and DiGiorgio.

The night before the election I got home late, turned on the TV news and bigger than life there was this story from Las Vegas, where they set the odds six to ten against us. I called Fred. He said, "We'll win, don't worry. Get some rest. You'll need it for tomorrow's celebration." We hung up. A moment later he called back: "César, remember this is only a battle, and maybe a very small battle, in the history of this union. The war is yet to be decided." With that, I went soundly to sleep.

It was 1967. The grape boycott was having severe problems because boycotted grape growers were switching labels with growers who weren't being boycotted. I was caught in a strange moral dilemma. Somehow, I couldn't get myself to boycott growers we weren't striking—even though some of them were giving their labels to the struck growers.

Fred and Dolores [Huerta], in New York on the boycott, argued that it could be done—it had to be a generic boycott of all grapes. They made me see the light. And the boycott turned around pretty quickly.

Fred died of natural causes on September 27. He was eighty-two. His deeds live on in the hundreds of organizers he trained and inspired. Not the least of them is his son, Fred Jr., who made his father very proud.

I have been thinking through how best to memorialize Fred's contribution to society and have come to the conclusion that it would be most fitting to focus it around what I believe is his greatest contribution: developing the organizing of people for action into an art form.

That art form must now be preserved in aphorisms, so that future organizers can learn and be trained from the lessons Fred taught. While guarding this inheritance, we must take pains to keep it clean and pure—God forbid that it be corrupted by some PhD's analysis and interpretations.

At one point Dolores Huerta, David Martínez, and Artie Rodríguez and I got together and decided that we should mount a campaign to have Fred awarded the Nobel Peace Prize—and win it for him with the kind of campaign he taught us to run. We organized support from a number of U.S. senators and congressmen, bishops, and others.

I had to take it to Fred—and I knew it would be a hard sell. I came to see him, but when I talked to him about it, he furrowed his brow and said, "César, there's a lot of good work you can do instead of this nonsense."

Fred Ross gave me and so many others a chance. And that led to a lot of things. But he did more than discover and train me.

The other day, preparing for this memorial, I was reading though correspondence between Fred and myself from the early 1960s that I hadn't seen in thirty years.

We saw each other then infrequently. But we wrote as often as we could—often long letters—and Fred would usually include a modest contribution to help tide us over. Listen to just a few excerpts from some of our letters.

May 2, 1962. "Dear Fred: Sure happy to receive your letter this morning. Cheque or no cheque, your letters will give me that which I need so badly right now."

"Dolores [— Dolores Huerta—] was here . . . I filled her in on all of the plans and asked her to join the parade. As you know, she is all for it and will begin . . .

soon . . . [W]e did some work on the list of towns to work . . . throughout the Valley. Helen, [Dolores] and I decide[d] on the name of the group. 'Farm Workers Ass[ociation].'"

". . . I have in fact done some work in the fields. Driving Grape Stakes, Chopping Cotton and Suckering Vines. After about two hours out there I felt about 80 years old. Like Los Viejitos that come to the CSO for Pensions."

". . . Will be moving to another house, lower rent, on the 15th of May . . . But for the time being, keep your letters coming to this address."

". . . Am very sorry to hear about the ulcer. If I'm going to follow in your footsteps, I guess I'll have to get one myself, if I don't already have one and more. Seriously, I hope it isn't too bad."

". . . Am expecting the Income Tax Return [check] any day now, I hope. Also received the shirts [you sent]. Muchas gracias. [D]on't have a telephone. [P]robably won't get one just now."

". . . Please write whenever you can. As ever, César.

". . . P.S. Birdie-boy says hello to Fed Oss." (Birdie or Anthony, our youngest son, was then two years old. He couldn't pronounce the "Rs.")

June 4, 1962. (From Fred to me.) "Hola! Mi General: This'll be a short one because I've seen you so recently and . . . I want to get the little propina [Spanish for gratuity or contribution] in the mail. This time it'll have to be a bill because Frances went off with the cheque-book. Should have sent it yesterday, but got so busy putting the bite on others—forget to bite myself."

". . . When I get to Stockton [I'll] try to get a few of them to maybe start a "Buck a Week" Club and assign one of them to collect the money and send it to you. OK?"

"Well, you're the one with the news that sooths. So shoot some my way, eh? Warmest & best, Fred."

July 9, 1962. "Dear César:

". . . Well, I'm enclosing the usual & hope I hear from you soon with some more marvelous stories."

June 5, 1962. (Me to Fred.) "Estimado Jefe (Dear chief): Gracias muchas por su bondadosa oferta. [Many thanks for your generous donation.]"

". . . I have so many things to tell you that I . . . hardly know where to start. . . ."

August 7, 1962. (Me to Fred.) "Ola Jefe: Well, I'm up in Merced County now and things have been going my way. . . . After that Mendota failure, guess I got scared and really did some work. . . . My meetings haven't missed and my pitch [message] has finally developed so that I don't have to be changing around every time I give it."

". . . On the Peace Corps matter, I called Rockefeller. . . . He says that they are having their difficulties in getting good people for community development. Want[s] me to send him names of people whom I feel are qualified for this work.

Do you know anybody we don't particularly want around California for at least two years? Maybe we can outdo Saul [Alinsky] on this."

". . . Gracias mil por la contribución. [A thousand thanks for the contribution.] Su amigo César."

October 3, 1962. "Dear César:

". . . Well, viejo [old one], you've really done a [great] job! I know there's a long way to go, but with that miraculous mana of yours and judging by the glory I saw pouring from the eyes of the farm workers sitting around that table all afternoon, and with luck, you'll make it. I'm absolutely sure of it."

". . . Meantime, keep the old dream coming true and drop me a bit of news . . . Fred."

January 7, 1963. "Dear Fred: Sure enough I had your letter upon my return."

". . . I don't know whether I mentioned that both Corcoran and Hanford are go go go. Your latest silent contribution is being applied to the materials for Laton."

". . . Will see what happens as the drive progresses. Personally, I think it will get better as time passes."

". . . mejor deseo verlo que escribirle. [I prefer seeing you than writing to you.] Como siempre, César. Viva la Causa."

January 10, 1963. "Dear César: I hope you'll forgive me for letting you down this once. I didn't prepare the introduction to the petitions. . . ."

". . . On the roses, a couple of Pearl Scarlets would be nice, if you can get them (for me). Am sending along 20 maracas mas [20 dollars and more]. Best and warmest to you, Elena y los esquinlis [Helen and the kids], Fred."

March 11, 1963. "Dear Fred: Am terribly sorry for not writing. I've been chasing the rat for the past two weeks, not that I have accomplished very much. But nevertheless, have had to devote every bit of time to it."

". . . Before I forget, doesn't our bird [the union's Aztec-eagle symbol] resemble the N.R.A. (New Deal) bird of yesteryear."

"Financially we are still in the dust—but hope to get up and out gradually within the coming months. I think that if we can keep our present membership we can pay ourselves about $50.00 per week and pay for the gas expense. The great if, of course."

". . . Thank you very much for the contribution. . . . Hope this is the last one we have to burden you with. Regards to all, César."

May 14, 1963. "Dear César:

". . . Knowing how well things are going for you has both bucked me up & turned me a screaming shad of envidioso verde [envious green]."

"Mientras aqui va un cuero a de iguana. [In the meantime, I am sending an iguana skin—a $20 bill.] Como siempre, Fred."

January 3, 1964. (From Fred.) "Dear campanero de la pluma [Dear friend of the pen]: It's a good thing our pal-ship doesn't depend on la pluma or it would long since have withered away. And I certainly can't excuse the lapse by telling you how awfully busy and productive I've been, because, as you know so well, these holidays shoot hell out of everything in our line [of work]."

". . . There's little likelihood I'll be down in the Valley in the near future, and I don't suppose you'll be coming up to San Jose. But if you do, let me know and we'll have one at the "Hole in the Wall" for the sake of auld lang syne. Warmest regards, Fred." (The Hole in the Wall was a coffee shop in San Jose where we hung out 40 years ago.)

After hearing that Fred was very ill, David Martínez and I drove up to see him at the community where he was living in Mill Valley. I'm very grateful that we had a chance to spend time with Fred about a week before he died.

Fred Jr. had warned me that his dad might not recognize us. He was sitting on a chair in the hall when we arrived. He looked at me the way he did forty years ago, eyes and arms open in a big smile, and said, "Oh César."

We spent three hours walking around the grounds. We did a lot of reminiscing, spoke about his book, *Conquering Goliath,* spoke about the union and the boycott.

I told him how grateful we were for everything he had done for us. Fred, always humble and with no trace of ego, said, "Come on, I didn't do anything for you. You guys did it all."

"No," I replied. "We'll never forget the lessons you taught us. Every time we take a short cut, we get in trouble. There are no shortcuts in organizing, remember?"

We talked about the organizing techniques I first learned from him so many years ago. I wanted to keep them in my head. Fred was sharp as a tack. He remembered a lot of stuff. We talked about how it is that people understand the difficult things very quickly. It's the simple things that take a long time for people to understand.

Fred was lucid and animated. He was not one to complain about his health or much else. So on that day last month in Mill Valley it didn't occur to me that he would die soon.

And I didn't have a chance to tell him that in addition to training me and inspiring me and being my hero, over forty years he also became my best friend.

I shall miss him very much.

Eulogy for Nan Freeman, 1972

A transcript of this speech is in the United Farm Workers Papers, Wayne State University.

On Tuesday, January 25, 1972, Nan Freeman, a young Jewish woman from Boston, gave her life for Farm Workers. She was eighteen years old when she died.

To some she was a young girl who lost her life in a tragic accident. To us she is a sister who picketed with farm workers in the middle of the night because of her love for justice. She is a young woman who fulfilled the commandments by loving her neighbors, even to the point of sacrificing her own life. To us, Nan Freeman is *Kadosha* in the Hebrew tradition, "a holy person" to be honored and remembered for as long as farm workers struggle for justice.

How can we measure the gift she has given to our cause? Will God give her another life to live? God has given Nan Freeman just one life, and now that life is ended. Think of that, all who cherish our farm workers union: Nan Freeman, our young sister, has poured out her *one life* so that farm workers everywhere might be more free.

There is no way to repay her immeasurable gift. There are no words to thank her for what she's done. Some things we can do: our whole movement is declaring a period of mourning that will correspond to the traditional seven-day period of mourning.

We can remember Nan Freeman. We can honor her life and express our thoughts to her family. We can give more of ourselves just because she has given everything. We must work together to build a farm workers union that is worthy of her love and sacrifice.

Eulogy for Juan de la Cruz, Arvin, California, August 21, 1973

A transcript of this speech is in the United Farm Workers Papers, Wayne State University.

We are here to honor the life of Juan de la Cruz. On behalf of his family, we speak to all those who mourn here and throughout the country. Juan de la Cruz was a simple and a good man. He is gone and we miss him, and yet he is alive in our respect and love for his life. He was a humble farm worker and yet in his dying thousands of people have come to pay honor to his life. What is it about the life of our brother, Juan, that produces such a response in us?

Last night as we walked in a candlelight procession through Arvin, I was thinking about the earliest days of our union. I remember with strong feelings the families who joined our movement and paid dues long before there was any hope of winning contracts. Sometimes, fathers and mothers would take money out of their meager food budgets just because they believed that farm workers could and must build their own union. I remember thinking then that with spirit like that we had to win. No force on earth could stop us.

Juan de la Cruz is part of that spirit. He joined the union in its earliest days.

He could have held back. He could have waited to see which side was going to win. Instead he threw himself into our struggle with the DiGiorgio Corporation. He picketed. He worked on the boycott. He went to jail. He did not hold back. He gave himself completely so that all farm workers might some day be free.

It is hard to turn your back on such a person. His example of service and sacrifice reaches the spirit of each one of us. His life and his deeds of love pull on our best instincts and cause us to want to give something of ourselves.

Juan has not only given himself in life, but he has now given his only life on this earth for us, for his children and for all farm workers who suffer and who go hungry in this land of plenty. We are here because his spirit of service and sacrifice has touched and moved our lives. The force that is generated by that spirit of love is more powerful than any force on earth. It cannot be stopped.

We live in the midst of people who hate and fear us. They have worked hard to keep us in our place. They will spend millions more to destroy our union. But we do not have to make ourselves small by hating and fearing them in return. There is enough love and goodwill in our movement to give energy to our struggle and still have plenty left over to break down and change the climate of hate and fear around us.

We are going to win. It is just a matter of time. And when we win there will be a strong and vital service center and hiring hall and field office in the Lamont-Arvin area. It seems only fitting and proper that our union office here be named in honor of Juan de la Cruz.

Juan de la Cruz has not given his life in vain. He will not be forgotten. His spirit will live in each one of us who decides to join the struggle and who gives life and strength to others. Juan is a martyr in a just cause. He will give purpose and memory to his life and death by *what we do*. The more we sacrifice, the harder we work, the more life we give to the spirit of our brother, Juan de la Cruz.

Eulogy for Rufino Contreras, Calexico, California, February 14, 1979

A transcript of this speech is in the United Farm Workers Papers, Wayne State University.

February 10, 1979, was a day of infamy for farm workers. It was a day without joy. The sun didn't shine. The birds didn't sing. The rain didn't fall.

Why was this such a day of evil? Because on this day greed and injustice struck down our brother Rufino Contreras.

What is the worth of a man? What is the worth of a farm worker? Rufino, his father, and brother together gave the company twenty years of their labor. They were faithful workers who helped build up the wealth of their boss, helped to build up the wealth of his ranch.

What was their reward for their service and their sacrifice? When they petitioned for a more just share of what they themselves produced, when they spoke out against the injustice they endured, the company answered them with bullets; the company sent hired guns to quiet Rufino Contreras.

Capitol and labor together produce the fruit of the land. But what really counts is labor—the human beings who torture their bodies, sacrifice their youth, and numb their spirits to produce this great agricultural wealth, a wealth so vast that it feeds all of America and much of the world. And yet the men, women, and children who are the flesh and blood of this production often do not have enough to feed themselves.

But we are here today to say that true wealth is not measured in money or status or power. It is measured in the legacy that we leave behind for those we love and those we inspire.

In that sense, Rufino is not dead. Wherever farm workers organize, stand up for their rights, and strike for justice, Rufino Contreras is with them.

Rufino lives among us. It is those who have killed him and those who have conspired to kill him that have died, because the love, the compassion, the light in their hearts have been stilled.

Why do we say that Rufino still lives? Because those of us who mourn him today and bring him to his rest rededicate ourselves to the ideals for which he gave his life. Rufino built a union that will someday bring justice to all farm workers.

If Rufino were alive today, what would he tell us? He would tell us, "Don't be afraid. Don't be discouraged." He would tell us, "Don't cry for me, organize!"[26]

This is a day of sorrow but it is also a day of hope. It is a time of sadness because our friend is dead. It is a time of hope because we are certain that Rufino today enjoys the justice in heaven that was denied him on earth.

It is our mission to finish the work Rufino has begun among us, knowing that true justice for ourselves and our opponents is only possible before God, who is the final judge.

Eulogy for René López, Fresno, California, September 1983

A transcript of this speech is in the United Farm Workers Papers, Wayne State University.

On behalf of all of us here, we extend our deepest sympathies to René's family—his mother, Dolores, his father, Francisco, his brother, Efren, his sister, Lupe, his sister, Rebecca, his sister, Yolanda, his brother, Juan Francisco, and his sisters Iliana [and Grace], and his grandparents, Fernando and Tomas López and Ignacio and Virginia Robles.

Thanks be to God, René's mother, father, brothers, and sisters, whom he loved so much, were able to be with him at his bedside during his final hours. René left them a beautiful heritage of courage, a heritage that, please God, will sustain them, come what may, until they meet him again in paradise.

René López's good deeds are known to all of you and, especially, to the members of his family, good deeds, above all of charity and kindness and human compassion. These deeds go with him and live after him, and for that reason, his funeral this morning is an occasion not for gloom, much less for despair, but rather an opportunity to celebrate, in a spirit of Christian joy, René's life and the goodness and the mercy of God.

The Book of Wisdom tells us: "Length of days is not what makes age honorable, nor number of years the true measure of life. Understanding, this is a man's gray hairs. The virtuous man, though he died before his time, will find rest."

All who knew René López as a personal friend or more immediately as a member of the family, can vouch for the fact that he had understanding. By this I mean that he had the gift of faith, the gift of knowing what is truly important in his life.

It was not possible for René to shut his eyes to situations of distress and of poverty which cry out to God, or to keep silent in the face of injustice. *He was that kind of a man.*

René was young, but he was wise beyond his years. He died in the prime of his life, but the number of his years was not the true measure of his life. For this reason . . . regardless of the number of his days or the length of his years . . . he will find rest, for grace and mercy awaits the Chosen of the Creator, and protection awaits God's Holy Ones.

René was young, but he had already felt the call to social justice. His mother, Dolores, said that he came home one day with the stub of his union authorization card, showed it to her, and said, "Here is my first union card; now I am important, now I am a man."

But René's first union card was also his last, he will never enjoy the blessings of youth, he will never fulfill all the promises others saw in him, he will never pass on his great love to his own sons and daughters. René has been taken away from us in the prime of his life, before he could share the full measure of his talents and goodness with the world about him. René is gone because he dared to hope and because he dared to live out his hopes.

Rarely do men and women choose to die in the midst of their quest for freedom. They wish to be truly free and to live more fully in this life.

But death comes to us all, and we do not get to choose the time or the circumstances of our dying. The hardest thing of all is to die rightly. René López died rightly; he is a martyr for justice.

René is at peace with God. He has given all that he can give.

But how many more farm workers must fall? How many more tears must be shed? How many more martyrs must there be before we can be free? When will the day come when the joy becomes great and the grief becomes small?

The answer, my brothers and sisters, is in our hands. The answer is in *our* hands.

We who live must now walk an extra mile because René has lived and died for *his* and *our* dreams. We who keep on struggling for justice for farm workers must carry in our hearts *his* sacrifice.

We must try to live as he lived, We must keep alive his hopes, and fulfill, with our own sacrifices, his dreams. We must take René into our hearts and promise that we will never forget his sacrifice.

René's father, Francisco, looking down on his fallen son, said these words: "When he was born, I received him with a kiss, and, now I give him back to God with a kiss."

"Happy are those who died in the Lord: let them rest from their labor for their good deeds go with them."

Amen.

Notes

INTRODUCTION

1. Our scholarship on Chávez stretches back twenty years in a variety of journals and books. See John C. Hammerback, "The Rhetorical Worlds of César Chávez and Reies Tijerina," *Western Journal of Speech Communication* 44 (Summer 1980): 166–76; John C. Hammerback and Richard J. Jensen, "'A Revolution of Heart and Mind': César Chávez's Rhetorical Crusade," *Journal of the West* 28 (April 1988): 69–74; John C. Hammerback and Richard J. Jensen, "Ethnic Heritage as Rhetorical Legacy: The Plan of Delano," *Quarterly Journal of Speech,* 80 (1994): 53–70; John C. Hammerback, "The Words of César Chávez, Teacher of Truth," *San Jose Studies* 20 (Spring 1994): 10–14; John C. Hammerback, Richard J. Jensen, and José Angel Gutiérrez, "Teaching the Truth: The Righteous Rhetoric of César Chávez," in *A War of Word: Chicano Protest in the 1960s and 1970s* (Westport, Conn.: Greenwood, 1985), 33–52; John C. Hammerback and Richard J. Jensen, "César Chávez," in *American Orators of the Twentieth Century: Critical Studies and Sources,* ed. Bernard K. Duffy and Halford R. Ryan (Westport, Conn.: Greenwood, 1987), 55–62; John C. Hammerback and Richard J. Jensen, "'A Revolution of Heart and Mind': César Chávez's Rhetorical Crusade," in *Western Speakers: Voices of the American Dream,* ed. Susan H. Koester (Manhattan, Kans.: University of Kansas Press, Sunflower Books, 1989), 69–74; John C. Hammerback and Richard J. Jensen, "César Estrada Chávez," in *Leaders from the 1960s,* ed. David De Leon (Westport, Conn.: Greenwood, 1994), 54–61; Richard J. Jensen and John C. Hammerback, "History and Culture as Rhetorical Constraints: César Chávez's Letter from Delano," in *Doing Rhetorical History: Concepts and Cases,* ed. Kathleen J. Turner (Tuscaloosa: University of Alabama Press, 1998), 207–20.

2. Marc Grossman, interview by the editors, Sacramento, October 14, 1995.

3. Jacques E. Levy, *César Chávez: Autobiography of La Causa* (New York: W. W. Norton, 1975), 1.

4. Susan Samuels Drake, *Fields of Courage* (Santa Cruz, Calif.: Many Names, 1999), xvi.

5. "Chávez vs. The Teamsters: Farm Workers' Historic Vote," *U.S. News & World Report,* Sept. 22, 1975, 82–83.

6. "Chávez Jailed for Boycott," *San Francisco Examiner,* Dec. 4, 1970, 1.

7. "A Boost for Chávez," *Newsweek*, May 26, 1975, 68.

8. Evan T. Barr, "Sour Grapes: César Chávez 20 Years Later," *New Republic*, Nov. 25, 1985, 20; Jeff Wright, "Farmworkers' Leaders Advocate Boycott," *Register-Guard* (Eugene, Oregon), April 16, 1991, C-3; Matt S. Meier and Feliciano Ribera, *Mexican Americans/American Mexicans* (New York: Hill & Wang, 1993), 212; Bill Clinton quoted in "'Visionary' César Chávez Dead at 66," *Las Vegas Review-Journal*, April 24, 1993, 1.

9. Winthrop Yinger, *César Chávez: The Rhetoric of Nonviolence* (Hicksville, N.Y.: Exposition, 1975), 16.

10. Bob Vick of the California Farm Bureau Federation, quoted in "Visionary César Chávez Dead at 66," *Las Vegas Review-Journal*, April 24, 1993, A3

11. Luis A. Solis-Garza, "César Chávez: The Chicano 'Messiah?'" in *Pain and Promise: The Chicano Today*, ed. Edward Simmen (New York: Mentor, 1972), 304.

12. John Robertson, "Hispanic Leader's Message Transcended Ethnicity, Race," *Albuquerque Journal*, April 24, 1993, A-10.

13. Eugene Nelson, quoted in Richard Griswold del Castillo and Richard Garcia, *César Chávez: A Triumph of Spirit* (Norman: University of Oklahoma Press, 1995), 147.

14. "Inspiration, Si—Administration, No," *Time*, April 22, 1974, 94.

15. José Angel Gutiérrez, "César Chávez Estrada: The First and Last of the Chicano Leaders," *San Jose Studies* 10 (Spring 1994): 35.

16. Gutiérrez, 35.

17. Susan Ferriss and Ricardo Sandoval, *The Fight in the Fields: César Chávez and the Farmworkers Movement* (New York: Harcourt Brace & Company, 1997), 93.

18. Ferriss and Sandoval, 11–12.

19. Eliseo Medina, quoted in "The Struggle in the Fields," F. Arturo Rosales, *Chicano! The History of the Mexican American Civil Rights Movement* (Houston: Arte Publico, 1996), 130.

20. Dorothy Rensenbrink, "On Chávez, Women and Faith," *The Christian Century*, April 24, 1974, 444.

21. Ibid., 445.

22. For a more detailed discussion of Chávez's life, see John C. Hammerback and Richard J. Jensen, *The Rhetorical Career of César Chávez* (College Station: Texas A&M Press, 1998), 11–23; the entirety of both Ferriss and Sandoval, *The Fight in the Fields*, and Griswold del Castillo and Garcia, *César Chávez*.

23. Chávez, quoted in Ronald Taylor, *Chávez and the Farm Workers* (Boston: Beacon, 1975), 64.

24. Ferriss and Sandoval, *The Fight in the Fields*, 34; Griswold del Castillo and Garcia, *César Chávez*, 9–21.

25. Chávez, quoted in Levy, *Autobiography*, 50.

26. Chávez, quoted in Cletus E. Daniel, "César Chávez and the Unionization of California Farm Workers," in *Labor Leaders in America*, ed. Melvyn Dubofsky and Warren Van Tine (Urbana: University of Illinois Press, 1987), 358.

27. Chávez, quoted in Levy, *Autobiography*, 97, 99.

28. Fred Ross, quoted in Levy, *Autobiography*, 102.

29. César Chávez, interview, tape recording, at Wayne State University, Detroit 1980, ARC 2:48, copy in possession of the editors. Audiotape in the UFW Papers,

Archives of Labor and Urban Affairs, Walter E. Reuther Library, Wayne State University, Detroit.

30. César Chávez, "The Organizer's Tale," in *Chicano: The Evolution of a People*, ed. Renato Rosaldo, Robert A. Calvert, Gustav Seligmann (Minneapolis: Winston, 1973), 298.

31. Ibid.

32. Fred Ross, *Conquering Goliath* (Keene, Calif.: El Taller Grafico, 1989), 79.

33. César Chávez, interview by Nancy Padilla, Albuquerque, N.M., Dec. 7, 1981, 2.

34. Dolores Huerta, "Dolores Huerta Talks About Republicans, César, Children, and Her Home Town," *La Voz del Pueblo* (November– December 1972), reprint in *An Awakening Minority: The Mexican Americans*, ed. Manual Servin, 2d ed. (Beverly Hills, Calif.: Glencoe, 1974), 286.

35. For a detailed description of the events in Oxnard, see Fred Ross, *Conquering Goliath*.

36. Chávez, quoted in Daniel, "César Chávez and the Unionization," 362.

37. Chávez, quoted in Levy, *Autobiography*, 3.

38. César E. Chávez, "The Mexican-American and the Church," a paper presented at the Second Annual Mexican-American Conference in Sacramento, March 8–10, 1968, in *Voices: Reading from El Grito*, ed. Octavio Romano V (Berkeley: Quinto Sol, 1971), 101.

39. Chávez, "The Mexican-American and the Church," 104.

40. César Chávez, "Tilting With the System: An Interview with César Chávez," interview by Bob Fitch, *Christian Century*, February 18, 1970, 204.

41. César Chávez, interview by Nancy Padilla, 1.

42. Ibid., 2.

43. Ibid., 3.

44. Mark Grossman, interview with editors, Sacramento, October 14, 1995.

45. César Chávez, interview by Nancy Padilla, 4–5.

46. Ibid., 2.

47. Winthrop Yinger, *César Chávez: The Rhetoric of Nonviolence* (Hicksville, N.Y.: Exposition, 1975), 48.

48. Ibid., 47.

49. Ibid., 21.

50. Griswold del Castillo and Garcia, *César Chávez*, 49.

51. Daniel, "César Chávez and the Unionization," 351.

52. Hammerback and Jensen, *The Rhetorical Career of César Chávez*, 193.

53. Chávez, quoted in Levy, *Autobiography*, 148.

CHAPTER 1

1. For an in-depth discussion of the events of the years 1962–1970 and Chávez's rhetoric during that period, see Hammerback and Jensen, *The Rhetorical Career of César Chávez* (College Station: Texas A&M University Press, 1998), 62–100.

2. César Chávez, "Why Delano?" in *Aztlan: An Anthology of Mexican American Literature* (New York: Vintage, 1972), 203.

3. Judith Dunbar, "For César Chávez," in *1962–1982*, n.p, n.d. This is a booklet in honor of the twentieth anniversary of Chávez's beginning to organize the UFW. Copy in possession of the editors.

4. Ibid.

5. For an interesting discussion of community organizing, see César Chávez, "The Organizer's Tale," *Ramparts*, July 1966, 43–50. It was reprinted in *The Chicanos: Mexican-American Voices*, ed. Ed Ludwig and James Sántibañez (Baltimore: Penguin, 1971), 101–12, and *Chicano: The Evolution of a People*, ed. Renato Rosaldo, Robert A. Calvert, and Gustav L. Selgiman, Jr. (Malabar, Fla.: Robert E. Krieger, 1982), 273–78.

6. For an extensive analysis of the Mexican Plan in general and the Plan of Delano specifically, see John C. Hammerback and Richard J. Jensen, "Ethnic Heritage as Rhetorical Legacy: The Plan of Delano," *Quarterly Journal of Speech* 80 (February 1994): 53–70.

7. For a detailed analysis of this letter, see Richard J. Jensen and John C. Hammerback, "History and Culture as Rhetorical Constraints: César Chávez's Letter from Delano," in *Doing Rhetorical History*, ed. Kathleen J. Turner (Tuscaloosa: University of Alabama Press, 1998), 207–20.

8. The strike in Wheatland was actually among the hop workers on the Durst Ranch, the largest employer of agricultural labor in California. In August of 1913 over two thousand workers and their families were living on the ranch in terrible conditions. The IWW sponsored a meeting to protest the conditions and to call for a strike. The owners of the ranch asked the authorities to arrest the leaders. In the process of arresting the leaders, a gun battle broke out and four individuals were killed. The authorities used the incident to crush the strike. For further information, see Melvyn Dubofsky, *We Shall Be All: A History of the Industrial Workers of the World* (Chicago: Quadrangle, 1969): 294–300.

9. In 1955 the American Federation of Labor and Congress of Industrial Organizations joined to form one organization.

10. A scab is an individual who takes the job of someone who is on strike. In labor unions, being called a scab is one of the worst insults an individual can receive.

11. "Right to Work Laws" state that membership in a union cannot be required as a condition of employment. Labor leaders and supporters see these laws as antiunion, and they often exist in states where conditions are not favorable toward unionism.

12. During World War II there was a shortage of farm workers; so the federal government allowed the importation of braceros (meaning literally "a pair of arms") to enter the country to work as contract workers. They supposedly were only allowed to take jobs when resident workers were not available to fill them. The program was badly abused and often used to break strikes and hold down wages for farm workers. The program ended in 1964.

13. Green carders are individuals, usually workers, who are in the United States on a permanent resident status but who are not citizens. Chávez and the union were concerned because these individuals were often used as strikebreakers against the union.

CHAPTER 2

1. Ignacio M. Garcia, *Chicanismo: The Forging of a Militant Ethos among Mexican Americans* (Tucson: University of Arizona Press, 1997), 31.

2. For a thorough discussion of the events of this period and a summary of Chávez's public discourse, see "Rhetorically 'Working towards Creating the New Man,'" in John C. Hammerback and Richard J. Jensen, *The Rhetorical Career of César Chávez* (College Station: Texas A&M Press, 1998), 101–24.

3. Ibid.

4. Cletus E. Daniel, "César Chávez and the Unionization of California Farm Workers," *Labor Leaders in America,* ed. Melvyn Dubofsky and Warren Van Tine (Urbana: University of Illinois Press, 1987), 372.

5. César Chávez, quoted in Susan Ferriss and Ricardo Sandoval, *The Fight in the Fields: César Chávez and the Farmworkers Movement* (New York: Harcourt, Brace & Company, 1997), 162.

6. Chávez, quoted in Ferriss and Sandoval, 164.

7. Chávez, quoted in Richard Griswold del Castillo and Richard A. Garcia, *César Chávez: A Triumph of Spirit* (Norman: University of Oklahoma Press, 1995), 118.

8. Chávez, quoted in Ferriss and Sandoval, 172.

9. Ibid., 164.

10. Ibid., 173.

11. Chávez, quoted in Daniel, 372.

12. Ibid., 373–74.

13. Rev. Howard Matson, *1962–1982,* n.p., n.d.

14. Chávez, quoted in Ferriss and Sandoval, 184.

15. Ibid., 188.

16. This is a quote from the speech Chávez gave ending his fast in 1968. The full text of the speech is in chapter five.

17. Ripple was a very inexpensive wine so it was often drunk by individuals who had little money.

CHAPTER 3

1. For a summary of the events of this period and a summary of Chávez's public discourse, see John C. Hammerback and Richard J. Jensen, *The Rhetorical Career of César Chávez* (College Station: Texas A&M University Press, 1998), 143–55.

2. Richard Steven Street, "It's Boycott Time in California," *Nation,* March 23, 1985, 330; Rudolfo Acuña, *Occupied America* (San Francisco: Canfield, 1972), 370; Patrick H. Mooney and Theo J. Majka, *Farmers' and Farmworkers' Movements* (New York: Twayne, 1945), 176–78; Richard Griswold del Castillo and Richard Garcia, *César Chávez: A Triumph of Spirit* (Norman: University of Oklahoma Press, 1995), 129–30.

3. Chávez, quoted in Susan Ferriss and Ricardo Sandoval, *The Fight in the Fields: César Chávez and the Farmworkers Movement* (New York: Harcourt, Brace & Company, 1997), 216.

4. *Congressional Quarterly Weekly Report* 34, no. 29 (July 17 1976): 3.

CHAPTER 4

1. For an in-depth study of the events and Chávez's rhetoric during this period, see John C. Hammerback and Richard J. Jensen, *The Rhetorical Career of César Chávez* (College Station: Texas A&M University Press, 1998), 156–88.

2. Richard Griswold del Castillo and Richard A. Garcia, *César Chávez: A Triumph of Spirit* (Norman: University of Oklahoma Press, 1995), 135.

3. Chávez, quoted in Griswold del Castillo and Garcia, *César Chávez*, 135.

4. Matt S. Meier and Feliciano Ribera, *Mexican Americans/American Mexicans* (New York: Hill & Wang, 1993), 211.

5. Chávez, quoted in Griswold del Castillo and Garcia, *César Chávez*, 136.

6. Susan Ferriss and Ricardo Sandoval, *The Fight in the Fields: César Chávez and the Farmworkers Movement* (New York: Harcourt Brace & Company, 1997), 238–39.

7. Cletus E. Daniel, "César Chávez and the Unionization of California Farm Workers," *Labor Leaders in America*, ed. Melvyn Dubofsky and Warren Van Tine (Urbana: University of Illinois Press, 1987), 380.

8. Griswold del Castillo and Garcia, *César Chávez*, 172.

9. Ibid., 173.

10. Ibid.

11. The United Farm Workers Web Site contains the texts of only two speeches by Chávez. The Commonwealth Club speech is one of the two. It can be viewed at *http://www.ufw.org/commonwealth.html/*.

12. For a detailed discussion of the speech, see Hammerback and Jensen, *The Rhetorical Career of César Chávez*, 161–66.

13. The second speech in the web site is the Pacific Lutheran speech. It can be viewed at http://www.ufw.org/fast.html/.

14. César Chávez, "My anger and sadness over pesticides," *Sacramento Bee*, April 16, 1989, 1, 6.

CHAPTER 5

1. *The Rhetoric of Aristotle*, ed. Lane Cooper (New York: Appleton-Century-Crofts, 1932), 17; John Poulakos and Takis Poulakos, *Classical Rhetorical Theory* (Boston: Houghton-Mifflin, 1999), 61–62.

2. Celeste Michelle Condit, "The Functions of Epideictic: The Boston Massacre Orations as Exemplar," *Communication Quarterly* 33 (Fall 1985): 291.

3. Susan Ferriss and Ricardo Sandoval, *The Fight in the Fields: César Chávez and the Farmworkers Movement* (New York: Harcourt, Brace & Company, 1997), 141–42.

4. Ibid., 142.

5. Ibid., 143.

6. Ibid..

7. Ibid.

8. Quoted in Ferriss and Sandoval, *The Fight in the Fields*, 225.

9. Ibid., 198–99.

10. Richard Griswold del Castillo and Richard Garcia, *César Chávez: A Triumph of Spirit* (Norman: University of Oklahoma Press, 1995), 137.

11. "Chávez's Condition Worsens in Fast Over Grape Boycott," *New York Times*, Aug. 7, 1988, 23.

12. "Chávez Plans to End Fast Sunday at Mass," *New York Times*, Aug. 19, 1988, n.p.

13. Ferriss and Sandoval, *The Fight in the Fields*, 246; Griswold del Castillo and Garcia, *César Chávez*, 136.

14. Condit, "The Functions of Epideictic," 290.

15. César Chávez, "Full Text of the Speech," in Winthrop Yinger, *César Chávez: The Rhetoric of Nonviolence* (Hicksville, N.Y.: Exposition, 1975), 47. Yinger's book provides a thorough analysis of the speech.

16. Ferriss and Sandoval, *The Fight in the Fields*, 250.

17. Ibid., 252.

18. Ibid., 187; Jacques E. Levy, *César Chávez: Autobiography of La Causa* (New York: W. W. Norton, 1975), 505–8.

19. Griswold del Castillo and Garcia, *César Chávez*, 123.

20. Levy, *César Chávez: Autobiography*, 509–10.

21. "Rufino Contreras (1951–1979)," available at http://latino.sscnet.ucla.edu/ research/Chávez/themes/ufw/rufino.htm March 12, 1997. Copy of text in possession of the editors.

22. "Rene Lopez (1962–1983)," available at http://latino.sscnet.ucla.edu/ research/Chávez/themes/ufw/rene.htm March 12, 1997. Copy in possession of the editors.

23. Kathleen Hall Jamieson and Karlyn Kohrs Campbell, "Rhetorical Hybrids: Fusions of Generic Elements," *Quarterly Journal of Speech* 68 (1982): 147.

24. For example, see Chávez's address to a union organizing convocation in Pharr, Texas, February 25, 1979. Copy of the text in possession of the editors and in the UFW papers in the Reuther Library of Labor and Urban Affairs at Wayne State University in Detroit.

25. In the 1940s and 1950s Pachucos were young Mexican Americans who were rebelling against their parents and society. They had their own music, dress, and language. Chávez briefly affiliated with the group. In the 1960s young Chicanos expressed admiration for the Pachucos because they had challenged the establishment. For a description of Pachucos, see Griswold del Castillo and Garcia, *César Chávez*, 17–18.

26. These words are very similar to those uttered by Joe Hill, the famous songwriter of the Industrial Workers of the World, before he was executed for murder in Utah. Hill's words have become a battle cry for workers in many industrial conflicts.

Index

ISBN 1-58544-170-8

90000